THE FIRST

Roland S. Martin

THE FIRST

PRESIDENT BARACK OBAMA'S ROAD TO THE WHITE HOUSE AS ORIGINALLY REPORTED BY ROLAND S. MARTIN

THIRD WORLD PRESS
CHICAGO, IL

Third World Press
Publishers since 1967
Chicago

First Edition
Printed in the United States of America
by KingPrinting.com

Cover and inside text layout designer: Kenon White

Library of Congress Control Number: 2009930961
ISBN-10: 0-88378-316-9
ISBN-13: 978-0-88378-316-0

14 13 12 11 10   6 5 4 3 2 1

To the millions of Americans who volunteered and worked hard for their respective candidate in the presidential primaries.

Hats off also to the nearly 130 million Americans who went to the polls to cast a ballot. You didn't complain and take no action. You didn't whine about the state of the nation and stay at home. You practiced the most important function of our democracy and all of you are true patriots.

CONTENTS

Contents

Contents

Contents

Contents

Contents

Contents

Contents

Contents

Tatyana Ali
Holly Robinson-Peete
Chris Tucker
Blair Underwood
Spike Lee

Kevin Liles
Erika Alexander
Common
Hill Harper

Contents

Contents

Tichina Arnold   Kevin Liles
Holly Robinson-Peete   Common
Erika Alexander   Hill Harper
Malik Yoba

Contents

Contents

Kevin Liles   Cash Warren
Tatyana Ali   Common
Vanessa Williams   Hill Harper
Jessica Alba   Spike Lee

INTRODUCTION

I NEVER THOUGHT HE WOULD RUN.

Oh, don't act like you were such a prophet and knew a half-white, half-black man named Barack Hussein Obama, only in the United States Senate for a couple of years, would actually have the audacity to run for the Democratic nomination for president of the United States.

Years from now folks will think that all was well in 2007 and it was inevitable that Obama would run for the presidency, especially coming off his mesmerizing speech at the Democratic National Convention in 2004.

But the reality is that up to that point, he was a state senator in Illinois who had written a successful book and given an awesome speech.

And he was facing the Mike Tyson of politics—Sen. Hillary Clinton. She was the tough-as-nails politician who fought through the political wars with her husband, President Bill Clinton, facing down the right wing media and hard-nosed Republicans who delved into every detail of his life, while tearing her to shreds at every turn.

She survived all of that as First Lady, then became the junior U.S. senator from New York, often eclipsing the senior senator, Chuck Schumer.

In all of 2006, political watchers, pundits, newspapers, magazines and TV networks all proclaimed her "The Inevitable Democratic Nominee." It was considered suicide to even bother running against her.

But under the weight of all that, Obama continued to travel the country, watching as hundreds and thousands showed up at book signings, imploring him to run. Even the Queen of America, Oprah Winfrey, offered her view that after reading his book, *The Audacity of Hope,* he was the kind of candidate she wanted as president of the

United States. Up until that point, she had never even endorsed anyone, but he stirred up something in her that was emblematic of many Americans.

Yet with all of that positive movement, it still seemed implausible that he would run with such a thin record.

But on February 10, 2007, Barack Hussein Obama stood before thousands waiting in the cold in front of the Old State Capitol in Springfield, Illinois, and made his intentions known: he was running for president.

This book tracks this journey through my eyes as I covered the improbable road to the presidency of Obama.

It's funny because we first met in September 2003 at the annual Congressional Black Caucus Foundation's Legislative Weekend. Both of us were working the floor— me meeting contacts; him seeking out donors. We shook hands, exchanged cards and went on our merry way.

I frankly forgot about the exchange.

But as fate would have it, our paths crossed a few months later when in August 2004, I was hired as a consultant to revive the *Chicago Defender*, the nation's most historic black newspaper.

I went to the Roots Music Festival, an annual event hosted by then-Chicago Alderman Dorothy Tillman. When we sat down to hear a musical act, I sat on Tillman's right, and on her left was Obama, a state senator seeking the opportunity to become the junior U.S. senator from Illinois.

Tillman asked us if we knew each other, and then tried to introduce us. I said, "We've met before."

And then he said, "I like your columns."

I was surprised by that, considering my nationally syndicated column didn't run in Chicago. But then I remembered he gave me his card, and I must have put his e-mail into my e-blast program.

With that, I went on to run the *Defender*, and he won the U.S. Senate seat. And for both of us, well, the rest is history.

My aim in publishing this book is to offer an historical account of covering this stunning and exciting race, but to also offer in real-time the ups and downs of the

Introduction

campaign, and even take a look back at various moments from my perspective, as well as those of some of the entertainers and others I crossed paths with along the way.

If there is something you disagree with, fine. Just keep in mind, what you see and read was based on the moment, not a sort of post-look at the campaign.

Roland S. Martin

PART 1

THE PRE-SEASON

America's Love Affair with U.S. Sen. Barack Obama

AS ILLINOIS' DEMOCRATIC JUNIOR SENATOR travels the nation, raising large sums of money for his party while seriously pondering a presidential run, throngs of people view Barack Obama as the Messiah, rising up to rescue the nation from its partisan political battles.

Pundits are at a loss to explain why America has latched onto Obama the way it has over the last two years. For a man with a thin record in the U.S. Senate—again, he's only been there for one-third of his six-year term—he is being greeted in cities and towns across the nation like a seasoned politician who has come of age on the national stage.

"The man with the funny name"—a line he likes to use in speeches—is being called a rock star, rivaling—and potentially trumping—former President Bill Clinton and his wife, Sen. Hillary Rodham Clinton (D-NY)—for the affections of his party.

While watching this magnificent courtship play out, it must be noted—without a sense of throwing water on this burning hot love affair—that Obama is just one man who is trying his best to make a difference.

When CNN anchor Don Lemon and reporter Bill Schneider interviewed me recently, both repeatedly pressed me on what the deal is with America's reaction to Obama. People are waiting in long lines just to get him to sign their book; they reach out to him with affection when he visits town. Heck, even the apolitical Oprah Winfrey gushes over him, hoping that he will make that leap and run for president.

So what's the big deal? Frankly, it boils down to this generation longing for a politician in the mold of John and Bobby Kennedy, two individuals who captured America at its core, providing a tremendous amount of spirit and positive feelings during a turbulent period.

The major dilemma facing today's generation is that we have never had someone— or something—come along that allowed us to pour our hearts, mind and soul into. We long for a relationship with a person like the previous generation had with the Kennedys, the Rev. Dr. Martin Luther King Jr. or the Civil Rights Movement. What do we believe in? What have we invested ourselves in?

While everyone insists that we are a divided nation of red and blue states, that is simply sophomoric. There are a tremendous number of people who choose not to fall into an ideological lineup. We desire not to see attacks on candidates but dialogues. Instead of trashing someone else's political plans, there really is a willingness to want to flesh them out over coffee and arrive at a logical conclusion. The partisan bickering has turned so nasty that people have abandoned the political process.

The sense that people are giving is Obama isn't like the rest; that he could restore dignity and civility to the nation.

Anyone who has heard Obama will tell you that he can light up an audience like a southern preacher. When he talks, he's thoughtful and careful, seemingly searching for a comfort zone in his positions that is hard to establish in these highly partisan times.

It's ironic that as Obama rises to new heights, Emilio Estevez's movie, "*Bobby,*" is playing on movie screens nationwide. It tells the story of the death of the presidential candidate from the vantage point of individuals who were impacted by his assassination.

We must not lose sight of the fact that this is a movie based on the unrealized dream of a man who was on the verge of winning the Democratic nomination, and going on to become president. Adults across the country continue to assert that had Bobby not been killed, America today would be much different. The Vietnam War would have ended sooner; America would have truly dealt with the horrors of poverty; we would be healed of the racial strife that has been at the core of the country since its founding; and every other ill would have been solved.

It really is an unrealistic expectation that Bobby Kennedy would have been able to do all of that. His brother didn't before he was assassinated in 1963. Yet the feeling persists that somehow this is the guy who can complete what those two—along with King and so many other warriors of yesteryear couldn't do: unite a nation.

I'm already on the record as saying Obama won't run for president in 2008. Then again, he may surprise me and choose to toss his name in the hat. If he does, that connection people feel for him will only be heightened. And if he doesn't, many of us will be let down, afraid that we will go through this life missing out on the chance to trust again.

January 19, 2007

Obama's Black Problem

There is little doubt that Illinois Sen. Barack Obama is going to aggressively pursue the Democratic nomination for president in 2008.

The forming of his exploratory committee is simply the foundation to what will be a campaign that many are saying will be a formidable challenge to Democratic rivals such as Sen. Hillary Rodham Clinton (D-NY)

While Democrats across the country fall over themselves just to touch the man, he is being eyed suspiciously by the nation's black leadership.

For the first time in history, America will have an African American seeking the world's most powerful position—one who actually has a shot at winning, and you would think that black politicians, civil rights and religious leaders would be the loudest voices calling for him to run. But, no! We have folks playing coy, whispering behind the scenes, questioning his blackness, and in some cases, complete silence.

This is nothing more than black-on-black hate at its best.

The Rev. Al Sharpton, who offered nothing more than a few great quotes in his 2004 presidential bid, told the *Chicago Defender*: "I think that Obama brings to the race a fresh face with an impressive background. I think that all of us around the country will be assessing all of the candidates and seeing what they have to offer. It is then that we will be able to make more solid comments about Obama and other possible candidates and what they will bring to the table."

He added: "My own thing is that I don't know him that well, but I seek to get to know him," Sharpton said. "Then I can give you better impressions about him and I will be able to grasp what it is he is seeking and trying to do."

Grasp what he is trying to do? Rev. Al, he's trying to become the president of the United States!

On my talk show on WVON-AM/1690 in Chicago, the Rev. Jesse Jackson said he supports Obama, but added that many black leaders nationwide don't know the junior senator from Illinois.

"He will have to take time to build relationships," he said.

The Rev. James Meeks, who served in the Illinois Senate with Obama, told the *Defender* that ego and envy has a lot to do with the lukewarm response from black leadership.

"I only hope that African American elected officials and other African American leaders do not become jealous and force Barack Obama to kiss their rings before getting their support," he said. "Black people are going to have to be fair enough to let him campaign in the United States, and not just in the African American communities and on African American issues. This is the United States, and not the United States of African Americans."

Yet Dr. Ron Walters, one of the nation's pre-eminent political science professors from the University of Maryland, College Park, said the feelings about Obama have nothing to do with jealousy.

"It's clear that Barack Obama is ascending to the pantheon of black leadership, and the problem that we always have had historically is whites sort of picking African American leaders and then importing the paradigm that they represent in our community," he said on WVON-AM. "That was the old Booker T. Washington problem. There is a reticence on the part of some of our leaders to accept Barack Obama until he comes full force in terms of his program. I think that's fair. I want to see where he stands on the critical issues that black people face before I give him carte blanche."

Here is the rub for me: Obama is entering his third year as a U.S. senator. Prior to that he served seven years in the Illinois Senate. By the time the first primary rolls around, he will have double the legislative experience that George W. Bush had when he was elected. The man has been speaking on black issues for years. So why force a litmus test on him that is not being established for Sen. Clinton and other candidates?

Frankly, the real problem black leadership has is that Obama didn't come through "the civil rights system." And like it or not, there is tremendous jealousy that he has been able to do what so many others have not done: First, he actually got elected to something. Second, he launched a campaign that people actually believe can win.

Lastly, Obama's rise as the top black political voice in America supplants others who have served as the arbiters of black thought.

This is nothing but the old lion flexing his muscle in order to try to scare off the fearless young lion. But as with life in the jungle, the only way a species keeps surviving is if the young take the place of the old.

People like Obama and Massachusetts Gov. Deval Patrick represent 21st century black leadership, and it's time for the men and women who have been on the scene for years to stop fighting change, and rest on the fact that they are seeing their labor come to fruition. If not, they will look like old fighters embarrassing themselves in search of glory days.

January 26, 2007

Obama Is an Authentic African American

ONE OF THE INSIDIOUS RITUALS any high-profile African American must endure in order to establish his or her credibility with some other African Americans is show that they are "down with the brothers and the sisters."

See, you can't just be a Fortune 500 CEO, politician, civil rights activist or journalist who happens to be African American. In order to be fully accepted and embraced, you are required to show your "ghetto card" at the entrance of the black gates of Black America. Otherwise, you are forced to stand outside, proving your worthiness to the masses as if you are a sinner trying to convince Saint Peter that you are good enough to get to heaven.

This may be surprising to many of my white readers, and my black readers may get offended and accuse me of airing our dirty laundry, but this type of silliness has been seen time and time again. And as it relates to U.S. Sen. Barack Obama's decision to run for president, some are already demanding that he prove himself to the peeps.

While preparing for a segment in which I discussed his presidential chances on CNN's "Paula Zahn NOW," I read the transcript from a San Francisco radio show where a co-host said that Obama has to work overtime to get blacks to trust him because he doesn't have a "hood" experience. The other co-host went on to say that because Obama didn't grow up impoverished on the streets of Alabama, Mississippi, Louisiana, Texas, Arkansas or in the northern slums of Chicago, New York City or Boston, he can't truly identify with the black experience in America.

Because his mother is white and his father is Kenyan, and because he grew up in Hawaii (that's still the United States for the map-challenged folks) and Indonesia, his blackness is somehow under review.

No doubt this comes as a surprise to some, but this is the kind of nonsense that is pervasive in black communities nationwide, and yes, there will be those folks on the campaign trail and who call into radio talk shows and make similar statements.

On one hand, Obama has to convince skeptical white voters that he can do the job, even though he is an African American, because of their biases. On the other hand, he must convince skeptical black voters that he isn't some white creation who appears to be black, but if elected, will crush the aspirations and dreams of black folks once in the White House.

Don't think for a second that I'm making this up. I've already started receiving the e-mails and phone calls on my radio show on WVON-AM in Chicago, so there are some nut jobs who have taken this position.

This is offensive because anyone who has ever sat down and listened to Obama can tell that he fully understands what it means to be African American—because he is!

Now, for the people who question his race, I wonder how many of them will claim Obama as one of their own if he wins the White House? These are likely the same people who screamed with joy when that talented and fine sister, Halle Berry, won the Academy Award. Was she questioned, considering her mom is white and her dad is black? Are these the same folks who clapped loudly when Mariah Carey took home Grammy after Grammy, but refused to admit that her makeup is similar to that of Obama? Could it be that these brothers and sisters claim Tiger Woods as one of their own when he is winning major golf championships, even though he considers himself a "Cablanasian," a combination of Caucasian, black and Asian?

We have reached the day when black folks are going to have to quit forcing others to pass a black test to establish their worthiness.

Every black person in America doesn't have a "hood" experience. They all don't have the same story of their father leaving them as a child, having to grow up in a single-parent home in a public housing complex, their brother on welfare and sister twice pregnant by the age of 18. We all didn't belong to the Crips or Bloods and didn't have to fight our way out of the gang in order to go to college. No, we all didn't grow up in the black church, singing "Precious Lord" and memorizing the speeches of Dr. Martin Luther King Jr. We shouldn't assume that every black person had to work three jobs to pay their way through college.

Segregation no longer limits where we live, work and play. So if Jim Crow is dead, why do we allow the system to continue to pervade our minds?

The day has come when we judge a black man or woman for who they are, where they stand on issues and what they believe in. If Obama offers a political agenda that speaks to the needs of African Americans, good. If he chooses to offer one that is broad and more universal, that doesn't make him any less of an African American (truth be told, Obama is more African American than most of us can claim. At least his father hails from the Motherland, while his mom is an American).

There is too much work to be done to raise the collective black community in the areas of education, economics and healthcare. And worrying about whether Obama or anyone else is black enough to do so should not be a part of the dialogue.

February 9, 2007

Obama Can't Win Presidency on a Black-Focused Agenda

A FEW DAYS AFTER MY INITIAL COLUMN on the "black problem" faced by Sen. Barack Obama (D-IL) I received calls from a number of individuals wondering why I took exception to black leaders questioning his candidacy.

One of the consistent points they raised: "Where is his black agenda?"

There was a constant comparison to the 1984 and 1988 presidential campaigns of the Rev. Jesse Jackson Sr., the last serious campaigns by an African American for the most powerful position in the world. I reminded them that Jackson only received 8 percent of Democratic votes in 1988, but that didn't change their view that he "won" simply by running.

Sorry to disappoint, but in my book, winning means winning.

The most difficult job a black politician has is trying to run for higher office. Most minority politicians run in "safe" districts that are drawn along racial lines. It's easy to present a black, Hispanic or Asian agenda when the majority of voters are of the same hue—you can easily speak to their issues.

But when it's time to run for a citywide, statewide or national office, the agenda has to change, and that is disconcerting to a minority group.

One of the most damaging things that can be said of any minority is "selling out" for a bigger job. If you are black and you run for mayor, governor or president, the expectation is that you must carry the hopes of your people on your shoulders, and place their concerns above any other. It's the most delicate of political dances, and for a lot of people, it is tough to do.

When then-Rep. Harold Washington ran for mayor in Chicago in 1983, he had to appeal to a wide variety of interests. African Americans who had been shut out of city hall made it clear they wanted a black mayor, while white liberals were afraid of him being seen as the black candidate, and wanted him to speak to a broader constituency. When he spoke at rallies on the South Side of Chicago, he had one message. When speaking at a church on the North Side, he had quite a different one. He may have been talking about housing, but Washington had to master the art of speaking to different audiences. Some call it the political two-step; others consider it being politically bilingual.

In many ways, that's the dilemma Obama faces.

When he steps to the microphone, African Americans have an expectation of him, and others have a different one. He clearly has to connect with black voters, but he can't do it and alienate whites.

Rev. Jackson knows the feeling.

In 1984 he was asked to distance himself from Nation of Islam Minister Louis Farrakhan, who is perceived by non-blacks as being divisive. But among African Americans, he is largely a striking figure who speaks to black empowerment and is willing to point out white oppression. Jackson would have lost tremendous credibility among blacks had he distanced himself from Farrakhan, and he was under pressure from progressive whites to do so.

At the end of the day, he didn't, and there is no doubt he lost some white support as a result.

The delicate nature of this can be seen in the agenda that Obama is likely to advance. He has spoken traditional themes of the need for universal health care, leading our troops out of Iraq and ending the divisiveness that permeates Washington, D.C.

What won't you hear Obama speaking on constantly? Reparations. An aggressive federal affirmative action policy. Impeaching President George W. Bush.

If you listen to black radio stations and read black newspapers, you will hear many of these themes. But don't expect Obama to tout them on the campaign trail. They simply aren't looked on favorably, and he isn't likely to garner moderate votes with such rhetoric.

Understand, Obama's plan isn't to put an urban agenda on the table, something Rev. Jackson wanted to do, and the same thing Rev. Al Sharpton has talked about doing. Obama's goal is to win, and he has to manage the process as best as he can.

One question tossed to me had to do with former North Carolina Sen. John Edwards opening his campaign in the Lower Ninth Ward in New Orleans. "Why is Obama launching his campaign in Springfield, Ill.? Why not be like Edwards and go to New Orleans?"

Nice thought, but the reality is that Edwards needs to shed his label of being a rich trial lawyer, and New Orleans serves his purpose of focusing on poverty and the disenfranchised. Many voters may expect Obama to speak to issues of poverty and the plight of the poor—hey, that's what the black guy is supposed to do. Yet he must counter that by focusing on matters such as foreign policy.

Hey, it may not be the perfect scenario, and folks will undoubtedly be unhappy with his choices. But if Obama wants to be sworn in as president, he has no choice but to do the dance.

Remember, running isn't winning. Winning is winning.

February 23, 2007
Democratic Primary Changes Good News for America

THE THOUGHT OF SEEING THE DEMOCRATIC PRESIDENTIAL candidates, minus Sen. Barack Obama (D-IL) standing before a crowd in Nevada must have been a welcome sight to the party activists who have fought to break the stranglehold on the primary system by Iowa and New Hampshire.

I've never been a fan of having the candidates pour a ton of money into the two states, and if they don't do well there, their campaigns are kaput. That meant a candidate from California or any other Western state, and even some in the South, had to pray they stayed in the game until the campaign found its way to their territory.

By diversity, I'm not just meaning ethnicity. Even the casual observer could recognize that with both states being overwhelmingly white—Iowa is nearly 88 percent and New Hampshire is 96 percent—the issues sensitive to blacks, Hispanics and Asians would be virtually ignored.

Yes, education, economic development and the war in Iraq are all issues that affect us across the board. But even greater issues are those of state and regional concerns. While Iowa may care about ethanol and farm subsidies, those in the Western states will toss out mining rights and land development as primary issues.

This is the way we should look at our presidential candidates.

Instead of having them tailor a message to a few people, we should get a better representation of who should be president based on the interests of multiple states. It is a much more effective way for voters to discern who will represent America.

In fact, Democrats should be looking to expand the number of states that hold early primaries in 2012. What is the harm in having as many as six to 10 states hold their primaries in the first month or two? Yes, it will be more costly because candidates will have to spread their resources over multiple locations, but it will lend more credibility to having a candidate representative of the American people. We all know that money is already a major focus of the candidates this early, but it all serves us well.

This will no doubt hurt the feelings of residents in Iowa and New Hampshire. They take tremendous pride in their first-in-the-nation status, but they also can't deny that a ton of money drives the local economy. Radio and TV stations, as well as newspapers in both states, generate a significant amount of revenue and the hotels and coffee shops clean up because of the massive ground troops hired.

But the ego of residents in both states is immaterial. What we need to focus on is fairness and equality.

Democrats who want to stay wedded to tradition need to step back and determine what is best for America. The party will no doubt establish much better candidates for the general election, and by being inclusive, those candidates could very well drive more Americans to get interested in the process, rather than the process becoming an afterthought.

March 2, 2007
Blacks Don't Owe the Clintons a Thing

ONE OF MY ALL-TIME FAVORITE TV SHOWS is "The West Wing." On one particular episode, the Bartlet White House was pretty miffed that one of its past supporters, an influential Hispanic labor leader in California, was being courted by a potential rival.

When they see the man sitting courtside at a basketball game with their nemesis, they summon him to the White House. The White House aide (played by Rob Lowe) then begins to go after the guy, giving him menacing looks, and demanding to know why he was flirting with the other side when Bartlet's folks had done so much for him in the past.

"That was last time," he said. "What do I get this time?"

The storyline came to mind as I listened to many African American political leaders, as well as everyday voters, go on about what African Americans owe the Clintons, believing that what took place during the administration of Bill Clinton is enough to warrant their full support for Sen. Hillary Clinton in her run for the White House.

What a bunch of hogwash.

Anyone knows that in politics, what you did last year is nice, but today is a different day.

And seven years after Clinton left the White House is a long time.

There is no doubt that African Americans felt strongly about Bill Clinton. His poll numbers among blacks was sky high, and there was no group that he could count on more. He played the saxophone on Arsenio Hall's show, was as comfortable as an old-school preacher in black churches and relished when folks like Toni Morrison (foolishly) referred to him as America's first black president.

Now his wife is running, and the expectation is that the goodwill created by her husband should automatically go to Sen. Clinton.

You see, that's the kind of stuff that played well with the civil rights movement crowd. A (white) politician paid attention to a few black causes, and we provided them with lifelong support. Drop by a few black churches on your way to the ballot box, take a few pictures, and all is well. When that got old, a few political appointments here and there were enough to satisfy African Americans.

Some candidates have even run on the "my dad was good to African Americans" platform, leading ministers and civil rights leaders to toss their support their way, without demanding anything in return.

Today this generation is tired of the old games. "What have you done for me lately?" is the mantra, and it is one that various political constituencies demand of candidates.

Republicans spent a lot of time in the last election heavily courting Hispanics. But with so many in the GOP taking a strong anti-immigration stance, they are going to pay a dear price if they don't make amends before November 2008.

Mostly white evangelicals have held sway in politics the last 20 years, namely in the Republican Party. If a candidate doesn't speak aggressively to their issues—pretty much limited to gays and abortion—you can bet there will be political hell to pay.

Gays are a major force in the Democratic Party. Any presidential candidate who doesn't support gay rights—including civil unions, gay adoption or inclusion of sexual orientation in hate crimes legislation—can expect to feel the heat.

The point is everyone demands accountability, and if they don't get what they want, they make them pay at the ballot box.

Not African American political leaders, who have always talked loudly, but who run and hide when a few crumbs have been thrown their way.

That shouldn't be the case with Sen. Clinton. The love blacks have for her husband should be earned—by her. If some want to ask Sen. Barack Obama (D-IL), if he's "black enough," then they should have the courage to ask of Clinton, "What are you prepared to do for us?"

If she gives the same boilerplate speech, then they should go look for another candidate to support. She recently dropped $10,000 a month for the services of a prominent South Carolina state senator and pastor (Obama and others also tried to recruit him), hoping he will seal the deal for her with blacks in South Carolina.

Sen. Clinton, that's old school. And trust me, this generation doesn't play by the same rules as their mommas and daddies. They play for keeps. And as they say on the basketball courts in the 'hood, "You better bring it if you want to keep playing."

May 4, 2007

GOP Pro-Life in the Womb, Not Necessarily After

ASIDE FROM RUDY GIULIANI'S TORTUROUS EXPLANATION of his views on abortion, it was easy to discern after Thursday's debate that the candidates running for the Republican presidential nomination are staunch advocates of life, namely when it comes to abortion.

In fact, they were passionate on the issue, and some made it clear that nothing is more important than life itself.

Former Massachusetts Gov. Mitt Romney: "Well, I've always been personally pro-life."

When asked about the Terri Schiavo case, he replied: "I think the Congress's job is to make sure that laws are respecting the sanctity of life."

California Rep. Duncan Hunter evoked the memory of a late president to explain his position: "Ronald Reagan said, on the question of life, 'When there's a question, err on the side of life.'"

Kansas Sen. Sam Brownback was the most eloquent on the subject: "I believe life is one of the central issues of our day, and I believe that every human life at every phase is unique, is beautiful, is a child of a loving God, period."

He later added: "Her life is sacred. Even if it's in that difficult moment that she's in at that point in time, that life is sacred, and we should stand for life in all its circumstances."

On stem cell research, Brownback said, "It is not necessary to kill a human life for us to heal people."

That last line caught my attention because that is often something we hear from victims rights groups, law enforcement and prosecutors when someone is put to death for committing a crime.

But if you take the candidates at face value, then why hold the same view when it comes to the death penalty?

Now, for the purposes of getting everything out in the open: I'm pro-choice. Does that mean I'm marching in the streets advocating abortion? No. For me, it comes down to a woman choosing. And just like Giuliani, I hate abortion and prefer for women not to make that choice. Will some suggest that this is counter to my Christian faith? Absolutely. But it is a difficult position, and one that I have wrestled with and continue to do so.

Yet I also support the death penalty. There are individuals who should lose their life for committing heinous crimes. And yes, I have struggled mightily, and would certainly say that my position has softened on this issue, just like it has on being pro-choice.

But even with all that, it's still important to at least philosophically explore the issue of being a staunch pro-life advocate, yet stop the moment the child is born.

"I believe that every human life at every phase is unique, is beautiful, is a child of a loving God, period." Those are the words of Brownback, but does not that person— even that hardened criminal—fall under the same banner?

Folks, it's hard to say on one hand that every life—at every phase—is important, but then say, "Send them to the death chamber!" Those two are diametrically opposed to each other.

And I'll be the first to tell you that many Christians—especially right-wing conservatives—are staunch anti-abortion advocates on Monday. And on Tuesday, if there is an execution, they are right there supporting that one as well.

It would have been nice had debate moderator Chris Matthews forced the candidates to deal with this issue.

But let's also expand the pro-life dialogue. Where do the Republican candidates stand on funding Head Start for children? Is that not part of the development of human life? Are we going to see Republican candidates seek to change Medicaid laws to allow dentists to better care for those who get government assistance? Or are we willing to see another case like Deamonte Driver, a 12-year-old Maryland boy who died because his family lost their Medicaid, and the boy's abscess, which could have been cured with an $80 tooth extraction, led to his brain becoming infected?

Are the Republican candidates going to vigorously fight for expanded pre-natal care for mothers in many inner cities around America, where the infant mortality rate rivals that of some Third World countries?

What is needed—on both sides—is a full-scale discussion on actually what it means to be pro-life.

Life is indeed precious. And just as I have tussled with my personal views on being pro-choice and supportive of the death penalty, the pro-lifers should really examine whether they are as passionate about life beyond the womb.

May 11, 2007

Giuliani Must Confront Abortion Critics Head-On

FORMER NEW YORK CITY MAYOR RUDY GIULIANI has cultivated an image as a tough-as-nails guy who wasn't afraid to face down mobsters as a U.S. attorney; targeted rising crime in the city with tough initiatives and showed his resolve in the face of unbearable tragedy on Sept. 11, 2001.

So why is the guy looking like a bumbling fool when he has been pressed on whether he supports a woman's right to an abortion?

Rudy, stop with the mealy-mouth responses. You look like an idiot. It's time for some straight talk. So, just in case your advisers are on the fence and afraid to alienate the right wing of the Republican Party, I'm offering a speech for you to use. Free of charge.

"Ladies and gentleman. When I embarked on this run for the presidency, it was with the full intention of providing a vision of America that would put us in a better position for generations to come.

"We live in a world of uncertainty. American armed forces are engaged in a war against terror all over the world, namely in Iraq and Afghanistan. On the home front, we confront the reality of failing schools, the loss of manufacturing jobs overseas and reliance on foreign oil that clearly borders on an addiction.

"In short, all is not well in America.

"But despite all of this, we are a great nation. We are a country that fully respects the rights of individuals to make decisions that better their lives. Americans have led the world in innovation, and our shores continue to be sought after as a land of opportunity for people all across the globe.

"So that brings me to where we stand today on one of the most personal—and volatile issues—that we have confronted in our nation's history.

"When the U.S. Supreme Court ruled 34 years ago that various state laws that prohibited abortion violated the right to privacy under the Constitution's Due Process Clause in the 14th Amendment, it was hailed as a landmark decision. And those against it have continued to assert that the ruling is legally unjust, and that it has led to the deaths of millions of unborn children.

"We all must recognize that no matter what side we are on, abortion is one issue that forces us to choose.

"I realize that my party has historically been opposed to abortion, and I respect that. It is the right of the party, and its members, to state their intentions. But like it or not, I'm an American. I'm a Republican. I love my party; have always loved my party and will never leave the party.

"But I'm also pro-choice on abortion.

"I know that my statements over the past few months have led to intense criticism, and I'll admit that I have not been as clear on where I stand, partly in trying to appeal to longtime Republicans.

"Yet I have to be who I am. And the Rudy Giuliani who wants to represent the nation in the White House is the same Rudy Giuliani who has fought to protect that same U.S. Constitution that has guaranteed a woman a right to choose. Would I prefer a woman to make such a decision? No. I want to see children raised in loving families. But that is not always the case, and we have to simply be honest about this.

"I am who I am. And if there are Republican voters who feel so strongly about this issue, then they can feel free to support another candidate. But if you care about terrorism; if you care about an environmentally sound country; if you desire a strong economy that protects jobs and evens the playing field for workers and business; if you want to able to walk the streets of your neighborhood safely; if you want to see America prosper, then I'm the man for the job.

"We will never agree on every issue. That's called democracy. And make no mistake, we are the world's greatest democracy. But when making a choice on a candidate, study the totality of his or her views. And even with there being an issue like abortion, I'm confident the American people will see my deep and abiding passion for a stronger nation, and make the right choice.

"Thank you, and God bless America."

May 18, 2007
Paul's 9/11 Explanation Deserves Debate

FORMER NEW YORK MAYOR RUDY GIULIANI was declared the winner of Tuesday's Republican presidential debate in South Carolina, largely for his smack down of Texas Rep. Ron Paul, who suggested that America's foreign policy contributed to the destruction on Sept. 11, 2001.

Paul, who is more of a libertarian than a Republican, was trying to offer some perspective on the pitfalls of an interventionist policy by the American government in the affairs of the Middle East and other countries.

"Have you ever read about the reasons they attacked us? They attack us because we've been over there. We've been bombing Iraq for 10 years," he said.

That set Giuliani off.

"That's really an extraordinary statement," said Giuliani. "As someone who lived through the attack of Sept. 11, that we invited the attack because we were attacking Iraq; I don't think I've ever heard that before and I've heard some pretty absurd explanations for Sept. 11."

As the crowd applauded wildly, Giuliani demanded that Paul retract his statements.

Paul tried to explain the process known as "blowback"—which is the result of someone else's action coming back to afflict you—but the audience drowned him out as the other candidates tried to pounce on him.

After watching all the network pundits laud Giuliani, it struck me that they must be the most clueless folks in the world.

First, Giuliani must be an idiot to not have heard Paul's rationale before. That issue has been raised countless times in the last six years by any number of experts.

Second, when we finish with our emotional response, it would behoove us to actually think about what Paul said and make the effort to understand his rationale.

Granted, Americans were severely damaged by the hijacking of U.S. planes, and it has resulted in a worldwide fight against terror. Was it proper for the United States to respond to the attack? Of course! But should we, as a matter of policy, and moral decency, learn to think and comprehend that our actions in one part of the world could very well come back to hurt us, or, as Paul would say, blow back in our face? Absolutely. His real problem wasn't his analysis, but how it came out of his mouth.

What has been overlooked is that Paul based his position on the effects of the 1953 ouster by the CIA of Iranian Prime Minister Mohammad Mossadegh.

An excellent account of this story is revealed in Stephen Kinzer's alarming and revealing book, *Overthrow: America's Century of Regime Change from Hawaii to Iraq*, where he writes that Iran was establishing a government close to a democracy. But Mossadegh wasn't happy that the profit from the country's primary resource—oil—was not staying in the country.

Instead, the Anglo-Iranian Oil Company (now known British Petroleum, or BP) was getting 93 percent of the profits. Mossadegh didn't like that, and wanted a 50-50 split. Kinzer writes that that didn't sit too well with the British government, but it didn't want to use force to protect its interests. But their biggest friend, the United States, didn't mind, and sought to undermine Mossadegh's tenure as president. After all kinds of measures that disrupted the nation, a coup was financed and led by President Dwight Eisenhower's CIA, and the Shah of Iran was installed as the leader. We trained his goon squads, thus angering generations of Iranians for meddling in that nation's affairs.

As Paul noted, what happened in 1953 had a direct relationship to the takeover of the U.S. Embassy in 1979. We viewed that as terrorists who dared attack America. They saw it as ending years of oppression at the hands of the ruthless U.S.-backed Shah regime.

As Americans, we believe in forgiving and forgetting, and are terrible at understanding how history affects us today. We are arrogant in not recognizing that when we benefit, someone else may suffer. That will lead to resentment and anger, and if suppressed, will boil over one day.

Does that provide a moral justification for what the terrorists did on Sept. 11? Of course not. But we should at least attempt to understand why.

Think about it. Do we have the moral justification to explain the killings of more than 100,000 Iraqis as a result of this war? Can we defend the efforts to overthrow other governments whose actions we perceived would jeopardize American business interests?

The debate format didn't give Paul the time to explain all of this. But I'm confident this is what he was saying. And yes, we need to understand history and how it plays a vital role in determining matters today.

At some point we have to accept the reality that playing big brother to the world—and yes, sometimes acting as a bully by wrongly asserting our military might—means that Americans alive at the time may not feel the effects of our foreign policy, but their innocent children will.

Even the Bible says that the children will pay for the sins of their fathers.

June 1, 2007

Democrats: Ignore Critics, Take the Debate Fight to FOX News Channel

EMBOLDENED BY MOVEON.ORG and other liberal activists, the Democratic presidential candidates are running as fast as they can away from any debate that could potentially be shown on Fox News Channel, and frankly, that is a mistake.

We all know that FNC doesn't just tilt to the right; it is embedded on the political right. It has been the choice of the Republican Party, and the on-air folks there don't try to hide that. That nonsense about "We Report. You Decide" is clearly a joke, considering the fact that its talk show hosts are decidedly conservative.

And hey, if that's how they want to run their shop, fine. Rupert Murdoch has as much right to run something he owns the way he sees fit as I do.

But this has proved to be troubling for Democratic activists, who see Murdoch and the leader of his channel, Roger Ailes, as the devil incarnate. After MoveOn.org fired up its masses, it was effective in scuttling a debate in Arizona a few months ago that was to be aired on Fox.

Now MoveOn.org has gone after a plan by the Congressional Black Caucus to stop Democrats from having a debate on Fox because of its political stance (the institute has also scheduled a debate on CNN, where I am employed as a contributor).

As a result, the leading Democratic candidates—Sens. Hillary Clinton (D-NY), and Barack Obama (D-IL)—and former Sen. John Edwards, along with several others, have announced they will not participate in the debate. The only candidate with any cache who hasn't pulled out is Sen. Joe Biden (D-Del). This has pretty much ended any chances of the debate happening.

And frankly, that is a shame.

African Americans are the most reliable block of voters for the Democratic Party. But every election cycle, the presidential candidates often ignore issues that speak to the minds and hearts of African Americans. So the CBC's institute felt that this is one way it could have some sort of impact on the election. And if you include the CNN debate, and the two being hosted on PBS by Tavis Smiley, this will mark an unprecedented number of debates that are specific to black interests.

But the MoveOn.org folks—and members of a related group, ColorOfChange. org—are vigorously fighting to ensure that it doesn't happen. And they have so far succeeded.

I've had the leaders of ColorofChange.org on my radio show on WVON-AM in Chicago, and the concern about the representation of African Americans on the network is a valid one. But instead of running away, I say you look them dead in the eye and call them out.

Don't just say, "We won't show up." Demand that Fox change the representation to ensure that credible voices are at the table. And use their airwaves to put them in check.

I never understood folks who would say they would never go on Bill O'Reilly's show. Prior to joining CNN, I did his show nearly 10 times and was happy to go toe-to-toe with Bill. He rarely raised his voice; we always had a cordial conversation and I made my points as he made his. The only person who was afraid to take me on was Sean Hannity, and I threw down the gauntlet to him personally (Sean, I'm still willing to debate you anywhere, anytime).

Obama, Clinton and Edwards should go on Fox and show them up. They want to be president of the United States. Well, tell Fox viewers how you want to change America and show them what you are made of.

If the Democrats see Fox as a big bully, then go on the network and punch the bully in the mouth. The liberal bloggers should be willing to take them on when it comes to political philosophy. Otherwise, the Democrats will simply look like the cowards Republicans often accuse them of being.

June 7, 2007

Dems Must Find a Way to Embrace Faith On the Campaign Trail

ALL OF THE ATTENTION THIS WEEK has been focused on the two presidential debates that took place in New Hampshire, but perhaps the most substantive forum was that held by Sojourners/Call to Renewal at George Washington University.

Moderated by CNN's Soledad O'Brien, the non-debate—more of a discussion—featured the three leading Democratic presidential candidates, Sens. Hillary Clinton and Barack Obama, and former Sen. John Edwards. It would have been much better to have that group expanded to include the other candidates, but the drawback to speaking to eight candidates—10 in the case of the Republicans—would have made it unwieldy.

But to hear each candidate speak for 15 minutes on a variety of issues was a blessing in that we weren't forced to endure some of the silly bells, whistles and 60- and 30-second responses that we have come to expect.

O'Brien asked the candidates a variety of questions that have been typical in the debates—about the Israeli/Palestinian conflict, the war in Iraq and gays in the military—but to hear the three speak to issues of faith was important because many believe it will be a defining issue of this campaign.

Ever since the Rev. Jerry Falwell's Moral Majority kick-started its focus on politics in 1979, and was followed by the Rev. Pat Robertson's Christian Coalition, and now James Dobson's "Focus on the Family", the religious right has dominated the evangelical political landscape, which has mostly been a debate about abortion and homosexuality.

And while GOP members embraced Jesus about as much as they wrapped themselves in the U.S. flag, Democrats treated evangelicals as if they were lepers, isolating them as nutty Christians hell-bent on destroying the nation.

In fact, during a post-discussion on CNN's "Paula Zahn Now," Sen. Joe Biden (D-DE), essentially said Democrats acted more "agnostic" than understanding on matters of faith.

Yet it was refreshing to see Clinton, the most guarded of all the candidates, take the mask off and share more of herself with the public. Either she's one heck of an actress or she was really genuine as she discussed her faith and how it helped her get through her husband's affair with Monica Lewinsky.

Edwards did a good job dancing around the gays in the military question during Sunday's debate, but O'Brien forced him to further explain his position, which was vital to better understanding what he meant. Sitting across from the person asking the question—and being the only one on the stage—makes it tough to avoid it. Even that grin of his gave it all away. He knew he couldn't escape it this time.

When the forum's organizer, Jim Wallis, asked Obama about how to deal with poverty in America, the candidate gave him a detailed answer, although he went on way too long. His answer was about seven minutes, taking up nearly half of his allotted time. But at least he raised the point about providing education opportunities for inmates, helping women with pre-natal care and increasing the minimum wage.

As Wallis even mentioned, poverty didn't come up during the Dems' Sunday debate. And it should have.

What these three candidates—along with the other five—must do is not treat the issue of faith as if it is a side issue. The reality is that for some, faith is a part of who they are. But for many, it's the essence of who they are. Edwards, Clinton and Obama showed their humanity by allowing a peek into their views on the issue, and that's a good thing.

Democrats can do themselves a huge favor by casting many of our domestic issues within a faith and/or moral prism. When it becomes ideological, it's easy to dismiss what they say as rhetoric. But by making it personal, and connecting it with the religious teachings many of us have grown up with, then it can cause a certain level of discomfort and introspection.

Or as the Rev. Frederick Douglass Haynes III of Dallas would say, they need to "bowl down your alley and sit in your pew."

June 8, 2007

Obama's "Quiet Riots" Are For Real

CONSERVATIVE CRITICS HAVE BEEN LIGHTING UP the airwaves and blogs for the last 48 hours since Sen. Barack Obama's speech to the Hampton University Annual Ministers' Conference raised the combustible topic of the burning anger among the nation's poor African Americans.

Much of this was the result of a terrible story by Bob Lewis of the Associated Press, who wrote in his lead that "Democratic presidential candidate Barack Obama said Tuesday that the Bush administration has done nothing to defuse a "quiet riot" among blacks that threatens to erupt just as riots in Los Angeles did 15 years ago."

After seeing the story I was stunned to read such a thing, and immediately sought the transcript of Obama's speech. In reading it, Obama used the word "riot" nine times, the phrase "quiet riot" three times and never suggested that America was on the verge of seeing African Americans lash out like they did during the Los Angeles riots in 1992.

What Obama did try to do was give the 8,000 attendees and anyone else watching an understanding of what is a real problem in America's inner cities—and more importantly, his blueprint for fixing the problem.

"(Quiet riots) happen when a sense of disconnect settles in and hope dissipates," Obama said. "Despair takes hold and young people all across this country look at the way the world is and believe that things are never going to get any better.

"You tell yourself, my school will always be second rate. You tell yourself, there will never be a good job waiting for me to excel at. You tell yourself, I will never be able to afford a place that I can be proud of and call my home.

"That despair quietly simmers and makes it impossible to build strong communities and neighborhoods. And then one afternoon a jury says, 'Not guilty'— or a hurricane hits New Orleans—and that despair is revealed for the world to see."

We all saw what that looked like when Hurricane Katrina hit the Gulf Coast, and it was ugly and sad. Even worse was our government's response to the crisis.

But folks, this goes on every day. And we do a very good job of pretending that it doesn't matter.

Check out what often quoted conservative "thinker" Dinesh D'Souza had to say about this: "A quiet riot. Now certainly that's the best kind of riot, because no buildings get burned and nobody gets stampeded or knifed or shot. And if it's a really quiet riot, then we don't even have to listen to shouting and can continue to work or read or watch TV without disruption. It would really be nice if all riots could be quiet riots."

See, guys like D'Souza, who know nothing about the conditions of the nation's urban poor, want to sit in their ivory towers and pretend that if you just read, write and work hard, all will be well. And there is no doubt that work ethic and a willingness to do better are paramount, and encouraged—even by African Americans. But it's also critical to know that there are many who are working and working and working, and don't seem to be making any headway.

I don't sit in a think tank and write papers and books like D'Souza and these other wholly ignorant conservative bloggers. In fact, most of my time is spent at 1000 E. 87th St., in the heart of Chicago's South Side. That's the headquarters of WVON, where I host a morning talk show. When I ran the *Dallas Weekly*, it was on the South Side of Dallas on Martin Luther King Drive. (Why is it that the black parts of town are always on the south side? Maybe because north means going up and south means going down.)

And what Obama spoke of, I see every day. I can look out our bay window and see men and women going to work each day, trying to make ends meet, and they often don't. I see women walking their kids to school just to keep them safe, but inevitably, some don't come home, like the 31 Chicago Public Schools students who have been murdered this year. Oh, I definitely see the urban terrorists—gang members and drug dealers—who tear the fabric of the black community apart with their rampant violence.

People shouldn't have to endure "quiet riots." They should be shouting from the rooftops, and we should hear their pleas. See, if someone is stranded on a roof and the tides are rising, two things must happen if they want to be rescued: First, they must make themselves visible for the helicopter to see. Second, the helicopter must lower a line to help them up. The pilot can hook up the belt and do all the work, but the individual must be a willing participant.

Obama gave a voice to the voiceless. As he said, they must do their part. They must work hard to escape poverty by going to school, do a good job at work and not be involved in crime.

Let's not treat them as if they are non-existent. If we remain quiet in the face of chronic conditions, shame on us for saying, "God bless America," because we surely are not being a blessing to our fellow Americans.

June 15, 2007

Dems Should Invest in Poor Whites

WHEN SEN. BARACK OBAMA (D-IL) raised the issue of the anger and despair among poor African Americans due to failing schools and rampant poverty in several recent speeches, the general consensus among the media elite was "been there, heard that."

In fact, the focus in the aftermath of his speech wasn't actually on the problems of poverty, but on his mention of riots. That must have been sexier than the real issue he was raising.

Whether we want to admit to it or not, poverty is forever on the backburner in the minds of most people. That is, unless we are put in that position—or hit up for money by our poor family members.

The initial reaction to the cries of help after Hurricane Katrina was tremendous. But poverty isn't a one-shot deal; it must be dealt with in a much stronger and more sustained way.

Many may have assumed that after Katrina, the face of poverty is that of an African American. But to act as if whites, along with Hispanics, are not poor, is a huge mistake.

According to the 2005 U.S. Census, 37 million Americans lived in poverty, including 13 million children. Between 1993 and 2000, the poverty rate was on the decline. Yet from 2001 to 2005, it was on the rise.

The National Poverty Center reports that "poverty rates for blacks and Hispanics greatly exceed the national average. In 2004, 24.7 percent of blacks and 21.9 percent of Hispanics were poor, compared to 8.6 percent of non-Hispanic whites and 9.8 percent of Asians."

So is the nation's poor confined to Chicago, Detroit or Compton, Calif.? No. Under the headline "Vital Signs," the *Wall Street Journal* reported this week on the top 20 states with the highest percentages of individuals living below the poverty level in 2005. Those were: Mississippi, Louisiana, Washington, D.C., New Mexico, West Virginia, Texas, Arkansas, Alabama, Kentucky, Oklahoma, South Carolina, Tennessee, North Carolina, Georgia, Montana, Arizona, Oregon, Idaho, New York and South Dakota.

I'll be that if you took a tour of Montana, Idaho, Oregon, West Virginia, South Dakota, and significant portions of Georgia and Alabama, you would see a large number of whites who would raise their hands if a poverty count were done.

Now, we all know that no one is truly campaigning for the poor vote. Candidates may generally raise the issue, but poverty didn't come up in the first two Republican debates. The Democrats also conveniently ignored the issue.

I fault them, but also those moderating the discussion. They were in charge of asking the questions, and should have done a much better job of dealing with the issue.

I got to thinking about poor white Americans when I was talking with a friend about the 1984 and 1988 presidential campaigns of the Rev. Jesse Jackson Sr.

Although he was defined as "the black candidate," Jackson was often ignored when he raised the plight of farmers in Iowa, rural citizens in Alabama and the working poor in West Virginia. Ask political observers on the campaign trail and you will see a candidate who was equally at ease in the slums of Harlem as he was in the dilapidated portions of Georgia.

Yet among those top 20 poor states, Democrats often lose to the GOP. There are multiple reasons—God and guns are at the top of the list—but part of the issue is that Dems have not been able to connect with voters in those states on issues that truly affect them. If they are effective at reaching out to poor blacks, why ignore poor whites?

If I were Obama—or Sen. Hillary Clinton, former Sen. John Edwards or any of the other candidates—I would take time off from raising big bundles of cash in Los Angeles, New York and Chicago to take the campaign to those small, out-of-the-way towns that never get to see a presidential candidate. Go to the schools that look like they belong in a Third World nation. Visit the rural towns where the lone hospital has closed up, and the town's poor must drive miles just to see a doctor. Check out the areas where the infant mortality rate rivals that of developing countries.

Bring the cameras and notepads to these forgotten places and show America what it often ignores.

Many of these towns, especially in the South, are separated because of years of racial separation. You stay on your side of town, I stay on mine. But a poor white man may not realize that he may have more in common with his black brother, and that is a lack of economic and educational opportunities.

The skin of both may be different, but their different hues will never help them pay their bills. Broke is broke.

June 22, 2007

Bloomberg's America is Different from Ross Perot's

POLITICAL JUNKIES ARE EXCITED AND ELECTRIFIED over a potential independent presidential bid by New York Mayor Michael Bloomberg, and for good reason.

If the billionaire jumps into the race, he would be the 900th candidate to declare for the presidency; he is worth $5 billion—some say as much as $20 billion—and the thought of a serious third-party bid hasn't been a reality since diminutive billionaire Ross Perot garnered 19 percent in the 1992 election, helping Democratic challenger Bill Clinton beat President George H.W. Bush to win the presidency.

It is assumed that Bloomberg would have to drop $500 million of his own money to compete for the White House, and considering he spent $140 million on two successful campaigns for mayor of New York City, he has shown that he's not afraid to toss a few dollars around to get what he wants.

Clearly his run is being compared to Perot's bid in 1992, and on the surface, that make sense. Dissatisfaction with the Republican and Democratic choices led to Americans pining for a new voice 15 years ago. We wanted someone who eschewed partisan politics and who saw himself as bidding to save American from ruin.

While simultaneously declaring that he doesn't want the job, Bloomberg has worked feverishly to burnish his national appeal by giving substantive policy speeches about non-New York City issues; traveling the nation and speaking with numerous political leaders, revamping his Web site and now, ditching the Republican Party label (he was a lifelong Democrat) that he picked up prior to his inaugural mayoral run in 2001.

On paper, he has the bona fides to run for president, but other than being a billionaire and calling for change in America, there is a significant difference between a potential Bloomberg candidacy and that of Perot's: The nation clearly isn't the same today as it was then.

Go back to Feb. 20, 1992, when Perot appeared on CNN's "Larry King Live" and opined about a number of critical issues. The nation was in a mess. We were buried in a recession, Bush had gone back on his no-tax pledge and his Republican supporters were angry and out for blood.

In steps a tough-talking Texan who brought a no-nonsense approach to politics. His voice was fresh—albeit a bit squeaky—he didn't bite his tongue on the tough issues, and then, of course, singer/actress Cher phoned in and expressed her support for him running for the White House.

So Perot made it clear: Get me on 50 ballots and I'm your man.

That led to the creation of the Reform Party, a group of grassroots activists tired of the established political parties. The nation was begging for a change and Perot was their man.

Fast forward to today. There is no national clamor for a Bloomberg candidacy. He is a sitting politician who is known more for being a great manager than someone who will speak truth to power and generate attention with soaring oratory. In fact, he is downright boring in his speeches. America is just as dissatisfied today as it was in 1992, but this time, it's about the Iraq war. A lot of folks thought the nation spoke by giving Democrats the Congress in November, but that still hasn't changed the war. So how will Bloomberg fix the most critical issue facing the country?

Where is Bloomberg's constituency? Is it Republicans who are desperate for a standard bearer in the mold of Ronald Reagan? Bloomberg doesn't appeal to the GOP base—he's liberal, from New York and is Jewish (be honest, if he was a hardcore conservative and a Baptist, they would be falling over him).

He might appeal to disenchanted Democrats like Perot did, but the left is energized by the last election, and the last thing they want to do is back a candidate who may keep them out of the White House after eight years of George W. Bush.

The New York Times has reported that Bloomberg's camp has studied the Perot race, but that's technical stuff. There is no passion, excitement or a significant rallying point to jump behind a Bloomberg run. And with the possibility of Rudy Giuliani winning the GOP nomination, Sen. Hillary Clinton grabbing the Dems' top spot, the idea of choosing between three New Yorkers is too much to handle.

At the end of the day, Bloomberg is simply a rich guy looking to spend what it takes to move into 1600 Pennsylvania Avenue. And that simply won't cut it with the American people.

June 29, 2007

Obama Blows Another Debate Opportunity

FOR SEN. BARACK OBAMA, last night's Democratic presidential debate at Howard University should have been his version of a fastball hitter getting a perfect pitch down the middle of the plate with the count set at three balls and no strikes.

Instead of swinging for the fences, Obama took one looking.

I wasn't in Washington, D.C. because I was hosting Paula Zahn's show on CNN, but all of the folks I've talked with said the room was hot, the audience was packed with some of the biggest names in black America and there was a general feeling that many were there to shower Obama with the love and affection you would expect with him being the only African American in the race for president.

So, on my Chicago radio show this morning—on the only black-owned, black talk station in a city with the second largest collection of black folks outside of Africa—what was the first sound bite I played? Sen. Hillary Clinton's remarks about black women and HIV/AIDS. What was No. 2? Sen. Joe Biden, discussing the U.S. Supreme Court's decision on race and education. What was No. 3? Rep. Dennis Kucinich's denunciation of mandatory minimums.

Obama was trailing behind.

That is telling, because others who were in the room came away with the same conclusion.

But don't just rely on my analysis, go to www.messagejury.com.

On the Web site are sample results of how voters in early primary states watching the debates rated the candidates based on their statements.

Prior to last night, Clinton had a pre-debate score of 5.3. After? It was 7.0, a 1.7-point bump; the highest among the eight candidates. Sen. Christopher Dodd began with a 3.7 and ended with a 5.1 (a 1.4-point increase). Biden started at 3.5 and ended at 4.7 (a 1.2-point increase). The biggest winner of the night was Kucinich, who began at 2.3 and ended at 5.1, a jump of 2.8 points.

Obama began at 6.1 and ended at 6.6, just a bump of half a point (even former Alaska Sen. Mike Gravel had a larger increase—0.8—than Obama).

I didn't need an elaborate dial-up test to come up with those results (well, maybe for Dodd, who I've pretty much written off).

So what gives with Obama? How can a candidate who speaks so eloquently and passionately on the campaign trial come off as flat and unemotional during debates? (I thought that was supposed to be Clinton's role!)

Most of it lies in the fact that Obama dislikes debates. During my interview with him to air on Monday at 10 P.M. EST on TV One Cable Network, Obama admitted that he is not enamored with debates, saying they provide little time to speak on issues. He prefers to use his time to "inform."

And he really doesn't like the idea of sound bites driving a campaign. That's understandable; politicians prefer to expound.

But it's time for him to wake up to reality.

When he has a campaign rally that attracts 20,000 voters, that's one heckuva turnout. But when there is a debate and 2 million people are watching, you can influence a lot more people.

He is riding on being the anti-establishment candidate who wants to avoid the normal rules of the campaign. But common sense suggests that style *and* substance are required when people vote for commander-in-chief.

Based on all the current polls, Obama is running second to Clinton. This isn't a guy who needs to play it this safe. He has to know when to take his shot and go for it.

Because he was speaking before a nearly all-black audience, Obama had to tread carefully. Although he was speaking before what some may view as the "home team," he also has the most difficult job because he has to be inclusive and represent all Americans. He can't appear to be pro-black and alienate white voters. But he also can't be so racially non-threatening that black voters—who by and large don't know him as well as Clinton (by virtue of husband Bill)—are left puzzled by his lack of forcefulness when speaking to issues they hold near and dear.

His image-makers and debate-preppers are going to have to step up their game— or be replaced—if he is going to overtake Clinton. She has come out of each debate looking strong, speaking passionately and decisive on issues and appearing to be able to master the format better than Obama (and the other candidates).

My good buddy, former NBA player Spud Webb, says a great basketball player is a triple threat; one who can shoot, pass and dribble.

Sen. Obama, your game needs some work. You're good on the stump and you can raise money, but if you aren't able to master the debates and speak to the minds *and* hearts of people, then your speech in Denver at the Democratic National Convention next August won't be the final one we hear. That spot will be reserved for Clinton.

July 27, 2007

Clinton/Obama Throwdown A Good Thing For Dems

AFTER MONTHS OF DANCING, dodging, love taps and bear hugs, Democratic presidential frontrunners, Sens. Hillary Clinton (D-NY), and Barack Obama (D-IL), finally went after each other with gusto.

Sure, I know we're five months from the first primary and no candidate wants to peak too early—or get themselves into trouble with an early attack—but it's evident the two of them have created enough distance between themselves and the other six candidates that, barring a meltdown, they will duke it out for the nomination.

So it's time they stop fooling around, lob a few grenades and see what happens.

It all started, surprisingly, with a question from one of the more than three dozen people who had their questions aired on the CNN-YouTube debate Monday at The Citadel in Charleston, S.C.

Stephen Sorta of Diamond Bar, Calif., asked: "In 1982, Anwar Sadat traveled to Israel, a trip that resulted in a peace agreement that has lasted ever since. In the spirit of that type of bold leadership, would you be willing to meet separately, without precondition, during the first year of your administration, in Washington or anywhere else, with the leaders of Iran, Syria, Venezuela, Cuba and North Korea, in order to bridge the gap that divides our countries?"

Obama said he would meet with the leaders.

"The notion that somehow not talking to countries is punishment to them—which has been the guiding diplomatic principle of this administration—is ridiculous," he said, going on to acknowledge that even when President Ronald Reagan called the Soviet Union the "evil empire," he continued to talk to the nation's leaders.

That led Clinton to follow, not wasting time in trying to expose what some consider to be Obama's biggest drawback: lack of experience in national politics.

"Well, I will not promise to meet with the leaders of these countries during my first year. I will promise a very vigorous diplomatic effort because I think it is not that you promise a meeting at that high a level before you know what the intentions are," she said. "I don't want to be used for propaganda purposes."

Bringing up the rear—and that's becoming a consistent position for him—was former Sen. John Edwards, who said he also would meet with the leaders in his first year.

But instead of allowing her well-timed power shot at Obama to marinate, Clinton decided to continue the verbal assault, telling an Iowa newspaper the next day that the junior senator from Illinois was naive on foreign policy.

That gave Obama his opening. He questioned her Iraq vote, and then compared her position to that of Bush/Cheney.

It then grew surreal when Republican candidates Mitt Romney and John McCain seemed to slam Obama, thus agreeing with Clinton.

Is all this fascinating to political hacks and irrelevant to the voting public? Yes and no.

Clinton has maintained a sizeable lead from the outset of this campaign, and she is trying to protect that. Obama, although he has raised more money, is stuck in the polls. Although in second place, he hasn't chipped away at her lead.

Her goal is simple: portray herself as far above him in terms of dealing with worldly issues. For Obama, the goal's to cast Clinton as a throwback to the days of barroom brawls with the GOP that defined the two-term presidency of her husband.

But the real issue for the voter is that we get to see these two locking horns in an effort to see how they stand up to scrutiny, as well as challenge each other directly.

It's easy to say they must attack the Bush administration, but that is a given. At some point, Clinton and Obama must go after each other in order to show who has the mettle for the job.

This will not be the last time the two of them throw a few roundhouses. They have spent the past six months like boxers in the early rounds—dancing, bobbing and weaving, trying to stalk one another. Now it's time to start throwing some punches. And in a slugfest, you can bet the final rounds will be full of flurries, punches and counterpunches.

Like it or not, there can be only one winner. And that's not the person with the biggest bank account or the most endorsements. It's the one who has the heart, passion, stamina and willingness to use everything in his or her arsenal to win the job.

When thinking of these two and the fight for the Democratic nomination, all I can think of is what longtime boxing referee Mills Lane used to say to the boxers when he finished reading them the fight rules: "Let's get it on!"

July 27, 2007

YouTubers Show America What it Really Cares About

AMERICA, THANK YOU.

Thanks for advancing the critical issues facing our nation beyond Iraq, immigration and abortion.

Important? Yes. Absolutely the only issues we care about? No.

In the wake of Monday's CNN-YouTube debate, many of my mainstream media colleagues are throwing cold water on the debate, suggesting that it wasn't that big of a deal.

Julie Mason, *Houston Chronicle*: "Only a guilty sense of obligation forced the blog to watch that CNN/YouTube Democratic debate tonight." But she did admit the idea of voters asking questions was good, although it was "gimmicky."

David Hinckley, *New York Daily News*: "At evening's end, even the most hard-wired new-media enthusiast would have had a hard time selling this evening as the night the old system crashed."

Tim Cuprisin, *Milwaukee Journal-Sentinel*, "The Internet makes everybody a critic—social critic, political critic or entertainment critic. But it doesn't necessarily make those questioners good interrogators." A good number of people found the debate refreshing, although it's easy to find small quirks with things here and there.

What we must come to accept is that there is often a disconnect between what the pundits find to be important, as opposed to the general public.

My research team here at CNN determined that based on a lot of the submissions, the top questions sent in focused on education (16 percent); health care/insurance/obesity (9 percent); energy/environment (5 percent); Iraq (4 percent); immigration (3 percent); gay rights (2 percent); religion (2 percent); Darfur, Sudan (2 percent); drug trade/war (1 percent).

Of course, this isn't a technical breakdown of where Americans stand, but it sure is a good barometer.

The fundamental problems with debates in the past is that they have been the sole province of the media and political elite (meaning boring and drab), serving as a forum for them (okay, us) to decide what you need to be focused on. For instance, foreign policy is made to be a big issue in these forums, and the issue of experience, but it has been 47 years since we sent someone from the U.S. Senate—John F. Kennedy—to the White House. The only foreign policy trips then-Texas Gov. George W. Bush had under his belt were trips to Mexico (no, not spring break jaunts to Cancun).

Not only that, the smug media elite somehow believe they have a birthright to address candidates. We look down on the common man and woman, believing they don't have the requisite skills to ask the tough questions the candidates should answer.

Go to barbershops, salons, bars, community centers, churches and schools, and you will hear people going back and forth on the various candidates and where they stand.

Don't think for a second that I'm dismissing what we do as a craft. We have a certain skill set that others don't have, and that is vital. Holding a candidate accountable to the facts is critical. I slammed bloggers a couple of years ago when I said that they weren't going to supplant journalists. A guy sitting on his computer and banging out his opinion—without any basis of fact—with a blog is nothing but a glorified diarist. But when you actually put perspective behind it, along with interviews with those involved, then it's a different story.

When I interviewed Sen. Barack Obama (D-IL), for an hour on TV One Cable Network—you can see clips at www.tvoneonline.com—most of the questions came from viewers. Oftentimes subjects come on my radio show on WVON-AM in Chicago and don't want to take questions. I usually say no; the people should be able to talk to a CEO or a politician directly.

Life is much different when you have to answer directly to the voter. Looking at that father who has lost a son in the war on Iraq or a woman with breast cancer taking off her wig to show her balding head makes a big difference.

Not only that, CNN reported that the network drew 407,000 people in the hard-to-reach 18-34 demo out of a total of 2.55 million. That's the sector that needs to be more engaged in politics, and the fact that so many watched a debate is vital to the next generation stepping up in the political arena.

As the people with the bullhorn, we owe it to the public to try as many innovative methods to get them excited and focused on the election.

If not us, then who?

August 6, 2007, Essence.com blog

Enough With the "Is Obama Black Enough?" Nonsense

ARE BLACK FOLKS SO THOROUGHLY CONFUSED that when we have the first serious presidential candidate, we continue to be stuck with having to ask the silly—and yes, downright degrading—question over the blackness of the junior senator from Illinois, Barack Obama?

For the last six months we have seen a litany of intellectuals, columnists, pundits and radio talk show hosts decipher this issue, as if it is really a relevant one.

Oh, you think it's relevant? How about this: I haven't heard a single person ask if Sen. Hillary Clinton (D-NY) is woman enough to run for president. You don't find Catholics wasting precious airtime pontificating about the relevancy of former New York Mayor Rudy Giuliani, even though his position in abortion and gays certainly runs counter to that of the church. And with all the white guys running, no one white is asking if they are white enough for the White House.

This is dumb. No, it's insulting.

And it's time that Black America grew up.

For years we have heard our parents preach and preach about the need to stay focused on getting a good education and going to a good school. So we've seen a generation of African Americans head to the Ivy League institutions; the state schools that fought to keep us out; and the private schools that refused to admit us, even if some had the money.

Then we were told not to settle for what was given. So, an increasing number of Blacks ran for citywide and countywide positions. Others chose to go even higher and run for statewide office. In the case of L. Douglas Wilder, he became the first African American elected to the governor's mansion in Virginia. Last year, we saw Deval Patrick, a Harvard-educated PK—project kid!—from the South Side of Chicago be sworn in as governor of Massachusetts.

Since Reconstruction, we've seen three African Americans join the U.S. Senate: Edward Brooke, a Republican from Massachusetts in 1966; Carol Moseley Braun, an Illinois Democrat in 1992; and Obama in 2004.

Now, years after seeing blacks like the late Rep. Shirley Chisholm, Rev. Jesse Jackson Sr., Braun and Rev. Al Sharpton (OK, for racial sake, I'll mention Alan Keyes' run for the White House) run largely symbolic campaigns—Rev. Jackson did get 7 million votes in 1988 but only 8 percent of the delegates—Obama's candidacy has legs, and more importantly money.

I knew this would be an issue, so in February, I ran a front page story in the *Chicago Defender* asking this very question. That was followed up by a three-part series using my syndicated column to lay out the foolishness of the question.

Enough is enough.

There is no litmus test to determine if you are an African American. If you disagree with the policies of Supreme Court Justice Clarence Thomas—and I surely do—he is still a black man. Condoleezza Rice may be in lockstep with President George W. Bush, but the first Black female secretary of state is a Black woman. And yes, Obama may be speaking to mostly white audiences on the campaign trail, but when that U.S. Census form comes to his home, he checks the black box.

So why don't we accept the reality that he can't win the presidency by being contained to our black box. He can have an agenda that includes black folks, but he can't win on a black agenda. You know, so stop trippin'. There is no Black White House. He's not running for president of Black America. He is seeking the highest office in the land: The U.S. president. The commander-in-chief. The head man (or if Clinton wins, woman) in charge.

Trust me, if he wins, these same idiots who question his blackness will be doing their best to suck up to him, calling him "Brother Obama," as if they always saw him as one of their own.

August 9, 2007, Essence.com Blog

Clinton: "Madam President" Sounds Good!

LAS VEGAS—SEN. HILLARY CLINTON spoke for eight minutes in her opening comments, and it didn't take long for her to connect with her audience.

Recognizing that the two female candidates running for president of the National Association of Black Journalists, Clinton referenced them by saying that "however this election turns out, Madam President has a wonderful ring to it."

In an effort to connect with her audience, she also took a moment to recognize the death of Chauncey Bailey, the *Oakland Post* editor who was gunned down last week, allegedly by followers of a group he was investigating.

Also, she referenced author James Baldwin in her opening presentation.

CNN's Malveaux to Clinton: "Are You Black Enough?" to be President?

LAS VEGAS-CNN WHITE HOUSE CORRESPONDENT Suzanne Malveaux, who is moderating the session with Sen. Hillary Clinton (D-NY) at the National Assocation of Black Journalists national convention, led off with the question of "Are you Black enough?"

Prior to this session, NABJ held a panel where the question came up as to whether her challenger, Sen. Barack Obama was "Black enough" to run for president.

But Les Payne, the retired Pulitzer Prize-winning journalist from *Newsday*, asked if Clinton was Black enough to champion the interests of African Americans if she was elected president.

Malveaux thought it was thought provoking and used it to open the Q and A session, eliciting laughter and some applause from the audience.

Sen. Hillary Clinton Opens Speech at NABJ With Focus on Young Black Men

LAS VEGAS—SEN. HILLARY CLINTON (D-NY) is speaking right now at the annual convention of the National Association of Black Journalists, and in her opening remarks, she said it's time for America to have a national conversation about the plight of 1.4 million men of color who are in the nation's prison system.

Clinton, the first of two Democratic candidates to speak at the convention-Sen. Barack Obama (D-IL) will speak tomorrow-said that is a national crisis that needs to be addressed.

"That's the conversation that I want to have," she said, "it's a conversation that I believe in."

August 10, 2007, Essence.com Blog

Obama to Black Journos: End the "Black Enough" Talk

LAS VEGAS—SEN. BARACK OBAMA has made it clear that he doesn't like the debate formats, which are all about one-liners and the sound bite.

But up close and personal, it's easy to see why voters in small towns and communities come out in large numbers to listen to him expound on the issues of the day.

The junior senator from Illinois spoke to the National Association of Black Journalists convention Friday afternoon, and it was clear that he was the main attraction.

The cavernous ballroom was standing room only, a stark contrast to Sen. Hillary Clinton, who spoke to a half-filled room.

Belying his past job as a law professor, "Professor Obama" appeared relaxed and at ease, engaging in a easygoing discussion on a variety of issues—and often joking—with moderator Byron Pitts, a national correspondent for CBS.

There were multiple issues that I could have easily written on, but what stood out was his challenge to black journalists over this whole issue of whether he's black enough to run for president.

He's often answered the question by saying they never ask that question when he's catching a cab in New York—deftly used during the CNN-YouTube debate—but this time he demanded that the group of black journalists themselves are to blame for advancing the issue, and sought for them to offer some critical thinking on the topic.

It was the last question posed by Pitts, and when Obama answered, the room was eerily quiet. Not even the shutters of the cameras—in abundance when he walked in—were going off as he methodically challenged the notion.

Pitts asked what gives Obama the notion that America is ready for a black president, and Obama suggested that the question had nothing to do with his record as a state senator or U.S. Senator, and not even his work prior to elected office.

Instead, he challenged the view—not often discussed in black America—of a particular mistrust, even calling the question of his blackness "puzzling."

"What it really does is really lay bare, I think, that we're still locked in this notion that if you appeal to white folks then there must be something wrong," he said, even noting that blacks raise that issue if others go to Ivy League institutions like Harvard.

He challenged black journalists to put the issue out in the open, but also said that the idea of a black man running for president speaks to the fears in the black community.

But as he often does—his book is called *The Audacity of Hope*—he offered a bit for those who are ambivalent or scared of his winning the White House.

"Let's try. Let's see. Why defeat ourselves ahead of time? Why say we can't do something? Let's take a chance and see if we can."

September 7, 2007, Essence.com Blog

Oprah's Big Bucks Could Help Obama in a Big Way

IT'S BIG NEWS THAT THE GODDESS OF TALK, Oprah Winfrey, is throwing a huge shindig for U.S. Sen. Barack Obama at her California estate that is expected to bring in $3 million.

That is more than what Hollywood honchos Steven Spielberg, David Geffen and others raised in separate fundraisers for Obama and his chief rival, Sen. Hillary Clinton.

No one knows for sure what the effect will be with Oprah backing Obama because she has never thrown her full support behind a political candidate.

The Washington Post made it plain as to her influence on the general public, courtesy of her massive media platform: "the television program that reaches 8.4 million viewers each weekday afternoon, according to the most recent Nielsen numbers. Her Web site reaches 2.3 unique viewers each month, *O, the Oprah Magazine*, has a circulation of 2 million, she circulates a weekly newsletter to 420,000 fans and 360,000 people have subscribed to her Web site for daily "Oprah Alerts" by e-mail."

Although Winfrey is a billionaire, by law, all she can contribute to the Obama campaign is $4,600. She can contribute $2,300 to the primary and if he wins the nomination, she can contribute the other $2,300 to the general election campaign.

On CNN's "Larry King Live", she said that her support is bigger than any check she could write.

Not quite.

Although the Post reported that Oprah is in talks with the Obama campaign about taking an active role—appearing at rallies or cutting campaign commercials— she could instead choose to launch her own 527 political group that wouldn't have any spending restrictions.

Imagine this scenario: Oprah chooses to create the "O for Obama" 527 group. She then seeds it with $5 million, and plans a series of radio and TV ads touting Obama in Iowa, New Hampshire, South Carolina and Arizona.

In Iowa, she might shoot a commercial in a cornfield. In New Hampshire, the setting might be outside the state capitol. How about the Geechee islands in South Carolina? And for Arizona, the infamous (only because of its sheriff) jail in Maricopa County.

She could tailor each ad for residents of that state, and flood the airwaves as Obama is doing the same.

Now, the laws says the 527s can't coordinate their messages with the campaign, and there are other restrictions. But it could be a huge boost to a campaign lagging Clinton in national polls.

You don't think they matter? Ask Sen. John Kerry. The Swift Boat Veterans launched a 527 group that developed devastating ads that helped derail his message, and the campaign.

Oprah may get some heat for trying to buy the election, but many rich benefactors have used their money for partisan purposes.

The talk show diva has been on record that Obama is the first—and likely—last candidate she publicly backs. If that's the case, why not simply go all out?

September 28, 2007

Why Is the GOP Scared of Black Voters?

THAT'S RIGHT, I SAID IT. And mean it.

The GOP as a whole is completely scared of black voters, and the actions of the frontrunners for the party's 2008 nomination show that they are continuing the same silly political games the party has played for years.

Oh, don't bother tossing out the appointments of Colin Powell and Condoleezza Rice as secretary of state by Bush. Yes, they are black. But I'm speaking of the party.

Ever since Richard Nixon ran for the White House, the GOP has run on a "Southern strategy," meant to alienate blacks in an effort to garner white voters. They've worked the strategy to perfection. When he was head of the Republican National Committee, Ken Mehlman apologized for that strategy as he sought to make inroads among black voters.

Republicans will tell you they are the party of Abraham Lincoln, who signed the Emancipation Proclamation, but their outreach to black voters is lacking.

Oh, yes, I know. Democrats have a stranglehold on the black vote, receiving upward of 90 percent in national elections. A significant part of that is a result of the party seeing blacks as the backbone of the party. But the reality is that when you have only one party that truly makes a play for those voters, of course you will see such disparities!

That's why it's dumb, dumb and dumber that the leading candidates skipped Thursday's debate hosted by Tavis Smiley and aired on PBS.

Mitt Romney, Rudy Giuliani, Fred Thompson and Sen. John McCain all cited "scheduling conflicts" as the reason for their lack of attendance to debate at Morgan State University in Baltimore, even though Smiley personnel tell me that they first began discussions with then-RNC head Mehlman in February 2006. When the debate was announced earlier this year, along with a Democratic forum held in June at Howard University, the RNC promised their candidates would speak.

But those of us who follow politics knew that wasn't going to happen.

This summer, all of the Republican candidates, save Rep. Tom Tancredo of

Colorado, skipped the NAACP and the National Urban League conventions. OK, I get the former, but the Urban League? President Bush has spoken there several times as president!

The GOP keeps blowing a big opportunity by ignoring blacks. And look at the Univision debate! Only McCain accepted their invite.

Today's generation of blacks and Hispanics shouldn't be seen as the same as their parents. An increasing number of people are refusing to identify themselves with a party and are looking at issues. Hispanics have been a huge part of the Republican outreach, but the immigration debate is turning that in a different direction.

Why should the GOP talk to black voters, and what would they talk about? First, I can tell you that immigration is huge in the black community, and it gets folks riled up in a hurry (you ought to see my talk show lines when this comes up). Education and health care are also major. And every GOP debate has been about faith in the public square, and we know that plays well with black voters, especially on gay marriage.

Now, when it comes to the war in Iraq, the GOP can forget that tune. No one is listening. And they are completely uneven on the issue of civil rights.

Here is an example that further explains the GOP's stupidity on this topic: Several years ago, a Republican in the Dallas-Fort Worth area was trying to unseat then-Rep. Martin Frost, a heavily entrenched Democrat. That summer, a series of black churches was being burned. My good friend, Michael Williams, a third-generation black Republican, was planning to host a fundraiser at his home for the GOP candidate. He called the campaign and said it would be a good idea for the candidate to make a statement on the burnings, condemning them and saying it didn't make sense. The campaign said no. Michael called back and made the suggestion again, and the response was they didn't want to seem as if they were pandering to the black community. He laughed at that because the campaign was bringing then-Rep. J.C. Watts of Oklahoma in to visit black churches with the candidate. Hello! That's pandering. So Michael told his wife what the candidate said. Donna replied, "Any man who is such a coward that he can't speak against churches being burned is not welcome in my home." The fundraiser was called off.

Here was a simple opportunity to show that you actually care, but the candidate was so scared to say something, he turned off a campaign donor.

Will speaking at one debate turn around decades of black support for the Democrats? Nope. But not speaking will just mean business as usual, and the GOP needs less of that.

October 5, 2007

Black-Brown Coalitions Are Tough to Sustain

WITH HISPANICS BEING THE NATION'S largest minority group, the general assumption among many political and social pundits is that they will align themselves with African Americans to represent a potent political force on the local, state and national levels.

But as someone who has seen this so-called phenomenon up close, I can tell you that forging a multiethnic coalition will be very difficult.

As a native Houstonian, a longtime resident of the Dallas-Fort Worth area and now a resident of Chicago, it has been interesting to watch as a number of local leaders have tried to establish such a connection.

Back in 1989, when I interned at the *Houston Defender*, the city's top black newspaper, we ran a front-page story about a black-brown coalition. The city's black and Hispanic leaders announced their effort to seek a variety of appointments in the city's fire and police departments, as well as in the city's school district.

Yet it was always a fragile coalition, as each party tried to establish supremacy over the other. And one move could bring it all crashing down.

That was the case in 1994, when Rod Paige, an African American member of the Houston Independent School District board of trustees, was tapped as superintendent. Hispanics were angry, saying they were shut out of the decision-making, and they vowed never to let it happen again.

I saw the same black-brown breakdown in 1997, when Yvonne Gonzalez, a Mexican-American woman, was chosen as head of the Dallas Independent School District.

Pre-Season

African Americans in the city squared off against Hispanics over whether someone from their ethnic group should be chosen as superintendent, and it continued repeatedly, with protests, charges of racism flying back and forth and complete mistrust between both.

Why such acrimony? Pure and simple: power.

In America, the nation's largest minority group carries significant weight. It's sort of like being the daddy at the dinner table; you get the biggest piece of chicken or the largest slice of cake.

Political power means jobs and resources. And the one group with the most power wants to benefit their own and sacrifice everyone else.

For years, African Americans have argued that their sheer size in terms of numbers requires that they get a seat at the table. Coupled with African Americans leading the civil rights movement, they say Hispanics shouldn't easily benefit from their hard work and that blacks primarily should reap the benefits.

But that all changed when Hispanics became the largest minority, often exceeding African Americans in terms of the number of students in school systems, the primary battlegrounds in many cities.

Today, we see that spilling over into every area, even business. African American ad agencies and media outlets complain that the dollars set aside for blacks has been reduced savagely and shifted to Hispanic media.

So what you find is African Americans and Hispanics fighting it out over a piece of the pie, while the larger ethnic group—whites—remains the same.

Is it possible to see a true black-brown coalition that greatly benefits both minority groups? Maybe. But it's going to take a helluva lot of work between the leading organizations such as the NAACP, the National Urban League, La Raza and the League of United Latin American Citizens.

Instead of seeing one as taking from the other, what leaders in both camps should be exercising is a broader view. Blacks are not the enemies of Hispanics, and vice versa. The enemies are a lack of quality of education, being shut out of the economic levers, and poor health care. The resources of this nation should go where the need is. And if that means a larger portion going to one group instead of another, fine. But we can't sacrifice one for the other.

In cities across the nation, African Americans and Hispanics can find common ground on common interests. And where they differ, they simply should disagree.

But that requires trust, and neither group can afford to be egomaniacal and regard the other as irrelevant. Hispanics and blacks aren't going anywhere, and they better resolve their disputes, or watch both groups remain at a standstill. And that's not good for anyone.

October 9, 2007, Essence.com Blog

Are Black Women Feeling Obama?

HE HAS THE GREAT SMILE, smooth demeanor, and gorgeous wife, but will the ethnicity of Sen. Barack Obama (D-IL) come in second to the gender of Sen. Hillary Clinton (D-NY)?

A lot of political watchers talk about the importance of the black vote in the Democratic primary, and that is certainly the case. But it is women voters that will decide who gets the nomination. Women make up 60 percent of all Democratic primary voters, and with a woman on the doorstep of breaking the glass ceiling in the White House, women across the country and aggressively hyping the campaign of Clinton.

Emily's List, the top female political action committee, has thrown its full weight behind Clinton. As it stands, Obama is some 40 percentage points behind Clinton in the polls when it comes to women, and he's going to have to make a strong move to close that gap.

One place where he can do some serious damage is South Carolina, where 40 percent of black women are undecided. Considering African Americans make up nearly 50 percent of Democratic primary voters, when they do, this race could be over.

Obama's political team says they have a robust strategy to reach out to women, but for some reason, it's not breaking through.

October 12, 2007

It's Time for Voters to Get Their Heads in the Game

FORGIVE ME FOR BEING A BIT CRANKY. A week ago, I had three wisdom teeth removed, and with all the prescriptions and tight stitches in my mouth, I've been unable to do any radio or TV this week, and that has me all wound up.

But I've gotta get a few things off my chest, and none is more important than this ridiculous sentiment that people don't have time to worry about the presidential race and that it's too early to spend an inordinate amount of time worrying about the candidates.

Folks, that's about as dumb a comment as any I've heard.

Oh, I know we're all so busy with our lives, but really, does it make sense that we spend more time fantasizing about our dream car than investigating who the next president of the United States will be?

You might say I get paid to be wrapped up in all of this stuff. And while that might be true, I'm not checking Politico.com every five minutes and recording all the Sunday morning news shows. But when I see research that suggests the average person spends five minutes a month—total—on the presidential race, I go stir crazy!

Here we are in a war that is costing $275 billion a day, and we don't have any clue when it will end, and we have more things to be concerned with?

President George W. Bush vetoed a children's health care bill that would have cost about $35 billion annually, but the Republican-led Congress passed a prescription drug bill a couple years ago that cost $100 billion more than advertised. Hey, maybe had we gotten the full truth then, we could pay for the State Children's Health Insurance Program.

We've got an illegal immigration problem that is out of control. The borders aren't secure, big business is grabbing as much cheap labor as possible, and our attention is more on whether to buy a 45-inch or 50-inch HDTV for Christmas?!

For three hours a day on WVON in Chicago, I host a daily radio show and try to give people as much information as possible. Why? Because in a year, we'll be voting on the friggin' president of the United States! You know, the person who can decide whether our troops invade another country or not?

But the presidency goes beyond just the war. Anyone thought of the Supreme Court? I'm reading a great book by my CNN colleague Jeffrey Toobin called *"The Nine: Inside the Secret World of the Supreme Court."* Even though the Senate votes to confirm a justice, it is the president who chooses one of the nine most important jobs in the world.

Some expect the next president to choose three justices. And with the court on the cusp of having a solid conservative majority, evangelicals and conservatives are salivating at the chance of overturning *Roe v. Wade*. That also could drive liberals and women to the polls to push their candidate into the White House. That's a pretty big deal.

What I'm trying to say? This next election has huge implications, and we all should be more actively engaged. With candidates running a year ahead of time, spending millions of dollars and offering more policy positions, Web sites and talking points than ever before, *no one* can suggest they never had a chance to really get to know Sens. Hillary Clinton and Barack Obama, former Sens. John Edwards and Fred Thompson, former Mayor Rudy Giuliani of New York and former Gov. Mitt Romney of Massachusetts.

Each and every person should be asking his friends, family, church members and, yes, co-workers where they stand on the presidential race. If someone says, "I don't know much," point them in the right direction.

It would be great to see upward of 70 percent or 80 percent of Americans casting votes in the national election. But we'll never get there if people don't care.

And for that person who keeps saying, "My vote doesn't count," I say, "That's a bunch of crap." Whether it's a House or Senate race or even the race for the White House, the evidence is there that a few hundred votes here or there can make a huge difference.

The first primary begins in January. That's also when Fox's "American Idol" returns to the airwaves. The winner of that show gets a recording deal. The winner of the presidential election is the "leader of the Free World."

Which do you think is more important to the future of your children?

Barack Obama's Black Wake-up Call

IF THE ADVISERS AROUND SEN. BARACK OBAMA want to continue to delude themselves into thinking they have lots of time for black voters to get around to figuring out their candidate's record on issues they care about, then the latest CNN poll surely must be the kind of slap in the face they need to bring them back to reality.

There was a general assumption when Obama announced his candidacy for president that he was going to garner a lion's share of the black vote. In a normal presidential election, sure. But with Sen. Hillary Clinton in the race, the reality of the affection—real and perceived—that black folks have for the Clintons is clearly what has her storming out to a strong lead over Obama.

According to the CNN poll, Clinton leads Obama among black registered Democrats, 57 percent to 33 percent. Black women are backing Clinton to the tune of 68 percent, and 25 percent are for Obama. Black men favor Obama 46 percent to 42 percent for Clinton. The poll has a margin of error of plus or minus 6.5 percent.

On multiple occasions when I've interviewed him, Obama has reassured folks that his track record speaks for itself. He says with Clinton being on the national stage for 15 years, she has longevity. But he said he's confident black voters will come around the more they know about what he has done. That's nice and sounds good, but what the Obama campaign clearly has refused to recognize is that black voters are emotional, and you must speak to their core in order to reach them.

Obama has at times spoken passionately about issues blacks care about—the war, education, civil rights, social justice issues—but all too often, he has avoided engaging in a way that touches the consciousness of black voters. Voters have told me that he's sometimes sterile and not offering the kind of passion they desire.

But there are other reasons why black voters have been ambivalent about an Obama candidacy, and it's clearly having an effect on him being able to build momentum to challenge Clinton:

1. THE BELIEF THAT WHITE VOTERS WILL NOT ACCEPT HIM SO A VOTE FOR OBAMA WILL BE A WASTE. Forget the fact that there are thousands of black elected officials in the country. African Americans running for the White House are not the norm, especially one with his credentials. This is a real concern and one that can't be overlooked or dismissed easily.

2. OBAMA WILL BE "TAKEN OUT" IF HE WINS. *The New York Times* had a piece this past weekend where a black woman essentially said her way of protecting Obama from harm is by not voting for him. Sounds nutty, but again, it's real, and it's been said many times. I've heard this fear factor time and time again, and it speaks to the fears of blacks that America has not advanced enough to be comfortable with a black man in the White House.

3. OBAMA THE POLICY WONK DOESN'T MESH WITH BLACK VOTERS. This is not to suggest that black voters don't care about issues—they do. But Obama has a certain emotional detachment that has turned off black voters. You can't find one major moment where black voters have enveloped him and showered him with love. I was highly critical of his performance at the June debate at Howard University because that was his crowd. And he failed to ignite the room. One HUGE Obama supporter told me that his daughter went to the event backing him, and came out loving Clinton.

So what now, pack or go home?

No. He has an opportunity to make a move, but it must be done now.

First, the campaign must stop being afraid to put Michelle Obama on the road and let her rip. She has to be his major weapon in appealing to black women.

Second, having Oprah Winfrey's endorsement is one thing, but they must get her on the road. It also will help if he touts other black women who are backing him. Recently, former "Young and the Restless" star Victoria Rowell was stumping for Clinton in South Carolina, and other high-profile black women have been out front supporting her.

Obama just picked up the endorsement of Deval Patrick, governor of Massachusetts, and only the second elected black governor in history. Patrick's a former top Clinton administration official, but his state has a small black population, so that really doesn't help Obama with black voters.

Lastly, Obama must forget the national polls and focus solely on South Carolina. Nearly 50 percent of the Democratic Party primary voters there are black, and research shows that 40 percent of black women haven't made up their minds in the state. Even though research conducted by Clinton reveals that Obama's message isn't resonating with blacks, research done by the Obama camp shows that when black women have met and been engaged by Obama, he has been able to convert them into supporters.

BOTTOM LINE: Low black support means Obama is toast.

If his campaign keeps playing it safe, hoping not to alienate white voters, he likely will be on the campaign trail next fall.

But he'll be stumping for Clinton.

October 24, 2007, Essence.com Blog

Obama Pressed by Gays to Dump McClurkin, Mary Mary

THE ONE THING YOU'LL LEARN ABOUT POLITICS is that you can't please everybody, and even when you're trying to do something good, you can still tick off a lot of people. That's the case with a series of gospel concerts Sen. Barack Obama planned to launch around South Carolina with gospel stars Donnie McClurkin and Mary Mary.

But it's their views on homosexuality that has led gay activists and their supporters to denounce Obama, and even call for him to disavow their support of his candidacy.

Critics such as the Human Rights Campaign, the National Black Justice Coalition and others have expressed their disappointment with the concert, with some calling for him to cancel it outright.

The Obama campaign responded with the following statement: "I have clearly stated my belief that gays and lesbians are our brothers and sisters and should be provided the respect, dignity, and rights of all other citizens. I have consistently spoken directly to African American religious leaders about the need to overcome the homophobia that persists in some parts our community so that we can confront issues like HIV/AIDS and broaden the reach of equal rights in this country," Obama said in the written statement.

"I strongly believe that African Americans and the LGBT community must stand together in the fight for equal rights. And so I strongly disagree with Reverend McClurkin's views and will continue to fight for these rights as President of the United States to ensure that America is a country that spreads tolerance instead of division."

Here is the difficulty for Obama: McClurkin and Mary Mary are extremely popular among African Americans, and he is trying to increase his lead among black voters in South Carolina, who make up nearly 50 percent of the Democratic primary voters.

Second, the gay and lesbian constituency is huge in the Democratic Party, and they are not going to let the issue die down.

Lastly, African Americans are largely against homosexuality, and their numbers even exceed whites.

It is not a position that I envy, but a reality is that Obama has to walk this tightrope, like any other candidate. In fact, it's not shocking that he would have folks support him who he might disagree with on other issues. All the candidates are in that position. Individuals who have endorsed Sen. Hillary Clinton are also opposed to homosexuality, and if we look at the endorsements of other candidates, we'll find the same.

In the end, I don't believe that Obama will cancel the concert. He may choose to speak on the issue from the stage, or allow his statement to speak for itself. Normally, a controversial supporter would choose to back out, citing a need to not allow the event to overshadow the larger issue of the campaign. But with all three performers being ripped for their views on homosexuality, that means no concert.

We'll keep an eye on this one. It is sure to heat up.

October 31, 2007 Essence .com Blog

Obama, Edwards Go After Clinton With Gusto

WITH THE AVERAGE VOTER SPENDING FIVE MINUTES A MONTH—total, and not consecutive—on the presidential campaign, I won't assume that you watched last night's Democratic presidential debate on MSNBC.

But it was clear that former Sen. John Edwards and Sen. Barack Obama, needing to knock Clinton off kilter as the frontrunner, took dead aim at her, and did a very good job at it.

Clinton has been so on the mark in all the debates that she has come out sharp. But last night, whether it was providing driver's licenses to illegal immigrants in New York or the release of documents when she served as First Lady, Clinton was unclear in her answers and sometimes confusing.

Obama and Edwards used her dancing to their advantage, questioning her word, which is huge because one of the big negatives against Clinton is her credibility.

The Clinton camp will certainly take notice of what the punditry has to say, and expect her to smooth out the rough edges, but it would be wise for Edwards and Obama to keep the pressure up if they want to make a dent in her huge lead in the polls.

November 1, 2007

Sen. Barack Obama on The Roland S. Martin Show, WVON-AM/Chicago

Roland Martin: Right now we are joined by U.S. Senator Barack Obama. Of course, he is running for the Democratic nomination for president. Senator Obama, welcome back to the show.

Barack Obama: Good to talk to you Roland. What's happening?

Roland Martin: Before I ask you a couple of question about the campaign...on

Saturday there is going to be a march in West Virginia for a Hate Crime rally in the case involving Megan Williams, and one of the points that I have raised even coming out of Jena, is that I think we as Americans are extremely good at expressing our frustrations. We do it on talk radio, on blogs, and letters to the editor, but all too often we stop there. It does not translate in to actual action. One of the things that you have done throughout this campaign is constantly encourage people not to just sit there and be frustrated and be angry and upset, but to do something to make a difference in this country.

Barack Obama: Well, look, there is no doubt that whether we are talking about the criminal justice system or we are talking about doing something about the healthcare crisis out here, or we're talking about our education system that still leaves too many kids behind that the first stage is always recognition of the problem and protest to the problem. But it always has to translate in to some sort of concrete action. We started seeing that with the Jena 6. I think that had a real impact when young people went down there and folks from all across the country made it one of their issues, and I think that the same pattern of action has to be implemented when it comes to all the issues that are happening.

Roland Martin: Democratic debate took place on Tuesday night, hosted by Brian Williams and Tim Russet of MSNBC, and you as well as John Edwards stepped up the campaign in making some critical comments and targeting your differences with Sen. Hillary Rodham Clinton and this whole immigration issue; the license issue has really forced a hand as well. And so you made a point that you are going to not be personal in attacks but get more aggressive and show them the differences between the two of you.

Barack Obama: Well look, now is the time when people start focusing on the campaign and we wanted to make sure that they start focusing that they understand what the differences are between myself and Senator Clinton. And at the debate I think it was pretty clear that one of those differences is that I have consistently tried during the course of this campaign to tell the American people what I think. Here is how I would fix Social Security. Here is how I would approach dealing with immigration. Here is what I think we need to do when it comes to Iraq and Iran, and I think Senator Clinton, unfortunately, just has not been willing to clarify where she stands on stuff, and I think at the debate this week that it became apparent that that pattern of going back and forth on things can often times not only be confusing to voters, but I think actually makes you vulnerable long term. If you want to take on Republicans, you need to be clear about where you stand on issues.

Roland Martin: Well, just like I thought during the debate when the questions were asked about the documents in terms of her correspondence with the president. At one point, I was hoping you or someone else would say, Senator Clinton can you just answer the question? Yes do you want documents released or you do not.

Barack Obama: Well, as you know, I was pretty confused, particularly when she started saying, we have done everything we can, and I thought, well no, this is your president's library—this is your husband's library. So you cannot tell me that if you said to your husband, go ahead and release the papers, that they wouldn't be released tomorrow. So, I do not know who they were that she was referring to that somehow they were holding things up, or they were moving as fast as they could. But that's my point, I think that right now folks are really looking for clarity when it comes to what their leaders are going to do. They want to have some trust in our government, and that kind of campaigning doesn't instill trust and it doesn't solve the big problems, because if you are all over the map on various issues, then you are not going to be able to mobilize the support that you need to get things done. You might get elected but you are not in a position to govern.

Roland Martin: I saw you on the "Tavis Smiley Show" and you addressed the point head on, this whole issue that black folks fear for your safety and fear that whites are not going to support you, so therefore a vote for you is wasted. I mean, you addressed it head on, because that has sort of been just hanging out there and I think has been a serious problem that black folks have this whole notion of . . . well, I just think it might be wasted.

Barack Obama: Well, look what I said on Tavis and what I told you myself, Roland, is that we can't defeat ourselves. Now, obviously safety is an issue for every presidential candidate. I've got Secret Service protection; the best protection there is and we then need to move on. Michelle has moved on with it, I have moved on with it, and we need voters to move on with it, because this is something that we made the decision to do, and we are comfortable doing. But there is something more I think pervasive and that is people fearing, you know what? White people aren't going to vote for a black candidate or we are worried about him disappointing us, or et cetera, et cetera. Fear of failure, fear of that we cannot make this happen, and one thing I firmly believe is that we have made progress as a people throughout our history because we did not accept the notion that we couldn't do something or that it was too hard or the barriers were too high. We tried, we made an effort, and this is an opportunity where two months away from the first caucus, I have an opportunity to win the nomination of the Democratic Party for president, and if our people decide that this is important then it's going to happen, and if we say we cannot do it before we even try then that could be self-defeating. So, I hope everybody gets over that attitude.

Roland Martin: You took a lot of heat from folks over the gospel concert, Donnie McClurkin, but you did not drop him from that concert. Isn't it critical that, I do not care what campaign it is Republican or Democrat, you are going to have people who support your campaigning who come from opposing views. And that shutting someone down or keeping someone quiet or, no pun intended, trying to put someone in the closet so they cannot say anything, does not serve the general public well in terms of a dialogue.

Barack Obama: Oh absolutely, I mean, look, especially for a candidate like me. I am trying to reach out to all walks of life. I refuse to accept that the Republicans have a lock on church folks, because I go to church and there are lot of Democrats up in there. But I also know that if I am going to be doing the kind of faith outreach that we've been doing, well, there are going to be some folks in the church who have particular views on certain issues that may not jive with mine. But the flip side of it is, when Rick Warren major mega-church pastor, the guy who wrote *The Purpose Driven Life* had an AIDS conference, he invited me out there and took a lot of heat from his evangelical friends because they said, look this guy is pro-choice, he is pro-gay rights, you shouldn't have him in the pulpit. He said, I do not agree with him on that but I agree with him on AIDS. And so he extended the courtesy of allowing me to have a forum to speak and listen. And I can't operate in a different way just because I am running for president. If we are serious about reaching out to all walks of life and trying to find common ground, that applies even when you are running for president.

Roland Martin: Senator Obama, you hit the campaign trail hard, you are going to be in North Carolina, Iowa, New Hampshire, Nevada, South Carolina and so we surely appreciate the time. Final comments we've got about 30 seconds.

Barack Obama: Roland it is always a pleasure and it is just good to be back on 'VON because you know that is my family there.

Roland Martin: We certainly appreciate it, and again we are going to keep watching the campaign we will be following you closely.

Barack Obama: Talk to you soon, bye, bye.

Roland Martin: Thanks I appreciate it.

November 6, 2007, Essence.com Blog

Former VP Candidate Ferraro Plays Gender, Race Card

"GAME RECOGNIZES GAME."

That phrase certainly sums up my feelings regarding some recent comments advanced by a big supporter of Sen. Hillary Clinton's bid for the Democratic presidential nomination.

In an interview with the *New York Times* that ran on Monday's front page, 1984 Democratic VP candidate Geraldine Ferraro made some comments in her defense of Clinton after last week's attacks during the presidential debate aired on MSNBC.

"John Edwards, specifically, as well as the press, would never attack Barack Obama for two hours the way they attacked her. It's okay In this country to be sexist. It's certainly not okay To be racist. I think if Barack Obaba had been attacked for two hours—well, I don't think Barack Obama would have been attacked for two hours."

She later said, "We can't let them do this in a presidential race. They say we're playing the gender card. We are not. We are not. We have got to stand up. It's discrimination against her as a candidate because she is a woman."

Excuse me? How in the hell is Clinton being discriminated against?

She is leading all polls. She has raised more money than all the other candidates. She is leading likely GOP challengers in the polls, and Ferraro is mad because she's getting criticized? Give me a break!

Remember former Sen. Carol Moseley Braun? She ran for president in 2004, but no one went after her. Why? Because she's a woman? No. Because she was so low in the polls it served no purpose. The frontrunner always has a bullseye on their back.

It is insulting for Ferraro and other Clinton supporters to decry the fact that she is being pressed on her policy decisions. I've always thought it was stupid when folks talked about her pantsuits, her steely demeanor, willingness to mix it up with adversaries, and the notion that she should have been one of those first ladies who just focused on beautification projects.

But now that she is getting some heat, Clinton is coming off as the woman who cries, "don't hit me because I'm a girl."

And shame on Ferraro for injecting race into this. Do you recall Clinton calling Obama "naïve" for saying he would meet with Iran, Venezuela and Cuba with no pre-conditions? Did he respond by saying, "don"t hit me because I'm black?"

All women should be disgusted with this blatant play on gender. What does it say to women that you fight all these years to be seen as an equal, but when the heats comes, you want to fall back on you being a woman?

Look, we all know this is politics. When Clinton went to Wellesley and decried the "all boys club" of presidential politics, she was making a clear gender issue. She tried to clean it up by saying they are attacking her because she's the frontrunner, but that was after the fact.

Sen. Clinton, you want to be president, fine. If you win, you will be the first woman, and that will be wonderful. But tell your surrogates to cut the race crap. None of the men running have shown they are sexist. And none are racist.

You want the job? Earn it. Go through the fire like the men. But stop playing the victim. It's unbecoming of a commander-in-chief.

November 8, 2007

Will Evangelicals Choose Giuliani Over God?

"I WILL NEVER VOTE FOR ANYONE for the president of the United States who supports abortion or gay marriage."

Those were the words spoken to me three years ago by a prominent pastor in Dallas who has led a number of rallies on those two issues.

But the endorsement yesterday by the Rev. Pat Robertson—founder of the Christian Coalition, a tour de force during the 1990s, and a former Republican presidential candidate—of former New York Mayor Rudy Giuliani, who continues to lead national polls regarding the GOP race, puts front and center the day conservative evangelicals have long said we would never see: a pro-choice, pro-gay candidate as the Republican nominee for president.

On CNN's "AC 360," conservative commentator and CNN contributor Bill Bennett and CNN's senior political analyst Gloria Borger said they didn't anticipate Robertson making such an audacious move.

But I wasn't surprised. Why? Because the late Rev. Jerry Falwell signaled such a move was possible during the CNN special I hosted in April, "What Would Jesus Really Do?"

When I asked him whether there is a litmus test on abortion and homosexuality for the Republican nominee, Falwell said the most important issue of the day for the nation is national security, and he would prefer someone who has experience in that area rather than a Sunday school teacher.

Had Falwell not died, it would not have shocked me to see him standing next to Giualini and speaking of absolving people of sin, encouraging them to admit their mistakes and put the greater good of the nation before their principles.

This is definitely the blessing Giuliani needed. Evangelicals cursed, screamed and called President Bill Clinton everything but a child of God when he had his affair in the White House, but it's clear they are willing to overlook the past marital failures of Giuliani, his fractured relationship with his children and his support for abortion and gay rights when he was mayor of New York. Those are not the family values they have beaten into the nation's consciousness for nearly the past 30 years.

This isn't the rapture, when Christians say Jesus will return to earth, but it is the day of reckoning for conservative evangelicals. Will they abide by their faith and absolute opposition to abortion and homosexuality being first and foremost, or will they bend to the will of the party?

For years, I have maintained that the focus of evangelicals was never really principles of the faith; it was the Republican Party. By aligning themselves with the party, they've put themselves in the position for this day. And with 25 percent of the GOP base being evangelicals, this is going to cause some serious problems.

As for a possible third-party candidate, as suggested by Tony Perkins, head of the Family Research Council, that's not going to happen. Remember 1992? The barrage of attacks from Ross Perot against President George H.W. Bush allowed Bill Clinton to stay above the fray and focus on his agenda. Clinton garnered 43 percent of the vote, compared to Bush's 37.4 percent and Perot's 18.9 percent. Even the movement of 10 percent could spell doom for Giuliani if he becomes the nominee. Democrats are still angry at Ralph Nader, suggesting that his 2.74 percent of the popular vote in 2000 pulled away critical votes in some states and led to a George W. Bush victory.

Sure, there will be some evangelicals who will be so adamant that they will not support Giuliani, but the vast majority will fall in line because of what Robertson said: Giuliani "has assured the American people that his choices for judicial appointments will be men and women who share the judicial philosophy of John Roberts and Antonin Scalia."

That's code to the base that he won't be a Hillary Clinton. The idea of the New York senator, if she is able to win the nomination, appointing federal judges is too much for them to bear. And with conservatives on the cusp of having a majority on the U.S. Supreme Court and the next president likely appointing three justices, evangelicals will hold their noses and eat their words.

So I guess in the end, instead of allowing God to lead them in their choice for the nominee, they'll just pray to the Lord that Giuliani keeps his word.

Talk about a test of faith!

November 9, 2007

Clinton Camp Wrong to Play the Gender Card

WHEN WE WERE KIDS, my brother and I always used to get our butts whipped by my dad for hitting my sister LeVita. As the only girl at the time, she would run to daddy and tell him we hit her. So, believing his baby girl, he took it out on us.

But one day, he was at the kitchen table watching us play in the front yard, and his eyes lit up; he saw his baby girl hit Reggie and me, and when we hit back, she ran screaming into the house to tell him the usual tale. This time, Daddy spanked her for instigating the fight and then for trying to get us in trouble. Daddy had to explain to LeVita that when you hit boys, sometimes they hit back.

That story came to mind as I read how Geraldine Ferraro blasted the Democratic presidential candidates for their tough questioning last week of Sen. Hillary Clinton during the latest presidential debate.

Clinton herself kicked off the "woe is me" routine when her campaign accused her rivals of "piling on" when they took exception to her multiple answers to the question of illegal immigrants getting driver's licenses in New York and the release of her papers to the president during the two terms of President Bill Clinton. Then, of course, she went to Wellesley College, her alma mater, and talked about the school preparing her for the "all-boys club of presidential politics."

She has asserted that the criticism wasn't about her being a woman, but being the front-runner for the nomination. But her gender dance wasn't lost on her supporters, who took the cue from their fearless leader and went into action on talk radio, on blogs and in political circles.

But no one has been more egregious and offensive than Ferraro, the Democrats' vice presidential candidate in 1984. In a front-page story in Monday's *New York Times,* Ferraro didn't just play the gender card, she also combined it with the race card. "John Edwards, specifically, as well as the press, would never attack Barack Obama for two hours the way they attacked her. It's okay in this country to be sexist. It's certainly not okay to be racist. I think if Barack Obama had been attacked for two hours—well, I don't think Barack Obama would have been attacked for two hours."

She later said, "We can't let them do this in a presidential race. They say we're playing the gender card. We are not. We are not. We have got to stand up. It's discrimination against her as a candidate because she is a woman."

Excuse me? How in the world is Clinton being discriminated against? She is leading all polls. She has raised more money than all the other candidates. She is leading likely GOP challengers in the polls, and Ferraro is angry because she's getting criticized? Give me a break!

Remember former Sen. Carol Moseley Braun? She ran for president in 2004, but no one went after her. Why? Because she's a woman? No. Because she was so low in the polls it served no purpose. Front-runners always have bullseyes on their backs.

It is insulting for Ferraro and other Clinton supporters to decry the fact that she is being pressed on her policy decisions. For years, women have said that what matters are the issues, not their hair, nails, pantsuits vs. dresses or whether they can bake cookies.

But now that she is getting some heat, Clinton is coming off as the woman who cries, "Don't hit me because I'm a girl."

And shame on Ferraro for injecting race into this. Do you recall Clinton calling Obama naive for saying he would meet with Iran, Venezuela and Cuba with no preconditions? Did he respond by saying, "Don't hit me because I'm black"?

All women should be disgusted with this blatant play on gender. Ferraro essentially said that all the men who are running against Clinton are sexist and they should be ashamed of themselves for questioning her. I suppose Ferraro wanted the race to be a coronation, and Edwards, Obama, Joe Biden, Christopher Dodd, Bill Richardson and Dennis Kucinich were supposed to step aside and sing, "Hail to the queen."

But don't be fooled; this is a crafty ploy by the Clinton campaign to further solidify their female base. Remember when she ran for the U.S. Senate in 2000 against then-Rep. Rick Lazio? He made the stupid move of confronting her in a debate, wagging his finger in her face and demanding that she sign a campaign pledge not to use soft money. Lazio came off as a brute who was callous to attack a woman, and women who weren't enthralled with the first lady all of a sudden rose to her defense. That was Clinton's checkmate against Lazio, and she went on to crush him.

Edwards and Obama aren't dumb enough to pull a Lazio, but they must tread carefully and make substantive attacks rather than personal attacks. I talked to several prominent Democratic women—some of whom support Clinton—who made it clear that any attack on her could backfire and drive more women to her campaign.

Sen. Clinton, you want to be president. If you win, you will be the first woman to be president, and that will be wonderful and historic. But tell your surrogates to cut the race and gender crap. None of the men running has shown he is sexist. And none is racist. You want the job; earn it. Go through the fire like the men. But don't try to play the victim; it's unbecoming of a commander in chief.

November 13, 2007, Essence.com Blog

Michelle Obama Doesn't Hold Back On Issue of Race, Husband's Campaign

I'VE LONG MAINTAINED THAT MICHELLE OBAMA is the best weapon her husband, Sen. Barack Obama, has in his effort to win the Democratic presidential nomination.

Like most candidates, their spouses play a critical role in serving as their chief surrogate.

Obama's interview on MSNBC was an important one because instead of running away from the critical issue that is preventing a number of African Americans from embracing her husband's candidacy, she took it head on.

In an interview with Mika Brezezinski, news anchor for the network's "Morning Joe" program, Michelle Obama said the following:

Mika Brezezinski: The polls are showing your husband is trailing Hillary 46 percent to 37 percent in the African American community. What is going on here?

Michelle Obama: First of all, I think that's not going to hold. I'm completely confident. Black America will wake up and get it, but what we're dealing with in the Black community is just the natural fear of possibility. You know, when I look at my life, you know, the stuff that we're seeing in these polls has played out my whole life. I've always been told by somebody that I'm not ready, you know, I can't do something. My scores weren't high enough. There's always that doubt in the back of the minds of people of color. People who have been oppressed and haven't been given real opportunities that you believe somehow, someone is better than you. You know, deep down inside you doubt whether you can do it because that's all you've been told is, no, wait. That's all you hear. And you hear it from people who love you, not because they don't care about you, but they're afraid. They're afraid that something might happen.

Mika Brezezinski: It's interesting you say that, excuse me, because a stewardess yesterday, 52-year-old African American, and I asked her if she was interested in Barack Obama and if she would vote for him and she said, like this, (sigh) "I don't think so because he probably can't win because he's black."

Michelle Obama: That's right. That's the psychology that's going on in our heads, in our souls. And I understand it. I know where it comes from. And I think it's one of the horrible legacies of racism and discrimination and oppression.

On my radio show today, I had a blogger, Kevin McCullough, who wrote a piece ripping Obama. He even penned it with the headline: *NEW* Race Pimp Michelle Obama: Whites keeping Blacks from voting OBAMA!

What I tried to explain to McCullough is that Michelle Obama wasn't blaming whites, she was speaking to the real issue of self-doubt among African Americans.

He countered that young blacks called his New York radio show saying they don't have doubts, but believe they can do whatever they want.

But it's clear that McCullough missed the boat on the black voters. First, the prevailing fear is really there among older African Americans. Where does Sen. Hillary Clinton's black lead come from? Mostly older black voters.

In his column, McCullough tried to use Secretary of State Condoleeza Rice to counter Obama.

"Sure she might be couching it in 'generational effects' of blacks being told they aren't good enough. But that didn't seem to stop Condoleeza Rice from speaking six languages fluently, becoming an accomplished concert pianist, an Olympic competitive figure skater, the Provost of Stanford University, and oh yes—the first ever black female National Security Advisor and Secretary of State."

But I quickly reminded him that in Marcus Mabry's book on Rice, *Twice as Good*, her father, John, refused to even participate in the Civil Rights Movement because he never thought whites would change. So Condoleeza Rice benefitted from the work of other African Americans, despite her fathers fear of change.

Hell, when I was in high school, and word got around that I was going to attend Texas A&M University, one of the teachers at Jack Yates High School came up to me and asked if I thought I was prepared for A&M, and then countered that I should go to Prairie View A&M University first.

I said, "Hold on! Are you telling me that this school hasn't prepared me for mostly white A&M, so I need to go to black PV?"

See, doubt. Fear.

Like it or not, this is exactly what Obama is speaking about. African Americans need to confront our fears of success. Of going to the next level. We can't hold on to the doubts that have held us back for years. It's time to let that go.

And just go for it.

November 16, 2007

A Few States Shouldn't Decide the Race for President

THE NATION'S TWO POLITICAL PARTIES have done a pretty good job over the years of keeping voters in line by deciding the order in which states will vote on their presidential candidates.

But that respect for tradition—Iowa and New Hampshire always have been first in line—has gone out the window, and the Republican and Democratic national committees have struggled to keep order.

Folks, this cat is out of the bag, and it's never going to be the same again. And frankly, it shouldn't.

I've listened to many of the pundits this election season remark that if Sen. John McCain doesn't win New Hampshire, his candidacy is toast. Former Sen. John Edwards has put a lot of the emphasis on Iowa, and the prognosticators say that if he doesn't bag the state, he might as well hang 'em up. Michelle Obama has said on the campaign trail in Iowa that if her husband doesn't win that state, the campaign of Sen. Barack Obama is also toast.

But former New York Mayor Rudy Giuliani is attempting to defy conventional wisdom by ignoring the early states and focusing on delegate-rich states such as New York and California.

As a result, we've seen many states jockey for position by moving up their primaries. Michigan, Florida and others have seen their state officials change the laws to force their primaries to the top of the election calendar so that they may have a greater say in who is president. These moves have led both parties to threaten to strip the rogue states of delegates to the national conventions.

While these changes have created a huge mess for the campaigns—they are not sure exactly when the voting will take place—I must admit I'm on the side of the rogue states. It is grossly unfair for the first four states—Iowa, New Hampshire, Nevada and South Carolina—to pretty much decide the nominations for president. But in all honesty, it boils down to the first two.

If candidates don't do well in Iowa or New Hampshire, the media attention turns away from them, and then the political dollars dry up and the packing begins.

Yet this is no way to choose a president. Fine, I know all about that tradition crap, but honestly, no one should have such a stranglehold on the process. Of course, the hard part is coming up with a plan to which everyone will agree.

Instead of having one primary or caucus one week and another the next, why can't five states vote each week during January? That means by the end of the month, we will have nearly half the states make their choices for president, and we can have a much better idea what the will of the American people is. There is no doubt that will cause the campaigns to raise more money to run national campaigns, but hey, you've got to have a trade-off.

The folks in New Hampshire won't be happy because their constitution calls for them to be the first state in the nation to hold a presidential primary. I'm still trying to figure out how in the world one state believes it can usurp every other state and the political parties go along with this nonsense.

Iowa and New Hampshire residents want to keep saying it's about tradition. I think it's about money. The TV stations, newspapers, hotels, restaurants, sign companies and other businesses make a ton of dough off these candidates, and they don't want that cash cow to feed others.

Unless the political parties come up with a solution that incorporates more states and get away from this exclusivity, the other states will get even more aggressive, and we potentially will have every state trying to hold its primary the first week of January.

Americans want fairness, and there is nothing fair about fewer than 10 percent of the states in America choosing the next president for the rest of us.

November 26, 2007
Oprah Hits The Campaign Trail For Obama

AFTER HOSTING A $3 MILLION FUNDRAISER a couple of months ago at her palatial California estate for Sen. Barack Obama's presidential campaign, Oprah Winfrey will take her star power to the people to see if it can bolster him in the polls.

The Obama campaign announced Sunday that Winfrey will tour Iowa, New

Hampshire and South Carolina on December 8 and 9. The two will hit Des Moines and Cedar Rapids, Iowa on the 8th and Columbia, S.C. and Manchester, N.H. on the 9th.

Political watchers have often stated that endorsement from celebrities mean nothing. But with Oprah, who knows?

First, she has never endorsed a candidate for office, and told CNN's Larry King that she is sure she won't do it again.

Second, no celebrity has her daily cache. Look, if Will Smith, Angelina Jolie or someone tosses their support, it doesn't resonate because we see them on the big screen once a year. But Oprah is beamed into our living rooms five days a week courtesy of her talk show; her web site is hugely popular; and her magazine is a force to be reckoned with.

We know that she sells books, but can she sell Obama?

Frankly, I think Oprah gives Obama a heavy dose of media attention. When she shows up, so does the media. This will mean free exposure in a state where he has dropped $4 million already.

Oprah can also help Obama with women voters. That's her base, and she knows it. If she speaks at rallies where 10,000 to 20,000 folks turn out, Oprah can speak to the possibilities of an Obama presidency, and connect with women. Many have flocked to Sen. Hillary Clinton's campaign because if elected she will be the first woman president. So Obama needs to cut into her huge lead in the most important voting bloc in the Democratic primary.

Some say Oprah can't help Obama. But if I'm him, I sure want her on my side and not on Clinton's.

November 27, 2007

Good News for Clinton and Obama in Joint Center Poll

THE JOINT CENTER FOR POLITICAL AND ECONOMIC STUDIES, the nation's leading think tank on African American issues, released their "2007 National

Survey of Likely Black Presidential Primary Voters" and it bodes well for Democratic frontrunners, Sens. Barack Obama and Hillary Clinton.

BACKGROUND: The survey is a national survey of 750 black likely primary/caucus voters, and was done between Oct. 5 and Nov. 2, 2007. "Respondents were asked their views on important national problems, issues in the campaign, and candidates for both the Democratic and Republican presidential nominations. The survey methodology is described in an accompanying appendix. The Joint Center conducted the survey with the support of the AARP."

HERE ARE THE HIGHLIGHTS:
- Clinton had the highest favorable rating of any presidential candidate with 83 percent of black likely voters. Only 9.7 percent saw her unfavorably. Of that, 86 percent of black women viewed her favorably and only 7 percent unfavorably. Obama? He drew 74.4 percent favorable and 10.1 percent unfavorable.
- Black voters aren't too high on the Republicans. Former New York City Mayor Rudy Giuliani was tops among the GOP, but only 27.1 percent viewed him favorably and 42.7 percent unfavorably. The least negative among black voters? Former Tennessee Sen. Fred Thompson.
- Most important problem facing the nation? War in Iraq at 28 percent; healthcare came in at 20 percent; and jobs came in at 15 percent. Education was fourth at 10 percent. Interestingly, less than 1 percent chose immigration as "the most important national problem." This stands in stark contrast to the center's pre-2004 survey of black adults—"not likely voters," they said—that showed jobs and the economy tops and the war in Iraq second.

Clinton has been touting her experience as the most important factor in the race, but for black voters, that isn't the most important issue.

"A strong majority (63 percent) of black voters said what matters most to them in the presidential candidate is a commitment to change; less than a third indicated that a candidate's experience in elective office mattered most to them," according to the survey.

That should be good news to Obama, who has made change the leading focus of his campaign in an effort to distinguish him from Clinton.

Now when it comes to President Bush, "abysmal" was the word the Joint Center used to describe his ratings among likely black voters with "only 11 percent rating his work excellent or good, while 87 percent give him negative marks—including 58 percent who rate his work as poor. Black women voters (61 percent), those with more than a college degree (72 percent), and those making more than $75,000 (72 percent) were most negative toward the president."

Ouch!

When it comes to African Americans and their views about Democrats, it is no contest.

- "African Americans favor the Democrats over the Republicans on healthcare (75 to 11 percent), Iraq (72 to 14 percent), the economy and jobs (70 to 15 percent), terrorism and national security (60 to 23 percent), Social Security (72 to 13 percent), immigration (60 to 19 percent), taxes (71 to 15 percent), education (72 and 14 percent), and moral values (63 to 17 percent). Democrats are favored over the GOP even on the GOP's signature issues of terrorism and moral values."

- "African Americans continue to identify strongly with the Democratic Party with 84 percent being self-described Democrats and 11 percent identifying with the Republicans; 54 percent of those surveyed described themselves as strong Democrats, while only seven percent were strong Republicans. In 2007, likely black primary voters were also strongly liberal in their political orientation with 41 percent describing themselves that way; 36 percent were self-described moderates and 21 percent conservatives. Conservatism has lost some of its brand strength among African Americans: In Joint Center surveys of black adults conducted during the late 1990s, between 35 and 40 percent described themselves as conservative in their political orientation."

BOTTOM LINE: Democrats have lots of good news in this survey, and the GOP has a lot of work to do. But it also bodes well for both Clinton and Obama, who are far and away the preferred choices among likely black voters.

November 27, 2007, Essence.com Blog

Clinton Camp Has Problems Doing Their Math

I JUST FINISHED WATCHING THE ABC NIGHTLINE piece from Monday night on Sen. Barack Obama and anchor Terry Moran read a comment from the Clinton campaign that said if the junior senator from Illinois was elected president, he would have less experience than any president in the 20th century.

Here is what Deputy Communications Director Phil Singer wrote today after an Obama foreign policy speech:

"With the critical foreign policy challenges America faces in the world today, voters will decide whether Senator Obama, who served in the Illinois State Senate just three years ago and would have less experience than any President since World War II, has the strength and experience to be the next president. Senator Clinton, who has travelled to 82 countries as a representative of the United States and serves on the Armed Services Committee, is ready to lead starting on Day One."

Really?

George W. Bush was only in elected office for six years before he ran for president. He was elected governor of Texas in 1994 and won the presidency—okay liberal bloggers, the Supreme Court ruled in his favor—in 2000.

Obama is in his 11th year as an elected officeholder—eight years in the Illinois State Senate and in his third year as a U.S. Senator. Clinton is in her seventh year of elected office.

So the question has to be asked: Is the Clinton campaign struggling with their math or hoping we all can't add?

If the Clinton camp is saying state experience doesn't matter, does that apply to Bush, who never served on the federal level prior to coming to the White House; President Jimmy Carter, who was governor of Georgia before residing at 1600 Pennsylvania Avenue; and even her husband, Bill Clinton, who was governor and attorney general of Arkansas before being elected in 1992.

Make a decision, Sen. Clinton. Either state experience matters or it doesn't. History shows that it does.

I sent Singer an e-mail asking for a clarification. I'll let you know if he gets back to me.

November 28, 2007, Essence.com blog

Is Rev. Jackson An Obama Supporter or Not?

I CAN'T FIGURE OUT WHETHER AT TIMES the Rev. Jesse Jackson Sr. is truly a supporter of Sen. Barack Obama or not.

A couple of months ago he was busted for saying that Obama was "acting white" for his so-called refusal to speak out on the Jena 6 case. In fact, Obama did speak out on the case and was on record.

But yesterday, Jackson took all Democrats to task, except for John Edwards, for not addressing black issues.

In a column that ran in the *Chicago Sun-Times*, Jackson said: "the Democratic candidates—with the exception of John Edwards, who opened his campaign in New Orleans' Ninth Ward and has made addressing poverty central to his campaign—have virtually ignored the plight of African Americans in this country. The catastrophic crisis that engulfs the African—American community goes without mention. No urban agenda is given priority. When thousands of African Americans marched in protest in Jena, La., not one candidate showed up.

"Democratic candidates are talking about health care and raising the minimum wage, but they aren't talking about the separate and stark realities facing African Americans."

Now I get Jackson's position; he ran as a black candidate for president in 1984 and 1988, and we all knew he couldn't win. He ran as a "statement candidate" who had a tremendous effect on down ballot races.

But Obama isn't running to make a statement. He's actually trying to get the nomination. He's raised $80 million, and is now leading in the polls in Iowa, and is cutting into Sen. Hillary Clinton's lead in New Hampshire.

Now, Clinton and Obama have both made speeches, and issued policy statements on a variety of issues of concern to African Americans. So what in the world is Rev talking about?

Jackson mentioned education, poverty, the plight of black men and the criminal justice system in his column. I've heard multiple speeches from Obama and

Clinton on those issues. So how are they not getting addressed? Now how on one hand can folks say he hasn't said a word about black issues, when the record disputes that.

I get why Jackson is making a mountain out of a mole hill. This is in his focus. But him becoming the story is ridiculous because right now, Obama has momentum, and when I turned on CNN on Tuesday, all I heard was Jackson criticizing the Democratic candidates.

After Jackson's "white" comment in South Carolina, he issued a statement reaffirming his support for Obama. And what did he do yesterday after his column? The same thing.

This back and forth with Jackson over Obama points to a serious problem, and frankly, it's one that Rev is going to have to deal with. He wants a much larger role in the Obama campaign, but Jackson has to accept the reality that Obama has to be careful as to this issue.

Like it or not, Jackson is a volatile figure outside the black community. And Obama has to clearly appeal to non-black voters for him to have any chance of winning the Democratic nomination. I concur that he has to speak to black issues—and have written as such—but he can't run as the "black candidate."

When the Democratic candidates, and specifically Obama, discuss healthcare, the Iraq War and the economy, does that not include black folks? At one point are we going to wake up and realize this?

December 21, 2007

A Few Presidential Stocking Stuffers

WHAT IN THE WORLD IS GOING ON with these Christmas ads from the candidates for president?

First, former Arkansas Gov. Mike Huckabee garners a ton of attention for what his critics called an over-the-top, cross-lovin' Christmas ad. Forget the fact that it was a bookshelf. They suggested it was lit to look like a cross and that's wrong. Wow.

A Southern Baptist preacher having a cross in an ad is shocking. Give me a break.

Now lo and behold, nearly all of the candidates have gotten in on the act. Sen. Barack Obama sits with his family; Sen. Hillary Clinton, sans Bill, wraps gifts tied to her health care plan; former Sen. John Edwards talks about poverty; Sen. John McCain draws a cross in relating a Christmas story when he was a prisoner of war in Vietnam; Rep. Ron Paul has a ton of family members in his ad; and former New York Mayor Rudy Giuliani yucks it up with Santa.

I'm not impressed. They were all nice and sweet, but why not really have some fun?

So if I had done my own commercial, I would have enlisted former Sen. Mike Gravel of Alaska to don a red suit and play Santa as I dished out a few gifts to each of the candidates.

For Sen. Hillary Clinton, a cup of spiked eggnog and a helping of holiday warmth. She has struggled to be as tough as nails and present herself as sweet as lemonade.

For Sen. Barack Obama, a name change so we don't have to hear even more "Hussein Osama" flubs. When your last name is linked with No. 1 on the world's most wanted list, that's not a good thing.

For Sen. Chris Dodd, a one-way ticket back to the U.S. Senate. He has no chance in hell of winning, so why keep going?

For Sen. Joe Biden, one of those "Back to the Future" cars Michael J. Fox used in those great movies so Biden can run all over again in 1988. That was his best shot. He knows it. We know it. But his mouth got him in too much trouble. I love the guy, but his time has passed.

For former governor, congressman, ambassador and energy secretary Bill Richardson, a CareerBuilder.com account because he'll need one in a month. Plus, he spends more time in the debates reciting his resume than he does reciting his positions.

For former Sen. John Edwards, a lifetime membership to Supercuts. Who the hell pays $400 for a haircut?! It's kind of hard to talk about poverty and then have to answer for that haircut.

For Gravel, a personality. I haven't seen a man that out of sorts since the movie *"Grumpy Old Men."*

For former Gov. Mitt Romney, more hair spray. Does his hair ever move? Reminds me of former Dallas Cowboys coach Jimmy Johnson and his perfectly coiffed mane.

For former New York Mayor Rudy Giuliani, more hair. Remember when he did the "combover"? Yikes!

For Sen. John McCain, how about a teddy bear? Because he's coming off kind of abrasive, as if he grits his teeth while talking.

For former Sen. Fred Thompson, a case of the energy drink Red Bull. This man has the most BORING campaign in history! Hey, somebody wake Fred up and shout, "Ready? Set? Action!"

For former Gov. Mike Huckabee, the George W. Bush foreign policy primer from his 2000 campaign. He's a little weak in that area. Maybe a few prayers will help.

For Reps. Tom Tancredo and Duncan Hunter, an all-expense-paid trip to Cancun, Mexico, for two. These two despise illegal immigrants, so why not let them learn a little bit more about life on the other side?

And for Reps. Ron Paul and Dennis Kucinich, round-trip tickets on UFO Airlines. Some of their ideas are out of this world.

So with that, have a merry Christmas and a happy new year!

Reflections: Joining Team Obama/Team Clinton

TATYANA ALI

"I had been following him through *O Magazine*…because Oprah was talking about him for a very long time, and that really made me want to get involved. And after looking at his policies and doing my own personal research, I wanted to be more than just a voter this time. And what I was hearing from my peers scared me. They were so beautiful and I mean, young black people would say things like, 'This will never happen. And even if it happens, something will happen to him,' and just basically saying, 'This will never, ever happen.'"

HOLLY ROBINSON-PEETE

"Well, having spent time with the Clintons during their presidency, having been invited to bring our then two-year-old twins to the White House, and Roger was playing for the Redskins, I mean, they treated us so well, as the Clintons did so many people, and so we were very torn when Obama and Clinton both came in to the race and we felt the sense of loyalty.

"But then there was the mother factor, the grandmother-mother-mother-in-law factor, meaning Dolores Robinson, who had met the senator about five, six years ago and … came back to us and said, "I just met the first black president of the United States." And we said, 'Hey Mom, no offense, but you're 71... That probably won't happen in your lifetime.'

"And so that is what made us sort of say well, she's really on this and with each step and entering the race and all that, we got intrigued. And then we met him at Oprah's Legends Ball event, him and Michelle, and then I spent a little bit more time with Michelle in Chicago. We were both on a panel and we had all these friends in common—Juanita Jordan and all my Chicago crew and it just started—it was just popping up all over my radar and I was just feeling that this was the direction that I was going toward.

"So we gave money to both of them. We wrote checks. We felt like we owed it to definitely the Clintons to support in that way. But when it came down to it … Rodney and I just felt like he was better suited for the job coming in with less baggage and we just sensed the victory."

Tichina Arnold

"As soon as I found out, of course, that he was African American and just his history, just his humble beginnings made me more interested in seeing what he was all about.

"I think my number one issue was that thank God, (George W.) Bush is gone. I mean, this is his last term so I was excited about whoever was coming into it, but to know that it was an African American man running and really just watching the whole process, and watching and learning about men like David Axelrod and David Plouffe, and how they so amazingly put together his campaign that I don't think anyone will ever be able to redo."

CHRIS TUCKER

"I met Barack before he was senator. He was in L.A. and he was in a fundraiser and we rode in a car to another fundraiser together and that really impressed me and showed me what kind of person he was, by being down to earth, because he suggested it because I didn't have a chance to meet him at the fundraiser because I got there a little late and he was like, "Come on and ride with me to the next fundraiser," and we talked in the car.

"He signed a book for me and my impression was he was just a humble guy and a down to earth guy and just that gesture and that time I spent with him, I knew that— that made me determine my decision."

BLAIR UNDERWOOD

"I felt that the country was going to very different directions, polar opposite directions if John McCain had won the election as opposed to Barack Obama winning the election. I always try to vote on the issues. So it wasn't Republican or Democrat. It was about who's the best candidate, Barack Obama. It was everything he said. I don't agree with everything he said, but I agreed with most of what he said, but most importantly, it's like people vote from their gut.

"The sense I got from him, what I saw publicly over the years and also just personally, just spending a little time with this person in a room, I read people and I kind of go from my gut and I feel like he's a person of substance. I think he's a person of intelligence and someone who would lead with integrity and would look outside of the issue but wise enough and smart enough to really see everything on different levels."

JESSICA ALBA, AND HER HUSBAND, CASH WARREN

CASH: "We had been supporters of his a solid year before he announced he is running for President and then when he announced he is running, we did some (fundraising).

JESSICA: "I did a more bipartisan push in just getting people to vote knowing which way people were going to vote… they are more likely going to vote for Obama."

VANESSA WILLIAMS

"I got to be honest and tell you that I was very, very skeptical about whether a black man, no matter how qualified, could really win over the rest of the country, so I was a little bit doubtful. Then I was torn between my sort of feminist/womanist position because men had been running this country since it began so I was like, well, you know, since we're going to do a change, let's see what a woman would do. So I initially started out vacillating and leaning kind of toward Hillary but feeling very, very conflicted with that.

"I went to a rally where Hillary was speaking and some other really good friends and colleagues of mine were with her and it was kind of cool getting like a "Madam President" shirt and I was like, 'Wow, this is getting kind of cool.' But as I said, since I was still on the fence, I was really looking for her to really win me over, to really, like, change my mind about—that it was going to be different. But I still hadn't completely, completely turned around. I wasn't still leaning toward her after meeting her and it wasn't anything necessarily that she said. She spoke to a small group of Hollywood people and we had to wait a long time. But she was on the trail so I'd give people a break."

MALIK YOBA

"At the outset, I was definitely a Clinton fan, a Bill Clinton fan and I liked the idea that Hillary was running and I liked the idea that Barack was running. And from the beginning, I always felt like I'm kind of cool with either one of them and then I thought like if he won, she should be vice president. If she won, he should be vice president, that kind of thing.

"And then I saw Michelle Obama speak at UCLA and I felt like whoever is married to that woman, I got his back. And so that's when I started campaigning and then that's when I bought my Facebook and my MySpace page. I said, "I got Michelle's husband's back." And I was selling the Obama T-shirt, the one I had at the DNC. I started selling those to raise money for the campaign."

SPIKE LEE

"It was a pivotal moment in world history and I cannot just sit by the side on the side and wait 'till it was safe. And a whole lot of people, a whole lot of Negroes were waiting by the side before they stepped out. They want to make sure it is cool because they do not want to do anything that is going to impact you know, the bottom line. They eventually came aboard, but only when the coast is clear; when it became apparent that history is going to be made. And there are others... some people, no names need to be mentioned

"Look, people are going to vote the way they want to vote. But I would discuss how did they come to their way of thinking. You know, what are they basing their thinking on? A lot these guys felt that we are beholden to the Clintons, that we owe them something. I just could not understand that thinking."

Kevin Liles

"It was the first campaign that I directly got involved in as far as going out day to day, with the... for the president, but it is not the first campaign that I have ever been involved in.

"I felt as young America we had been disengaged for the last eight years. I felt that we are not a society of people that sits back and watch things happen for us, and the last election eight years ago was very disappointing to us. The one four years ago was very disappointing to us, so no longer were we staying around talking about woulda, coulda, shoulda. It was time for us to go out and make something happen ourselves."

Erika Alexander

"I found it a little difficult and I think it's difficult because so many people had started off, I'm sure, in support of Hillary Clinton. I don't think they knew who Obama was at the time. A lot of my friends certainly had not heard him speak, and his name had not come up.

"When I did an event here for Hillary, they came to the event and Hillary had just put out her record. She put out her record and her results. People were blown away. They had known her as a first lady but they didn't even know what she had done.

"It was interesting for people to be on board at first but then suddenly, when he won Iowa, it was like the support vanished in terms of the African American community, which I thought was as just exciting in one way because I think they were excited to have a candidate that reads the Bible that looked like them. But I thought that the support in what she was advocating and what she stood for and the things they said that were in their interest had not changed and that, to me, was, I think, a disappointment and that there was only one way to put it because it was very difficult to suddenly be on a side where people were whispering in my ears when I visited churches, because I was a national surrogate as well for Hillary and I went all over for her."

COMMON

"Well you know, being from Chicago, when I would go home, my mother and my stepfather would have an Obama sign up in the window.

"I could not say I was really politically astute or just really a big supporter of politics…Just because my mother was supporting him it did not necessarily mean that I was full-fledged, but…I heard more about him and I got to meet him and at the Hip Hop Summit. I am a real energy person (and) I felt like there is a positive energy from this person."

HILL HARPER

"My first meeting with him was 20 years ago when we were in a law school and we weren't thinking about who is going to run for president. We played a lot of basketball together in Harvard Law School.

"There is no question about it when I first met him in law school that I looked up to him and that is not just because he is taller than me. I looked up to him because he had a sense of gravitas to be quite honest. He was older than everybody else and certainly older than me. He had been out doing community organization in Chicago for five years and here he is going back to school. I went straight from undergrad to grad school, still trying to figure out if I was going to be in the government. He knew; he had a very clear sense that he knew exactly why he was there.

"He is so extremely intelligent, extremely hardworking, but the one thing that I think never came across as much during the campaign is really him and his personality and how funny he is. He has a great wit and is sarcastic. He can tell a good joke and he picks up on something and does a zinger."

PART 2

THE PRIMARIES

Back Story: Iowa

IT'S ALWAYS FUNNY TO ME WHEN I TRAVEL around the country and folks tell me they enjoyed my commentary on primary nights. But what many of them don't even remember is that on the very first night—the Iowa caucuses—I barely made it on CNN.

It was a crazy day. We were all running around, getting prepared for the big night. Elections are like that; it's sort of like a grand opening or a big party. Everything has to be in place because when 7 pm. hits, there is no looking back.

The fifth floor of 1 Time Warner Center, home of our Election Center set, was buzzin'. Crews were still assembling the set, dozens and dozens of people were running back and forth, peering at computer screens, looking at polling data, all to get ready for the first night.

Folks, election nights are sort of like the Super Bowl for sports journalists. Fortunately for us, we had at least 20 Super Bowls in 2008!

After checking it all out, I decided to head back to my office to prepare for a few more shows and get ready for the big night.

Now, I changed clothes before coming downstairs for the 7 P.M. show because after you've been on TV in the daytime, who wants to be seen wearing the same thing in prime time?

When I came downstairs, the place was even noisier. I brought my Comrex portable access unit, which allowed me to broadcast back to WVON as if I was sitting in the studio. I wasn't sure when I was getting on that night, so I decided to do a little double duty.

As we were waiting for the broadcast, Lou Dobbs walked by and I decided to do a quick interview with him. Then I sat down for the show.

Then 7 P.M. struck and we were off and running. Our A-team of The Best Political Team on Television were all on the set, and I was one of several political contributors waiting in the wings.

I was watching our coverage and working my sources in the Sen. Barack Obama campaign.

I knew his every move and what he was doing at that moment because I was communicating with several of his top folks.

At one point I heard one of our reporters say they weren't sure where Obama was watching election returns, and I sent an e-mail to my "handler" Stephanie Kotuby, "He's having dinner with friends and family."

As the night progressed, it was clear Obama was heading for an upset victory.

When he won, folks were stunned. Forget the professionals. No one thought this black political upstart from Chicago was going to defeat the likes of former VP candidate John Edwards and former first lady, Sen. Hillary Clinton.

But he did, and folks were going on and on about what it meant for an African American candidate to win nearly all-white Iowa.

I was talking to Obama's political operatives and getting the skinny on how it happened and shooting it directly to Stephanie, who began to press folks about getting me on the air.

But nothing happened.

Then one of our reporters talked about Obama coming to the victory party and saying they weren't sure when he was going to arrive.

I e-mailed Stephanie, "He's leaving in 15 minutes."

Stephanie asked me to land Obama for an interview with the network, but Obama's folks wanted his speech to be the only sound of him that night, and we were a no-go.

Finally, after much pleading and begging—she even pressed Jon Klein, president of CNN/U.S. (and she had never met him before!)—Stephanie got the green light to put me on the air. It was nearly four hours after our coverage began, and I was on the air for no more than 1 ½ minutes. Yea, I got in the game, but that was the equivalent of running down the field on a kickoff. Sorry, I wanted more action, and what took place the next day ensured that was the last time I was ignored on an election night.

January 4, 2008

Obama's Iowa Win Proves He's Electable

YOU MAY FIND A BUNCH OF POLITICAL OPERATIVES who will suggest today that they always believed a black man named Barack Obama would blow away his competitors in Iowa and would destroy the inevitably of a former first lady who is a member of the U.S. Senate.

If that's the case, just walk away because they are lying.

I was there on that frigid February day in Springfield, Ill., when Sen. Obama, standing in the shadows of the old Capitol where Abraham Lincoln delivered his famous "House Divided" speech on June 16, 1858, and while his soaring rhetoric was warmly received, it was assumed that, if he could just survive the first two states, maybe he wouldn't embarrass himself.

But the game has changed, and all of a sudden, there is a sense that Obama actually could win this thing.

Yet even after getting dusted by 9 points in Iowa and watching Obama walk away with more female voters than she got, Hillary Clinton continues to assert that it will be impossible for Obama to get elected in November against a Republican challenger.

When I asked Obama about that in an exclusive interview for my radio show on WVON in Chicago and for CNN, he couldn't help but laugh.

"Look at what happened in Iowa," he said. "We had Republicans who crossed over to vote for me. We had more independents caucusing for me than anybody. That's the reason why the polls show I'm the only Democrat that beats every Republican.

"What I think they are suggesting is that being engaged in this brutal brawl with the Republicans, that that's somehow the recipe for Democrats to win. I disagree. The strategy is to pick off Republicans and independents by having a positive agenda for change."

He later added, "You can't say someone's not electable when they keep on winning elections."

But there is something else going on here; and that is Obama is the first candidate of his generation to truly be a change agent who inspires, motivates and ignites the passion in a large segment of America that had ignored politics because it was unseemly and didn't move people to action.

My e-mail inbox and my talk show lines filled up with people who say that listening to Obama empowers them to get involved; that he is able to connect with them on an emotional and spiritual level that is reminiscent of John and Robert Kennedy and Martin Luther King Jr.

Sure, for a significant segment, Ronald Reagan represented that kind of hope in 1988. Gary Hart had the potential to do that, until his personal issues derailed his campaign in the '80s. And Bill Clinton touched the hearts and minds of the baby boomers in 1992.

But this appears to be something different. Obama seeks to serve as a bridge between the divisions in America that exist between young and old; haves and have-nots; liberals and conservatives; Republicans and Democrats.

It's reminiscent of Lincoln's speeches and Dr. King's book, *Why We Can't Wait,* a compilation of his essays including his "Letter from Birmingham Jail."

At the end of the day, Obama is trying to speak to the core of America that says we can overcome all the barriers that exist between us if we simply are willing to trust in one another.

Now he takes his campaign to New Hampshire, another predominantly white state, where there are a ton of independents who could vault him to the top of the field. Will residents there buy the hope of Obama and send him to South Carolina with another victory? Will African Americans who fear whites not voting for Obama now see his Iowa win as validation that those fears are unfounded?

Simply put, will America be willing to walk away from what some say is a sure thing of a Clinton in the White House and embrace a man who says we can do all things if we just believe enough in ourselves?

It all might sound like New Age mumbo jumbo. But the more Obama speaks and the more goose bumps that are raised, the more he makes the eight years Bill Clinton spent in the White House seem like ancient history and an Obama White House as the dawn of a new day for America.

Back Story: "No, It's a Roland Martin and WVON Exclusive"

AS SEN. BARACK OBAMA WAS GIVING HIS WINNING SPEECH in Iowa, I was working the hell out of the phones.

Man, I must have called every contact in his campaign to try to get him to do an interview that night.

And all I heard was, "No."

"Fine, can you get him to do my radio show tomorrow morning?"

Being from Chicago, and knowing that African Americans were his base, it was natural for him to do my morning show on WVON. It was the only black-owned station in Chicago, and he used to have a show there several years previously after the owner, Melody Spann Cooper, put him on the air to build his profile in the city.

His folks kept saying they would try, but not making any promises.

The next morning, he never called. He had gone straight from Iowa to New Hampshire and got virtually no sleep. The next election was five nights away and every moment counted.

But around 10 A.M., deputy press secretary Candice Tolliver called me and said, "I've got you eight minutes with the senator." Yet there was a catch: it was radio-only.

You might say that's no big deal, but I was already off the air! Yet there was no way I was going to let that stop me. So I agreed to do the interview and we would run it in it's entirety on the afternoon drive show hosted by Cliff Kelley.

So I had an idea. What if I did the interview on the CNN Election Center set, put his photo on the wall, had him call the control room, and did the interview that way? I shot an e-mail to the higher ups. One, they were shocked that he consented to an interview, and likely stunned that the only interview he gave to a journalist the day after his historic Iowa win would go to me.

But they agreed to the deal.

So that afternoon, it all came together. Here was the guy folks assumed was just a radio talk show host from Chicago, standing on the same set where Wolf Blitzer reigned supreme the night before, about to interview Mr. Upset and the Democratic frontrunner for president, Sen. Barack Hussein Obama.

Yea, I was feeling it, and knew what it meant for the rest of the election.

His team gave us eight minutes, but I kept going, and almost took about 15 minutes. Obama was gracious, even though he barely had a voice.

Once the interview was over, our folks were scrambling to get it on the air. Yes, it was an exclusive. No network, print or broadcast outlet had an interview with him that day, and we wanted to milk the heck out of it.

But remember that catch? CNN couldn't air anything without it running on WVON first.

I'm sure someone reading this will say, "Man, CNN is bigger than that 10,000-watt radio station on the South Side of Chicago!" That's true. But the interview was promised to me and WVON, and I wasn't going to leave my radio audience out in the cold. So they took the audio from the interview, put it on a flash drive, and I uploaded it to my computer, and went live with it on Cliff's WVON show.

WVON's owner, Melody, was happy as all get out, and so was I.

When it came time to brand the interview a CNN exclusive, I had to tell them, no, it could be called a Roland S. Martin/WVON exclusive. That was the deal. And thankfully for CNN, I was also working there, and they benefitted from my relationship with WVON.

The next week, I was a part of Monday's pre-election show, and got a lot more airtime Tuesday night for the New Hampshire primary.

Suffice to say, Iowa put Sen. Barack Obama on the path to the presidency, and Iowa and Obama put me on the path to assume a much more prominent role as a member of The Best Political Team on Television.

January 4, 2008

Sen. Barack Obama on The Roland S. Martin Show, WVON-AM/Chicago

Roland Martin: We are joined right now by Senator Barack Obama after his huge win last night in Iowa. Senator Obama, welcome. How are you sir?

Barack Obama: It is great to talk to you Roland even though my voice is a little hoarse my spirits are high.

Roland Martin: I take it folks will tell you drink a lot of hot water and lemon, I am quite sure.

Barack Obama: That is what I am doing. I am turning yellow with all this lemon I am drinking.

Roland Martin: I understand. Now given the Iowa win, do you now consider yourself to be the frontrunner, or you are still operating as the underdog in this campaign?

Barack Obama: If your name is Barack Obama you are always the underdog in a political race, but obviously we had a big night last night, and the American people had a big night. Because what we showed was that if the American people are offered a chance for real change and coming together, somebody with a track record of overcoming the special interest, somebody they trust to be straight with them about how we are going to solve problems like healthcare, energy, our education system, bring our troops home from Iraq, then they will respond, and they responded in record numbers. What was best about it, Roland, was it was not just one group. We won among union voters, we won among women, we won among African American and whites, we won among older voters who had not participated in the caucuses before, we had independents coming in, we had Republicans who decided to change party affiliation, the caucus force, and most importantly we have young people. We, for the first time I think in election memory, had the 17 to 30 age group voting the same rate as the 65 and older age group. It never happened before.

Roland Martin: I want to talk about that, because I talked to Cornell Belcher, your lead pollster, and he said that you guys exceeded expectations in all those categories. What specifically do you think was it that caused you to sort of bring all of these different niche groups together to support your candidacy in Iowa?

Barack Obama: I just think that people are looking for something hopeful, something real, and they want to feel like they are being listened to. And that we are operating on the basis of practicality instead of ideology, and that's what we've been offering throughout this campaign and I think that really is going to resonate here in New Hampshire where a majority of the voters are undeclared, meaning they are independents. What they just don't want to see is a repeat of the same old partisan group right in Washington. That's what we really pushed off against.

Roland Martin: Let us talk about electability. Senator Hilary Clinton has really been talking today about the issue of being able to beat the Republicans. How are you able to beat the Republicans compared to her in a general election campaign?

Barack Obama: Look what happened in Iowa. We have Republicans who crossed over to vote for me. We got more independents to caucus. We have more independents caucusing for me than anybody. So, that is the reason why the polls show I am the only Democratic who beats every Republican. I mean, what I think they are really suggesting is somehow that being engaged in this brutal brawl with the Republicans that that somehow is the recipe for Democrats to win. I disagree. I think the strategy is to pick off Republicans and independents by having a positive agenda for change. And that is what we did last night; that's how I won my U.S. Senate race. You can't keep on saying that somebody is not electable when they keep on winning elections.

Roland Martin: Let us talk about this whole notion of you being an African American winning in Iowa. They've never elected an African American in any statewide office. And it is an interesting dynamic with that state being 90 plus percent white. You, a black candidate running in Iowa, what does that say about the state? What does it say about white voters embracing your campaign?

Barack Obama: I think it says that race is still a factor in this country, but that we've made enormous progress and that people right now are looking for somebody who can lead, and they are less concerned about what color they are than whether or not they are going help them provide healthcare to people who need it. Are they going to be able to deal with the enormous foreign policy issues that we confront. Whether they could lower gas prices; help people get jobs with good benefits and a decent retirement. And if they feel that that candidate is somebody who is going to perform for them then race is not the issue that they are going to vote on.

Roland Martin: We got a ton of phone calls on this issue on my radio show today, WVON, of course you are quite familiar with in Chicago and that is, it is interesting that African Americans somehow were waiting for white voters to validate you as a candidate before many of them would embrace your candidacy. You and I talked about this. How do you explain that... this notion that... well, we do not think white voters are going to vote for Obama so therefore we are going to hold our support and go to someone else. How does this now change the dynamic, especially in South Carolina?

Barack Obama: Well, I think that, if there is any African American voter out there who still thinks that whites won't vote for him, they just need to read the papers this morning. That should put that to rest. Now if they are African American voters who think that there is somebody else out there who could represent their interests better, then that's not a problem. I don't think there's a candidate out there who has been more invested in making sure that the African American community succeeds and prospers and has taken risks and chances to make that happen. But if an African American voter is selecting another candidate on the platform or just because they like that person better, that's fine. But they certainly shouldn't use the excuse that whites will not vote for me. We have shown that wasn't the case with my U.S. Senate race, we showed it last night in Iowa. I believe that we are going to show it in New Hampshire and so we are ready to move forward.

Roland Martin: And speaking of moving forward, let us advance this conversation in one year. Let us say you become president. If you are elected, what is the very first thing you focus on as commander-in-chief of this country?

Barack Obama: We will call in the Joint Chiefs of Staff, I will give them a new assignment, and that is to bring our troops home in a careful, responsible way, but to end this occupation in Iraq. I will call my Secretary of State and initiate the diplomacy that is needed to make sure that that exit is accompanied by negotiations between the Shiites, the Sunnis and the Kurds.

Roland Martin: So you believe the way to end it is to be able to negotiate between those rival factions in Iraq?

Barack Obama: Absolutely, and I said that consistently. Part of the reason we need to begin a withdrawal is to trigger a different set of actions among those in power in Iraq. We have not yet seen the central government in Iraq behaving in a responsible fashion and until that happens, we are going to continue to see instability in that country.

Roland Martin: You spend a lot of time talking about bipartisanship on the campaign trail—a huge issue in New Hampshire. How do you actually do that? How can you as president actually bring Republicans and Democrats side by side to find common ground on some of the most difficult issues facing this country?

Barack Obama: We are not going to be able to find common ground on every single issue, I mean there will be some issues. But there is a certain wing of the Republican Party, for example, that thinks that no matter what, cutting taxes for the rich is always good. I just profoundly disagree with it. And so my strategy is to pick off enough fiscally responsible Republicans who are willing to say, you know what, probably more tax breaks for millionaires isn't the way to go because we need to balance the budget for future generations. So, you are never looking for 100 percent agreement, the question is can you get the 60? Can you get the 60 percent and if you got a mandate for change from the American people then I believe that that mandate can be achieved.

Roland Martin: Could we possibly find a Republican or two operating as a cabinet member in the Obama administration?

Barack Obama: That's certainly possible. I want the best people.

Roland Martin: Now, let us do this whole issue of you and your experience and operating from day one. What is your response when you hear your opponents talking about being able to run the country on day one?

Barack Obama: You know, I just find it remarkable that these are the same people that we're out-organizing in a presidential campaign. We started from zero and 11 months later are competing against organizations that were built over six years, 20 years, with all these great managers and leaders, and somehow they can't keep up. So, I think that we have shown the ability to set a tone, a positive tone in the campaign, to organize people and organize money to accomplish goals, to get a message across, to inspire the American people, to lead, and that's what I intend to do as president.

Roland Martin: Senator last question. I've been listening to your speeches over the last several months and especially that speech last night and I got the sense that you are channeling Abraham Lincoln's "A House Divided" speech, of course, you launched your campaign in front of the old capitol in Springfield, Illinois. But I am also hearing King's *Why We Can't Wait* and his "Letter from Birmingham Jail." Are you really pulling from those sources by saying that you are the bridge that somehow is able to bring young and old together, Republican, Democrat, liberal, conservative, red state, blue state? Am I on the right track when I hear those elements?

Barack Obama: I think there is no doubt Roland. I would not make those comparisons. Those are some of the greatest Americans in history. There is no doubt that I read their speeches and that they inspire me and that they represent the best moments in our history, and so, not surprisingly that you hear echoes of them in some of my speeches just because I believe as they believed that this is not a perfect union, but we can make it more perfect. That if we are willing to work hard and imagine something better then we can achieve something. We have to hope and we have to dream and put some hard work on it. So, that is what I think the American people believe as well, that is why I think we did well last night, I believe that is why we will do well in the weeks and months to come.

Roland Martin: Well, we will certainly follow the campaign and now is an opportunity for you to rest your voice because our time is up. Senator Barack Obama, I certainly appreciate it and we will see you in New Hampshire.

January 8, 2008

WVON-AM/Chicago: Susan Rice on The Roland S. Martin

Roland Martin: Let us go to Susan Rice. She is a former senior Clinton administration official and she was, I believe, Assistant Secretary of State in the Clinton administration and she is now senior adviser of foreign policy to Senator Barack Obama. And I could tell you this folks, I would not be surprised if there is a President Obama, there is going to be a second Secretary of State named Rice and that will be Susan Rice. Susan, welcome to the Roland S. Martin Show.

Susan Rice: Thanks, Roland you give me too many props.

Roland Martin: No, no, no, I understand but no, on this show the only black station in Chicago, we certainly give black folks their props with some significant accomplishments and you are certainly one of those folks. Let us talk about the senator for a second here—big lead in New Hampshire. What do you believe the American public is saying with this embracing of a politician? It is now a phenomena, and as someone has called it yesterday, it is becoming a movement.

Susan Rice: Well, what I would demonstrate, and we will see today in New Hampshire obviously, those New Hampshire voters need to have their say, but there seems to be this ground swell of feeling that our country needs fundamental change, that we are tired of the divisiveness and pitting against one another, that we need to come together to make our country as good as it can possibly be and to renew our relationship with the rest of the world. And I think there is a hope and a hunger and an optimism that hasn't been tapped into and that is what Barack Obama is doing and people are passionate for the first time about their politics and their ability to change their own political prospects.

Roland Martin: This whole issue of him not having foreign policy experience. You know, first of all, I am struck by several different things, I really am, and that is that George W. Bush, he was governor of Texas six years, he runs for the president, his top foreign policy adviser, Condoleezza Rice, and then there are people who are shooting here saying, well no foreign policy experience. When you look at our history, Jimmy Carter did not have much when he ran in '76, Reagan did not have much when he ran 1980, Clinton did not have much when he ran

1992, Bush did not have much when he ran in 2000. So the American people have never really said that foreign policy is the be all to end all. It seems to be something else that they say is important.

Susan Rice: You are absolutely right. You know this notion that he does not have foreign policy experience is wrong. He has more traditional foreign policy experience than all those former presidents you just named. He served three years, had been a leader and a very effective legislator on the Senate Foreign Relations Committee. He has traveled to the former Soviet Union, to the Middle East, to Africa, to Europe. He has passed legislation on critical issues like non-proliferation and securing our loose nuclear materials. He is on the Veterans Committee, the Homeland Security Committee, but Roland, the real thing about foreign policy experience if you have it and it works well for you, it should give you good judgment. Now, we saw what Dick Cheney and Don Rumsfeld, with all the years in Washington aside, it didn't give them good judgment. But Barack Obama innately has the good judgment and the wisdom to be able to see what is in our national interest. So, he was wise enough to see in 2002 that this war in Iraq would be disastrous for our national security. He was wise enough to say and endure ridicule that we need to be willing and never fear to negotiate with our adversaries, and that he would play a leadership role in trying to negotiate directly with countries like Iran. He was ridiculed and told he was naïve and irresponsible. Now, the other candidates are echoing that theme and the national intelligence estimate validates it. On Pakistan, he said we shouldn't put all of our eggs in Musharraf's basket. We need to be on the side of the democracy movement. And he said that many, many months ago, and now we've seen that perspective validated tragically. And so, you know he has the judgment and the wisdom to make the right decisions. He has more traditional foreign policy experience than virtually all of his predecessors in the last two or three decades. And he also has a life experience having lived abroad, continuing to have relatives who live in the developing world in Kenya. That sort of perspective gives you a unique understanding of what America looks like to people who are living on the bottom of the heap instead of the top of the pile, and that's crucial as we try to renew our relationships with the rest of the world.

Roland Martin: Last question, Susan. Lots of people, lots of people say that, Hey former Clinton administration officials were getting behind Senator Hillary Clinton, I know you do not have much time but 40 seconds, what was the one thing for you to say, this is why I am behind Senator Barack Obama?

Susan Rice: It has nothing to do with the Clintons. I have enormous respect with them. It's because I believe with all my heart that Barack Obama is the man we need to transform our country at this critical moment and renew and reinvigorate our relationship with the rest of the world. Nobody can do it better than he can.

Roland Martin: Okay folks, great, great conversation. I certainly appreciate it. Susan Rice, former President Clinton administration official, top dog in the state department. Well, like right underneath. Of course, she is now senior adviser foreign policy to Senator Barack Obama. Susan, thanks a bunch.

Susan Rice: Good to talk to you.

Sen. Dick Durbin on The Roland S. Martin Show, WVON-AM/Chicago

Roland Martin: You are listening to the Roland S. Martin show on The Talk of Chicago 1690/WVON. Certainly glad you could join us. You get a sense of what's going on don't you? Seems like every time it— one thing we are doing because of this feeling, these things that are going on in this race, what we do is anytime the—what we do with Obama, we are playing that song because indeed folks, something is going on. I don't think we can deny that, that there is something that is much seem to be bigger than politics that's going on in this campaign, which is why I think people are so taken aback. And the reality is if you look at Senator Hillary Clinton, frankly in a traditional year, she would be doing well.

Right now I have someone on the phone that I want to hear from. I have not talked to him in a while and I certainly want to get him on the show a lot more regularly. Senator Dick Durbin, senior senator from Illinois, somebody who early on, early on, was really encouraging Senator Barack Obama to run for president. Senator Dick Durbin welcome to the show.

Dick Durbin: Good to be with you.

Roland Martin: Look how thing are going. Your guy is doing very, very well. People are very, very surprised at what is going on. How do you explain it? We here, well you know, you vote things along those lines, change, hope, inspiration but what do you think? What is he tapping into that is creating this excitement if you will?

Dick Durbin: Well, let me tell you that Barack Obama is a special person. I think we know that. Now, we saw what happened when he ran for the United States Senate. He ran in a strong field of candidates from the Democratic Primary. One of the candidates spent $40 million to win, and when all the dust is settled, Barack Obama had more votes than all the other Democratic candidates combined. And then of course they had a tough time on the Republican side finding a serious candidate to run against him in November. He is just a powerful force in our state, and I think now, around the country, people are getting to know him. As they get to know him and like him and they believe that his attitude, his approach to America and its challenges is just what we need at this moment in time.

Roland Martin: One of the things that I am noticing, and I have been getting some e-mails on this is, that there seems to be this framing somehow that Obama is, you know, the Clinton campaign seems to be saying rhetoric versus action. But Obama has though, has taken a lot of significant policy positions and so I—this is giving the sense of the oh-oh, you know the guy has to say anything about, you know, immigration, but he has.

Dick Durbin: He has. And I tell you what, if you want to spend the day, if someone will send in the food, go to his web site and start reading him. I mean he has published his positions on all of these issues, so that criticism I think is from people who really haven't tried. I can tell you that as his colleague in the Senate, that for years now we've been voting on these big issues. When he comes to the floor, we come together, we talk about them for a few minutes because folks back in Illinois want to know if we are going to vote in different ways, and it is rare that we do. But I know that he has given good thought to these things. I know that he has been leader on a lot of these issues and if the folks want to know the specifics, head on over to that Obama web site. There is plenty of information there.

Roland Martin: New Hampshire, you got some major things happening there. The next step obviously is Nevada. That does get much attention. South Carolina, but the biggie is February 5th. In your estimation how is Obama shaping up for super duper Tuesday?

Dick Durbin: Well, it is hard to say at this moment. Here is the problem that we faced in the campaign. Earlier on Senator Clinton's name is well known, certainly a household name among Democratic families. So there would be a national poll, she would do very, very well. Now those of us in Illinois who know Obama said, 'Well, doesn't everybody else?" And the average answer is no they do not, but they are getting to know him, and after the Iowa caucus, that surprise victory that he had there, even more people are paying attention. So, I noticed now that Senator Clinton's national lead over Barack has gone from about 20 points just a few weeks ago to 7 points this morning. It's an indication to me that as people get to know Barack and know what his message is all about, they feel good about it and they feel good about the idea that he'll be our next President of the United States.

Roland Martin: Okay, well again Senator Dick Durbin we certainly appreciate this, so thank you so very much for being with us. It is certainly an exciting time just as the song is saying, "You can feel it."

Dick Durbin: I can feel it. I am out here in New Hampshire. I was with him last night and as he said and you said, something's going on.

Roland Martin: All right Senator Dick Durbin, thank you so very much sir for your participation. Thanks a lot.

Dick Durbin: All right. Thank you.

January 9, 2008, Essence.com Blog

So, What Did Happen in New Hampshire?

ON MONDAY NIGHT, the campaign of Sen. Barack Obama was preparing for a blowout day as they would defeat Sen. Hillary Clinton, dealing a serious blow to her chances of winning the Democratic presidential nomination.

By Tuesday night, everyone was left stunned as a nine-point lead—one poll had it at 13—evaporated and it was Clinton giving a victory speech and Obama thanking her on a job well done.

So, was it Clinton's tears causing women to come out and prop her campaign up? Was it an over-confident, some say cocky, Obama campaign getting humbled? Did Bill Clinton pull it out for his wife like he did in 1992 when he came in second here and declared himself the Comeback Kid?

Let's go inside the numbers.

UNDECIDEDS MATTERED. All of the polls had Obama gaining 37% and Clinton winning 30 percent. The final results? Obama got 37 percent and Clinton 39 percent. What happened? Undecided voters spoke. Exit polls show that 15 percent of the voters on Tuesday made up their minds as they headed to the polls that day. And with a record number of voters, nearly 300,000, that means you had 40,000-plus who cast ballots that had not made their feelings known. If you assume Clinton won 60 percent of those voters, that's about 24,000 to Obama's 16,000. What was her margin of victory? About 8,000.

TEARS FOR FEARS. Clinton was down three points to Obama among women prior to the vote. After the vote, she beat him by 13 points. Many believe her newfound sensitivity, especially with the choking back of tears on Monday, caused women to be more sympathetic to her and vaulted her over the top.

TRADITIONAL VS. NON-TRADITIONAL. Obama took the risky strategy of going after independents, the young vote and Republicans. Clinton? She went after labor, older voters, women and blue collar. The result? She won the key categories, especially single females. She also dusted Obama in the big cities, winning by wide margins.

THE BILL FACTOR. I'm not sold that he pulled it out for her. I think he was used wisely, but it was her overhaul of her message that won the day.

WHITE FLIGHT FROM OBAMA. There is some speculation that New Hampshire, 97 percent white, said Obama was the guy, but once they got into the booth, changed their minds. Not sure if that was the case, and it's hard to quantify. Maybe New Hampshire just gave her the close victory.

WHAT'S NEXT. Nevada on Jan. 19, where Obama has picked up two huge union endorsements. Then the battleground of South Carolina, where the Clintons and Obama will duke it out for black votes. The key? *Black women.* They are 40 percent undecided. Bill will pour on the charm to get them to back his wife. The Obama campaign should unleash his wife, Michelle, and let the mother of two, professional lawyer from the South Side of Chicago rally sisters to her husband.

Then Tsunami Tuesday, when 23 states go to the polls on Feb. 5. Among them? California, New York, New Jersey, Georgia, Alabama, Tennessee, Virginia and Arkansas. Who dominates here will likely be the nominee.

January 11, 2008, Essence.com Blog

Clinton Working Overtime to Clean Up King-LBJ Comments

THE CAMPAIGN OF SEN. HILLARY CLINTON has been working overtime in trying to allay the concerns among African Americans that she meant no disrespect to the legacy of the Rev. Dr. Martin Luther King Jr. in her criticism of Sen. Barack Obama.

And judging by the story in today's *New York Times* on Rep. James Clyburn, the powerful South Carolina congressman who is possibly reconsidering issuing an endorsement in the race because of the comments, they have some more work to do.

Sources inside and outside the campaign tell me that stalwarts of the Civil Rights Movement, as well as the King family, have received phone calls reassuring them that Clinton was not criticizing the civil rights leader.

In an interview with Fox's Major Garrett, Clinton criticized Obama for his emphasis on inspiring words, as well as suggesting that he was similar in that regard to President John F. Kennedy and King (Obama supporters deny this, saying he was suggesting that they, too, used words to inspire).

She went on to state that blacks attaining rights wasn't solely about speeches and marches.

"Dr. King's dream began to be realized when President Johnson passed the Civil Rights Act," Clinton said. "It took a president to get it done."

On the campaign stump, she expounded on the remark, crediting King and others for their action to get the president to act himself.

But the King slap flap is spreading like wildfire on blogs targeting African Americans, as well as black radio talk shows.

The Obama campaign failed to respond to her comments, even though she gave them an opening. They could have responded, "Yes, LBJ did sign the bills into law. But had Clinton's choice for president, Sen. Barry Goldwater, won the election, no civil rights laws would have been signed."

She, of course, was called a "Goldwater girl," and we all know he was hostile to civil rights.

What Clinton is learning, and what other politicians have had to face for a long time, is that Dr. King is untouchable among African Americans. Whether called a prophet or The Great Black Hope, any attempt to lessen his impact on the nation will be met with stiff resistance.

If Clyburn chooses to endorse Obama because of this flap, Clinton will have paid a King's ransom for broaching this subject.

January 11, 2008
Clinton Redefines What Experience Is

A GOOD ASSESSMENT OF HOW A CANDIDATE successfully takes a message and makes a mark on voters is when you begin to read and hear the person repeat it over and over in calls, e-mails and on radio talk shows.

After getting blown away by Sen. Barack Obama in Iowa, Sen. Hillary Clinton knew that she needed to change her position to combat the agent-of-change language presented by Obama. It was clear that just talking about her experience as first lady wasn't enough because taking credit for all the good done by the administration of President Bill Clinton also meant assuming the bad.

But what Hillary Clinton has done is reframe her experience by expanding it beyond the seven years she's served in the U.S. Senate. Now you hear her talk about having 35 years of experience as a change agent.

The key part really isn't being an advocate for change, but the emphasis on 35 years.

And it has caught on because I've noticed the phrase taking foot among the electorate, and now they are repeating it.

Judging by her resume, the 60-year-old Clinton has decided to reach back and suggest that all the work she has done since graduating from college matters. The compare and contrast is that with Obama being 46, Clinton is suggesting that she has been working on issues since her chief rival was still in junior high school.

Ouch.

During the debate before the New Hampshire primary, Clinton forcefully made the point, seeking to establish her credentials over a long period of time.

That was evident during the final stages of the campaign in the Granite State, where she chose to go toward a policy-oriented stump speech, rather than hit all the usual talking points.

And now, with the economy roaring to the top of the agenda as to what concerns America the most, this is going to become even more critical.

The biggest knock on Obama's campaign has been Clinton defining him as being inexperienced, even though it is true that he's served longer as an elected official (11 years) than Clinton (seven).

The Obama campaign has failed to respond adequately to this change in Clinton's tactics. Even during the debate, Obama sat idly by as Clinton efficiently made the argument, allowing the point to be hammered home.

If his team continues to let experience become a strong anthem, they will pay for it because, for the most part, the rest of the states will require getting traditional Democratic voters out to the polls. New Hampshire was big on low-to middle-income and blue-collar voters, and they find Clinton appealing, while upper-income voters prefer Obama.

Now that South Carolina is coming up on Jan. 26, along with states such as Virginia, Alabama, Tennessee and others, pocketbook issues will be vital, and not the war. That goes up Clinton's alley.

One way for the Obama campaign to connect with these critical voters is to stop having Obama just say he worked as a community organizer. What does that really mean?

He has to paint the picture of going into the public housing complexes of Chicago, helping people get needed services. He must say that he drove a beat-up car to the West Side and South Side to sign people up to vote. He must say that his experience in the streets—laid out as explicitly as possible—is the kind of experience that he will reflect on and use when sitting in the Oval Office. He should explain how his mom had to go on food stamps to feed the family. He should tell the audience that he and Michelle paid off their student loans just three years ago.

Voters are worried about rising tuition costs and the ability to maintain a decent standard of living. They want someone who will speak from the heart, make it clear that he hears them and offer solutions to their problems when he gets to 1600 Pennsylvania Ave.

As of now, Clinton is winning the experience battle by changing the definition, and that could be the turning point as the election moves forward.

January 14, 2008

WVON-AM/Chicago: Bill Clinton, 42nd President of the United States, on The Roland S. Martin Show

Roland Martin: Let's go to the phone lines for our next guest, ladies and gentleman, the 42nd President of the United States, William Jefferson Clinton, President Clinton, good morning.

Bill Clinton: Good morning, Roland, how are you?

The Primaries

Roland Martin: Doing great, certainly glad you could be with us, sir. I want to jump right into this, lots of conversation the last several days, a very heated campaign, Senator Barack Obama. He wins in Iowa, your wife, Senator Hillary Clinton, wins in New Hampshire; it's sort of like one-one, lots more states to go. One of the things that really folks have been talking about is this whole notion about fairy tale, this whole issue about race in the campaign. I want to start with a comment that Bob Johnson made yesterday in Columbia, South Carolina when he introduced your wife. Let's go ahead and play that, Geneen.

Bob Johnson: *And to me, as an African American, I am frankly insulted that the Obama campaign would imply that we are so stupid that we would think Hillary and Bill Clinton, who have been deeply and emotionally involved in Black issues, when Barack Obama was doing something in the neighborhood, that I won't say what he was doing, but he said it in his book...when they have been involved, to say that these two people would denigrate the accomplishments of civil rights marches, men and women who were hosed, beaten and bled, and some died, to say, and to expect us now all of sudden to say, we are attacking a Black man?*

Roland Martin: Now, President Clinton, the statement that was released by the Clinton campaign quote, from Bob Johnson quote, my comments today were referring to Barack Obama's time spent as a community organizer, nothing else, any other suggestion would simply be irresponsible and incorrect. But when you listen to that tone and the inflection, he was not talking about community organizing. I mean that, it seemed to be very clear what he was implying. How do you respond to that, and were his comments inappropriate?

Bill Clinton: Well first of all, I think, ironically, this is the first time I've heard it, what you just said. I listened to it on the tape, and I think we have to take him at his word. But let me say my real response is, when I said what I did, the Obama campaign went right out and told everybody I had attacked his campaign or him or as being a fairy tale, which is not true. I've always personally complimented Senator Obama in hundreds of hundreds of appearances on Hillary's behalf. But, this is to me, another example of their wanting a double standard. When his campaign manager, after Benazir Bhutto was killed in Afghanistan, I mean, in Pakistan, David Axelrod says her assassination was quote, "Yet another manifestation of Hillary's poor judgment." Senator Obama himself went on Larry King and said that Bhutto's assassination was in parts a result of politicians like Hillary who have in quote, "Not made particularly good judgments." I mean that's a lot worse than anything Bob Johnson implied or said, and I don't believe anybody even asked Senator Obama about it. Oh, say she's responsible for something like that, that's fine. The only overtly racist remark that's been made in this campaign was the print-out that Senator Obama's campaign issued referring to Hillary as the senator from Punjab, India, because she had supported the Indian community.

Roland Martin: But let's...

Bill Clinton: You know, she didn't take it very seriously. But, nothing happened to the paid aide of the Obama campaign who did that.

Roland Martin: But...

Bill Clinton: Let me just say this. I've got before me a list of 80, 80 attacks on

Hillary that are quite personal, by Senator Obama and his campaign, going back the last six months that I had pulled. I don't believe anybody on these radio stations, I don't believe anybody's asked about it, she didn't complain about it, but it would seem, I mean the Bhutto thing by Senator Obama and David Axelrod was just appalling to me.

Roland Martin: But here's the...

Bill Clinton: She just disagreed and moved on.

Roland Martin: But here's the...

Bill Clinton: Now everyone wants to make a federal case of it...

Roland Martin: No, no, no, it's not a question of everybody, sir, I've gotten a ton of e-mails; we've been talking about this on the radio show. As African Americans, when Bill Shaheen made his comment, that was certainly perceived as bringing up this whole drug issue. Granted, Senator Clinton did apologize to Senator Obama, he resigned or was fired, one of the two. But when you take that, when you take the comments made by New York attorney general, Andrew Cuomo, the shuck-and-jive comment, he comes and says, no that's not what I meant, and then of course Bob Johnson saying that's not what I meant, you certainly have this back and forth. What is going on here with this whole issue? Is this—this whole notion of race, is this an attempt to draw Obama out to discuss it? Or is this just, in your opinion, them seeing it one way, and the Clinton campaign seeing it another?

Bill Clinton: No, I don't, first of all, I don't think that Bob Johnson said what he said yesterday. Nobody knew what he was going to say and it wasn't part of any planned strategy, and certainly, nobody had any advance notice of anything Attorney General Cuomo said.

Roland Martin: But, but, but Bob has defended his comment…

Bill Clinton: What?

Roland Martin: He tried to defend his, he tried to say, he tried to defend it by that's not what I meant, but anybody listening can know what he's talking about. He wasn't talking about community organizing. That was kind of…

Bill Clinton: That's something between Bob Johnson and Barack Obama. If you look at what, there have been three examples, two were maybe precinct people who may not have even supported it, just for sharing those e-mails that scurrilous attack on Senator Obama's religion and faults, claiming that he was a Muslim. Those people that shared it, they resigned as precinct captains. They were just minor people, but they weren't in the campaign. Bill Shaheen had an office in the campaign. He stepped down for referring to what he thought the Republicans would do with what Senator Obama himself had said in the book. Now that's her record. Now by contrast, let's look at Senator Obama's record on the same thing. I already told you, I got a list of 80 attacks on her going back six months. When his campaign referred to her as the senator from Punjab, on the very same day, they put out a three-page, printed release, attacking me for my business relationships and work with Teamsters and others to try and get investments back in poor communities in America. It was a hard hit, man.

Roland Martin: Mmm hmm.

Bill Clinton: I didn't say a word about it, and nothing happened to anybody who called Hilary the senator from Punjab. Then his top aide...

Roland Martin: Actually, actually that did generate some controversy in terms of the media...

Bill Clinton: It generated controversy, but the point is, it was dismissed and what he did was nothing compared to what she did, she got all of the folks out of her campaign. Then, Benazir Bhutto gets killed, a person that Hillary considers a friend, and both Senator Obama and David Axelrod get on television and imply that everybody in the Congress who voted for the Iraq resolution somehow is responsible for her death. I mean that was rough. And, oh some people noticed it in a day or two, but you didn't have people calling him saying, "Are you going to get rid of Axelrod for saying that Hilary killed Benazir Bhutto." And the reason this is being done now is because they're really good at this. It's very important to Senator Obama that he gets through the primary season with as few voters as possible knowing that his central claim, which is that he was always against the war, and he gave a speech saying, "I was against it in every year, 2, 3, 4, 5, 6, 7, that that is factually called into question by the fact in 2004 he said, "By this point there's not that much difference between my position and George Bush's on Iraq." He doesn't want people to know that. And that's why he hasn't talked about it, why his supporters didn't ask him about it in lots of debates. So I think that this is beneficial but I think it's very hard to make that case that Hillary is a racist, after all...

Roland Martin: No, no, no, no, that's the whole point though. I don't, no one, I'm not hearing people say that Senator Hillary Clinton is a racist. What I am hearing is that there is a belief among some folks, and I'm not talking about the campaign, I'm literally talking about people who have been writing in my Essence.com blog, who have been on this show that there is this sort of ploy, in order to have Obama address the issue of race. And frankly, they don't want to have a conversation about it, I can tell you point blank, because they were skittish about this issue of race, him being an African American candidate, some believe it's the benefit of the Clinton campaign to sort of draw this out. Now, whether or not it's true...

Bill Clinton: Now, now, now, can I address that?

Roland Martin: Go ahead.

Bill Clinton: First of all, I have said hundreds of times, I'll say again, he is an immensely impressive man, with an immensely impressive campaign. If I weren't married to Hillary, I'd be supporting her instead of him this time because I think she's done more good for people in the public jobs she's had, and she is better suited to be president at this particular moment.

Roland Martin: But if she, if she...

Bill Clinton: He is an amazingly talented man, and I think that the Democrats have proved, so far that neither race nor gender is going to keep them from picking somebody they consider to be the best president. So to me, this is a very happy moment in history. What they're trying to do, both of them, is figure out how they can end their disagreements in a totally new and uncharted field, loaded with minefields, where people are nervous about somebody playing the race card or gender card or whatever. I think we should just take what they say on the merits, and deal with them or anybody that supports them, what either one of them says, and just deal with it. Look, let's say something else too. Both of them want to change the domestic and foreign policy of this country. They have some differences that are not major, except on the health care thing I think it's a little substantial difference, but otherwise, these, what they're trying to do, is to argue who would be the best president based on their record and public life, their statements and their actions. And, almost because we're in new and uncharted territory, and because you can't say, "Well, they have drastic differences on their voting records and proposals on Iraq, Iran, health care," these little things tend to get blown up. And I think that the psychological tensions on everybody, they're considerable. They're a lot of people who are supporting Hillary who've always wanted to vote for an African American for president, there are a lot of people who are supporting Barack who always wanted to vote for a woman for president. There are a lot of people who are supporting one or the other who like them both, including me. So, I think that it's not surprising that these sort of things will happen.

Roland Martin: Well of course not.

Bill Clinton: The only point that I was trying to make is, they just happen, I think it's very important not to overreact to it.

Roland Martin: I got you, but I was reading a story on Politico.com, with Bill Lench, as quoted, a Harlem-based consultant to the Clinton campaign, when it came to the senator's comments regarding MLK, LBJ, to one of the Fox reporters, he even termed it a mistake and said his phone was ringing, from friends, quote around the country, voicing their concern, he said, quote, "I've been concerned about some of those comments and there might be a backlash." And so what do you make of that, he was someone, an African American in the campaign saying, "Look, even some African Americans supporting her, are bothered by this racial overtone.

Bill Clinton: I think, she, if you look at what she did on that, she was concerned that as you just read it, that you could say, well, did she mean it took Lyndon Johnson to complete Martin Luther King's work?

Roland Martin: Right.

Bill Clinton: And what she said was, they both played a role, and that it's important who's president, white or black. To make sure it wouldn't be misinterpreted, she went back and said some more things about to make absolutely clear that what she thought was important was that Martin Luther King and John Kennedy, two people who Senator Obama have at least implicitly compared himself to, had both soaring eloquence and a record of doing things that made a big difference, and so did Lyndon Johnson. And Lyndon Johnson actually became more eloquent as he became president,

Roland Martin: Right.

Bill Clinton: Because of what he had done. And I, I was concerned about it. I called Mary Frances Berry, who was head in the, in our administration, a very prominent African American leader, and she went through the whole history of that era with me, and said that she thought it was factually accurate. That Lyndon Johnson made it possible for Martin Luther King's dreams on the Voting Rights Act, on the Civil Rights Act, the Open Housing Act to be realized, and it didn't diminish either one of their achievements, and she thought Hillary had done a good job to try to clarify what she meant, and…

Roland Martin: President Clinton…

Bill Clinton: I don't think that's a big problem, I think she's made that pretty clear.

Roland Martin: Right, I've got a couple of quick comments, I know we don't have much time, I want to play a sound bite from "Meet the Press" and then I want to get your reaction from it, let's go ahead and play that.

Tim Russert: *Do you believe that Barack Obama is ready to be president?*

Hillary Clinton: *Look, this is up to the voters of our country to determine. But I want them to have accurate information about our respective records, what we've accomplished, the working that each of us has done when given a chance to serve, and I think it's relevant. I mean we face huge problems at home and around the world. Nobody can diminish those. And the next president is going to have to walk into that Oval Office on day one, having to end the war in Iraq, having to deal with what's happening in Afghanistan, the Middle East, and across the world, dealing with our tough problems from the economy going south to 47 million people uninsured, and I think we're going to need a president who has really prepared and thought about what to do on that very first day.*

Roland Martin: Mr. President, you were criticized for not having Washington experience in 1992, you won two terms. Ask the question to you, you said he was immensely talented along with Senator Clinton. Is Senator Barack Obama qualified to be President of the United States?

Bill Clinton: I think for this moment in history, Hillary has the better case. First of all, the national security issues are much more complicated than they were when I ran in '92. Secondly, in '92, America had a to chart a new economic course, and while I didn't have Washington experience,

I was the second-longest serving governor in America, had passed major economic and education reform legislation and had an awful lot of experience in the international economy, so I think she makes the better case, I'm with her, the voters have the final say...

Roland Martin: I think we know that you're with her, that's no doubt, but the question is, do you believe that he's qualified, but are you saying she's more qualified?

Bill Clinton: First of all, qualifications, the minimum qualifications are set by U.S. Congress.

Roland Martin: Absolutely.

Bill Clinton: So if you run, the voters get to decide. I think the most important thing to me is, that I think he's more qualified than Mitt Romney or these other Republicans? You bet I do. But I think she—it's more likely that she'll be a better president because of her unique experiences and how they fit in with this moment in history, I do. You don't, this is not a question of is he or is he not? It's always relative in politics, who's got the better case. I think she's got the better case.

Roland Martin: And if she wasn't in the race, if she was not running for president, and the crop of Democratic candidates were, would you be supporting Senator Barack Obama if she was not in the race?

Bill Clinton: Well now you're asking me to get into a fight with a man that's had two positions in my cabinet, Governor Richardson, and Joe Biden...

Roland Martin: They dropped out, they dropped out. So of the three candidates left standing, let's assume your wife was not running. Would you support Senator Obama or John Edwards? Just a hypothetical.

Bill Clinton: I don't think that that's fair to get me into that.

Roland Martin: I think we might…

Bill Clinton: Ask me that when it's over! I want to talk about the two of them, I think it's come down to the two of them, and I'll talk about that when it's over, I'll be glad to talk about that other question.

Roland Martin: Well President Clinton, I certainly appreciate it sir, first time we got a chance to talk on this show, certainly hope it's not the last.

Bill Clinton: I loved it, thank you, bye.

Roland Martin: Thanks a lot sir, thoroughly appreciated it. Folks that was the 42nd President of the United States, former president Bill Clinton, we'll get your reaction in a moment.

January 18, 2008

The Voters Beat Shameful Suit by Nevada Teachers

THIS YEAR'S PRESIDENTIAL CONTEST already has sparked massive voter interest in Iowa and New Hampshire, and for those of us who are embarrassed by America's low voter turnout the past few election cycles, it is something wonderful to watch.

So thank goodness a federal judge in Nevada didn't damage this excitement by siding with the state's teachers union, which filed a shocking lawsuit eight days before Saturday's primary in a clear effort to dilute the voting strength of working-class people.

When Democratic officials in the Western state wanted to have their voices heard in the presidential primary season, they decided nearly a year ago to create nine at-large caucus sites so thousands of workers in the gambling hotels along the

Las Vegas strip could cast ballots. Because they work 24 hours a day—and Saturday is the busiest day of the week for the state's biggest economic engine—they would have no shot at going home to caucus and getting back to work in time.

The plan was approved by the Democratic National Committee in May, and virtually nothing was said about the changes by anyone.

That is until after the 60,000-strong Local 226 of the Culinary Workers Union endorsed Sen. Barack Obama for president.

The largest and most organized union in the state, the Culinary Workers Union could play a large role in determining who wins the state. All the Democratic candidates fought hard for their endorsement, as well as the vast resources they pour into campaigns. Their decision was seen as a huge boost to Obama and a major blow to Sen. Hillary Clinton.

Then, three days later, the 28,000-member Nevada State Education Association chose to get their lawyers involved, filing the suit on behalf of six state residents. Their rationale? The at-large caucuses would give the culinary union an unfair advantage because other workers couldn't caucus at their jobs.

The teachers union hasn't endorsed anyone officially, but several of its high-ranking officers are backing Clinton, and the suit was seen as an effort to squash her opponent's biggest political "get."

Clinton and her husband, former President Bill Clinton, steadfastly argued they had nothing to do with the suit, that it was all up to the teachers, but in their talking points, they were siding with the teachers' suit.

In fact, after the ruling, the Clinton campaign said: "While we were not involved in this lawsuit and have always said that we would play by the rules that we're given, it has always been our hope that every Nevadan should have equal access and opportunity to participate in the caucus. Make no mistake—the current system that inhibits some shift workers from being able to participate, while allowing others to do so, would seem to benefit other campaigns. More importantly it is unfair."

Here's the rub, and it boils down to one thing: politics.

The teachers union and the Clinton campaign said *nothing* about these caucuses before the Obama endorsement. The Clinton campaign was holding out hope they would get the endorsement, and if they did, those at-large caucuses would be like holding an ace up their sleeves on election day. Do you actually think their "fairness" argument would have been made with the endorsement? Yeah, right.

Let me be clear: This is not about Hillary Clinton, Obama or even John Edwards. It's about democracy and wanting people to do what far too many Americans take for granted: vote.

I'm tired of these two-faced politicians and Democratic-leaning hacks run down Republicans with charges of voter suppression, and the Democrats and one of their biggest bases of supporters—a teachers union—turn around and do the same.

Frankly, I don't care whom the culinary union backed. If they had backed Clinton, and the Obama or Edwards camp encouraged this stunt, I would be all over them, as well.

Remember, the Clintons joined a chorus of Democrats who yelled, kicked and screamed against the Republicans about alleged massive voter fraud and voter suppression in 2000 and 2004. (That was a bit disingenuous, considering Vice President Al Gore was trying to get military ballots thrown out to help his cause in Florida in 2000.)

These kinds of pathetic actions by so-called believers in democracy are why so many people are sick and tired of politics. We have witnessed both parties claim they want an open voting system that encourages—not discourages—people from voting.

Americans love to criticize elections in other nations that we don't think are done aboveboard. We tell Pakistan that there should be fair and free elections, and we denounce Robert Mugabe in Zimbabwe for his strong-arm tactics to keep the opposition party away from the polls.

Is my comparison too harsh? No. They do it with guns. We do it with lawyers.

It's time that we, the people, let unions, political parties or anyone else know that we will fight like the dickens for the right to vote, and we won't be obstructed by some special interest looking to score a cheap political point.

January 22, 2008

Ignoring White Dems in S.C. Isn't Smart

EVER SINCE WE GOT INTO THE THICK OF THE PRESIDENTIAL RACE, candidates, reporters, anchors, pundits, columnists and writers have spent a considerable amount of time on the fact that nearly 50 percent of voters in the South Carolina primary are black.

Considering you have a black male candidate—he's really half-white (mom) and half-Kenyan (dad) but identifies himself as African American—and a white woman, who is the wife of a former president beloved by black folks, leading the pack for the Democratic nomination, everyone has been waiting to see how this fight will turn out.

But for the life of me, I don't understand—and I literally have been screaming this fact on CNN, on my Chicago radio show and on every possible platform I have— how we can focus on blacks making up nearly 50 percent of the voters and absolutely, positively, unequivocally ignore the other 50 percent!

Being a black man, I don't mind talking about the nuances of black politics—I've run three black newspapers, a black Web site and been the news editor of a national black magazine—but I also can count. And to suggest that white voters are immaterial in South Carolina is nuts.

It has been so stunning that I can't even recall the last time I've seen journalists spend a lot of time interviewing whites. The stories have focused on black preachers, the tough choice facing black women, and whether young black voters will come to the polls.

In some respect, there is a blackout when it comes to talking to white voters.

One of the reasons for this seeming disparity is that this is the first state where black voters will play a critical role. And on Feb. 5, we're likely to see a similar focus in Alabama, Mississippi, Virginia, Louisiana, Georgia and Tennessee, where black voters range from 20 percent to 50 percent of Democratic voters.

But this is a dangerous game to play because it is wrong to ignore half the electorate in a state. We also need to be analyzing the white vote to gain a better understanding as to what may happen in future states.

With that in mind, I reached out to CNN's Bill Schneider, and he shot me an e-mail with the results of the ARG poll taken Jan. 17-18. That poll revealed that among whites, Clinton is attracting 56 percent of the vote in South Carolina; Obama, 20 percent; and Edwards is polling at 16 percent.

For African Americans, Obama is receiving 73 percent, and Clinton is at 16 percent.

So, what does this tell us? First, while Obama is running a campaign that isn't based on race and is trying to connect with people across the political spectrum, this first Southern state test shows that he isn't even reaching one-third of white voters. Edwards being in the race could be a big reason, but his support conceivably could go to Clinton.

Obama did far better in Nevada—Clinton received 52 percent to his 34 percent—but when it comes to winning the South, he is going to have to do more to appeal to these voters if he wants to win enough delegates for the nomination.

Not every state moving forward has such significant black support as South Carolina. Sure, Obama won Iowa. But geography plays a role in how people vote, and the people of Georgia or Nebraska may not see him the same as those in Iowa.

And when we go further inside the numbers, we discover that Clinton has a man problem. She does not poll well among men—black or white—which means she is even more reliant on women to get her the nomination, the general election or both.

A lot of voters have told us that they don't care about race or gender—that the issues trump everything. Sorry, the numbers just don't lie. When large numbers of women, African Americans, whites or Hispanics fall to one candidate, then there is something about that group that is choosing the candidate. The issues could be the decider, but race or gender also could be at play.

At the end of the day, our job is to delve into every aspect of the campaign and go where the numbers take us. And to give short shrift to white voters who make up half a state party's vote total means that we aren't living up to our responsibility.

In the words of Paul Harvey, it's time for "the rest of the story."

January 22, 2008, Essence.com Blog

King Confidant: Candidates Must Stop Evoking King for Political Gain

The personal lawyer, draft speechwriter and confidant to the Rev. Dr. Martin Luther King Jr. said he is sick and tired of presidential candidates trying desperately to link themselves to the legacy of the civil rights leader.

Clarence B. Jones, a prominent businessman and attorney, told me this morning that with the recent disputes among Sen. Hillary Clinton and Sen. Barack Obama about King and President Lyndon Baines Johnson, as well as the discussion in last night's debate regarding who King would endorse, is silly.

"I don't understand this pre-occupation with Martin King did this, Martin King did that," said Jones, who accused candidates on both sides of the political spectrum of trying "to expropriate Martin's legitimacy for their own purposes.

"And I guess that's just the nature of politics. It's regrettable," Jones said.

During last night's CNN-CBC Institute debate, all three presidential candidates evoked the name of King and his legacy (It's worth noting that the debate was held on the national celebration of the King holiday).

When asked by CNN's Wolf Blitzer if King were alive today would he endorse any of them, Edwards said yes, he would back his candidacy.

Obama said King wouldn't endorse any candidate. But it was the answer by Clinton that piqued my interest that led me to reach out to Jones for clarification.

She suggested in her answer that Dr. King was a civil rights activist, but didn't shy away from being involved in politics.

"He campaigned for political leaders," Clinton said. "He lobbied them. He pushed them. He cajoled. He did everything he could to get them over the line so that they would be part of the movement that he gave his life for."

I e-mailed Phil Singer, a spokesman for the Clinton campaign, and he replied with an excerpt from the King papers at Stanford University backing up Clinton's assertion:

"Later that year, Johnson won a decisive victory in the 1964 election, garnering the widest popular margin in presidential history. King had campaigned actively for Johnson and welcomed the victory saying, 'the forces of good will and progress have triumphed' (King, 4 November 1964)."

But Jones, who is writing his memoirs while in residence at Stanford's Martin Luther King, Jr. Research and Education Institute, disputes that.

"What Martin did was he campaigned hard for voter registration, and he spoke about the dangers of possibly Goldwater election," he said. "He did talk about that. But he was not in any way part of the Johnson campaign.

"His way of doing it was to point out how important it was that as many black voters come to the polls as possible."

He did say he found Clinton's repeated mentions of LBJ to be interesting because "she was a Goldwater Republican in 1964," and a staunch opponent to civil rights.

Then again, Jones said, "We all can change."

But Nick Kotz, author of *Judgment Days: Lyndon Baines Johnson, Martin Luther King, Jr., and the Laws That Changed America*, told me that the Stanford papers and Jones are both right.

"At the Democratic convention in 1964, they had this big fight about seating the Mississippi delegation. And Dr. King was being very pragmatic about this thing. He didn't want to fall on his sword. He wanted Johnson to get elected president and for them to work on the voting rights law. Out of that conflict was a deal that King would go out and campaign, and he went to six, seven and eight cities—I've got the clips and so forth—and he was asking people to register to vote, but he was trying to get Lyndon Johnson elected.

"He wasn't just telling them to register to vote. He was talking at rallies in each city that were organized by the Johnson campaign. They (Stanford and Jones) are really both right. At each stop did he say, 'Vote for Lyndon Johnson?' He may not have done that, but that's what the whole thing was all about."

The Michael Baisden Show: Sen. Hillary Clinton and Roland S. Martin

Michael Baisden: Senator Hillary Clinton how you doing senator?

Hillary Clinton: Hi. I am doing great. It's great to talk to you, thanks so much.

Michael Baisden: I have been eager, and my listeners have been eager to talk to you. We are only down about six minutes left before we have to go into a mandatory break so let's get right to it. First of all, congratulations on your success up to this point. I know it is a hard fought battle. South Carolina is coming up, Super Tuesday is coming up, and our listeners, as I am sure many Americans are interested in what the real issues are. Roland Martin is on, what is from a correspondent from CNN contributed to CNN. Say hello, Roland.

Roland Martin: How are you, Senator Clinton?

Hillary Clinton: I am good. Great to have you on too.

Michael Baisden: One of the most interesting, should I say, important issues to me, as you know I had the chance to meet you at the Congressional Black Caucus about the Jena Six case?

Hillary Clinton: Yes.

Michael Baisden: How would your response have been different as president?

Hillary Clinton: Well, I think that the president should have spoken out and of course we should have an attorney general who actually takes justice seriously, and a civil rights division that should have intervened immediately. This should have been given serious attention from the very beginning and the situation should have been resolved short of having to have people take to the streets. It was just you know a missed opportunity to once again reinforce the lessons of how we have to remain vigilant and open against any kind of discriminatory and hate crime treatment.

Michael Baisden: Yes, we do appreciate and Senator Barack Obama did get back witness on that and we do appreciate it. The incarceration rate is a very important issue. In general, I would think that in particular an African American community. It has been said that the incarceration rate actually went up, and Roland and I were actually talking, during the Clinton administration, about the powder cocaine compared to the crack cocaine. And we need to talk about whether or not it is something that needs to be fixed.

Hillary Clinton: It does need to be fixed, Michael. I think that this is one of the most egregious examples of injustice within the criminal justice system. This should be a one-to-one ratio. There should not be a mandatory minimum sentence for non-violent in crack users the way they are currently—it's the only such drug treatment, I mean drug sentence that exists and we need more drug treatment. I mean the part of the problem here is that we are looking at the drug problem as separate from what we need to do to help divert people, help keep them out of prison, give them second chances, provide more treatment, and I have come forward with a Youth Opportunity agenda that I think would begin to really tackle this problem because we cannot continue to fill our prisons up with young people, particularly young man, who we should be looking to to be productive and effective citizens.

Roland Martin: Senator, the Supreme Court has ruled that judges can give shorter prison sentences for crack cocaine convictions obviously dealing with the whole disparity. The CBC has fought for this for quite some time. You say if you support shorter sentences the "in principle" but not retroactivity. Why?

Hillary Clinton: I am in favor of changing the sentencing and eliminating the disparity, but here's what I am worried about. If we have open retroactivity without the resources to help people re-enter society, without the preparation in community, I think that we are going to have problems. And I talked to a lot of my folks in New York and elsewhere who say, "Well, this all sounds good, but if we start releasing thousands of people without the programs to help them, we are going to end up with some real challenges." So, retroactivity is something in principle that I think you have to approach very cautiously, but it is going to happen and I am going to fight to make sure we got the resources so that this is handled as smoothly as possible. Because you know what has happened, Roland, is that our prison systems have become you know nothing but warehouses. A lot of the programs that used to exist for education and treatment and even rehabilitation, they've all been cut out and so we do not really give the young people coming out and those even who have been there a long time, much of a shot at making it and I would like to end the revolving door and I think we got to put more resources into doing.

Michael Baisden: Fifty-seven city strong is the Michael Baisden Show. Yes, ladies and gentleman she is back. Senator Hillary Clinton, thank you so much for joining us again on the show.

Hillary Clinton: It is my pleasure Michael.

Michael Baisden: We wanted you back. Roland Martin, she's is back with us.

Roland Martin: Yes indeed, I see that.

Michael Baisden: We are very excited. Let me tell you something. This has been the most exciting political season I have ever experienced in my life. I mean, it's really great that everybody is fired up about it and I think that we want to take advantage of this by keeping everyone interested in the process, and Roland Martin and I were just saying off the air, we wanted to clarify. We wanted to make sure that between you and I, Senator Obama today, we get you all's word. How did you phrase him, Roland?

Roland Martin: And that is, will you play as your rate, obviously your surrogates including former president Bill Clinton, that if the Obama campaign stops the attacks and focus on specific issues will you pledge to stop the attacks yourself.

Hillary Clinton: Absolutely, absolutely. You know, I got into public service 35 years ago working for the Children's Defense Fund because, I think you know, we can do so much better in this country and we can really demonstrate that we live up to our values and take care of people, and that is why I am running for president because I think we have had a disastrous seven years and we got to pull us back from the brink, and that's going to take a lot of hard work, and that's what I want to focus on.

Michael Baisden: You know, I appreciated your passion in saying the things that you said in regards to finding your voice and appreciating what the listeners, should I say, the voters and the citizens are talking about, and I think between you and Senator Obama, the first person that steps up and says, "It is a wrap. I don't want to deal with this mess anymore," is going to win real big with the public because we are not mad about it, we are not interested. We are just not interested.

Hillary Clinton: Well, you know, Michael, what we've got to do it is not only have campaigns and candidates, but, you know, the media that covers politics has got to understand it is not about them either. You know it is about us. It's about our people. It is about, you know, the woman without health care. It is about the manager who just lost his job and the family that's about to lose their home to a foreclosure, and we keep getting diverted and detoured. I was just in an event here in Anderson, South Carolina, and a woman stood up and she did not talk to me, she turned around and talked to the press over there and she said, "I want you all to understand that we are not interested in what you're interested in."

Michael Baisden: We are not interested. We are not interested. In fact...

Hillary Clinton: You know, we want to know what you are going to do to get us healthcare and get us out of Iraq and make college affordable.

Michael Baisden: And speaking of which, let me—I got to represent my listeners about a question they asked. They say, "What are your plans for alleviating the debt college graduates face once leaving school? College graduates finished school and are barely able to make ends meet because of their student loans."

Hillary Clinton: Well, number one, we gotta help relieve the debt, and I think one of the best ways of doing that is to give people a chance to go into a public service job like teaching or nursing or, you know, law enforcement or social work, or something so they can then do that work, and as they do it, they will have their debts forgiven. But we also need to avoid people falling into debt in the first place. College has gotten too expensive and it is shutting the door on so many young people who deserve to go but can't afford it. So, we got to get more Pell grants and more direct aid. We got to give more tax credit to families. We got to get the student loan industry out of this business. It should be a direct loan like I had when I went to school a hundred years ago. I got to borrow money directly from the federal government at 2 percent interest. Yes, I had to pay it back but I did not go into deep debt and come out like an endentured servant. I could go to work for the Children's Defense Fund. I didn't go to work for a law firm to make money to pay my debt, and I think we ought to give people a chance to do national service before they go to college to earn money to be able to afford it. But I am going to make college affordability one of the biggest accomplishments if I am fortunate enough to be president.

Michael Baisden: One of the things that I think is very challenging is that when presidential candidates pledge to do things, I think that for the most part they really plan on doing it. But what happens once you get there and you gotta deal with the, you know, with the partisanship, with the Republicans and trying to get your programs through the same thing with universal healthcare. Everybody gets excited when they hear you and all the other candidates say, "universal healthcare" but it's not that easy. If it was that easy it would have already been done. How do we know it is ever going to happen?

Hillary Clinton: Well, you are right, it is not easy but I think we have made a lot of progress towards understanding that our country has to work together. You know when I got elected to the Senate, there are a lot of people who said, "Oh my, she will never work with Republicans and Republicans will never work with her," but you know these were people who didn't know me. I figure it is job. It is a public trust so I got to work with people that I think folks thought I'd never talk to. You know I joined up with Senator Lindsay Graham from South Carolina to get healthcare for our National Guard and Reserve members and the White House didn't want us to do it and the president threatened to veto it."

January 25, 2008

WVON-AM/Chicago: Michael Eric Dyson on The Roland S. Martin Show

Roland Martin: This is Roland S. Martin Show on "The Talk of Chicago" 1690 WVON. Today is Friday. Of course tomorrow, South Carolina goes to polls; Democrats in that state to make their choice. According to the latest polls, the average poll has Senator Obama up by 11, though Zogby had him up by 13. He is down by 2 points. John Edwards appears to be picking up some voters there, especially some undecideds. And joining us right now on the phone line to talk about this campaign, Dr. Michael Eric Dyson now with Georgetown. Dr. Dyson what's happening?

Michael Eric Dyson: How are you doing Brother Martin? Oh, it is good to see you on CNN, to hear you on VON. You got the N's locked down, brother.

Roland Martin: Well, you know, absolutely… somebody has to do it. Somebody…

Michael Eric Dyson: Yeah, it might as well be you.

The Primaries

Roland Martin: Several different things here. Let us get right into it. This campaign has been hot and heavy over the last week, and I tell you, I have been reading some stuff online how many people in the media had been taking some really hard shots at the Clintons for what some call them "dirty tactics." I read the people at E.J. Dionne the *Washington Post* outlining the praise at Bill Clinton offer, but he was running in '92 for Ronald Reagan. Yeah, when you listen now, it is as if none that stuff ever took place. What is your analysis of what Senator Obama has had to deal with over the past 7 to 10 days?

Michael Eric Dyson: Well, just an extraordinary level of political attack. The Clintons are fierce and formidable political opponents. They know how to play this game. They know how to play the backroom spoil to politics as well as the front and center spotlight politics, by which I mean, they know how to play the game in a so-called straight-forward and clean way. And obviously with President Clinton he understands the deals brokered behind the scenes and the code words and the implications and inferences about things. So I think that when you are facing the Clintons, you are facing a very shrewd force who understand how to get the results, and I think that on the one hand saying that they did not praise Mr. Reagan, which is so patently dishonest in the sense that Mr. Clinton was seeking to extend the Reagan era so to speak. I think even Alan Greenspan said that the most effective Reaganite, the effective Republican president over the last decades since Reagan himself was Bill Clinton, and Mr. Greenspan of course is a Republican. So I think that he took many of his ideals, welfare reform, certainly borrowed a lot from the Republican ideology and certainly, even more directly from the supply-side economics of Mr. Reagan. They praised his ability to communicate the great Gipper, he knew how to turn a phrase in and articulate his vision. So when you put all that stuff together, it's just highly disingenuous and dishonest, I think, for that other side to pretend that they did not borrow from and pay a debt to the ideas that had a deleterious, negative, messed up, impact on black people undoubtedly, and Sen. Obama has had to face that. And in one sense having his hands tied because he looks as if he is attacking Senator Clinton when he simply tried to defend his own record, and at the same time they are allowed to engage in this very, very slippery battle of cold water throwing in implications. So he is taking the high road and does an extraordinary job in the midst of it.

Roland Martin: There is a story on Politico.com that says "black voters fear D.C. unready for Obama" and that is a gentleman interview. We discussed them yesterday and I really... it was amazing. It said this fear has caused Obama at least one vote already. Edwin Green, a 36-year-old director at an insurance company said concerns about Obama's race hampering his effectiveness are a key reason he does not back the candidate. "I think it is a matter of getting things done. He is going to run into so many obstacles being a black man. Every bill he tries to pass, he's going to get shut down." What is going on with what I describe as the invisible handcuffs that seems to shackle African Americans when it comes to this race?

Michael Eric Dyson: Yeah, and not just by people outside the race, that's the tragedy. You know, it is the plantation dirt doesn't just exist in geography. It exists in some people's minds, man. I think that black people have had such vicious and consistent lack of self-belief, the aching self-doubt that attends our every path and many of us impose it on ourselves. If we waited for what the white man thought, we wouldn't be out of slavery, we wouldn't have defeated Jim Crow. If we thought white opposition and white backslash was going to be real, we would have never thought for the civil rights bill, nor the voting rights bill, nor for fair housing. We would have never had freedom rides. We would have never taken up a responsibility to defend ourselves against the state that tried to impose it's will on us. Black people are going to really come to grips with the fact that we are doing more damage to ourselves wondering about what white folk might do as opposed to saying let's organize our own ability to support our own candidate for a good reason and then convince and persuade others that he is indeed the person. So it depends on if you see the glass half empty or half full, but it certainly is tragic that so many black people just can't get over the fact, as initially what's happening in South Carolina, but not just they are throughout the South, where black people would say well, he might get killed or he might get assassinated or white folks to get with him. Well, if you get with him and you determine that he's worthy of being gotten with, then you go and have some results that make a huge difference. Martin Luther King Jr. didn't have the white folks behind him in Montgomery, and had to convince the Negros to do it, but once they were on board they were able to change history. And I think that black people have to really have a transformation of our mindset here to understand we wield a greater deal of power and influence than others may realize.We are indeed swing voters in so many of these battleground states and we make the difference. We are going to make the difference in South Carolina, but we can make the difference in the nation if we would but except our greatness and the responsibility that goes with that.

Roland Martin: I was reading a story the other day in the *New York Times* and Bill Clinton, this is with the *New York Times* said. Mr. Clinton also suggested in public remarks that his wife might lose here because of race. Referring to her and Mr. Obama, he said, "They are getting votes to be sure because of their race or gender, and that is why people tell me that Hillary does not have a chance to win here." Do you believe the Clintons are using a southern strategy, that is to use race to divide;

to further divide and make people see Senator Obama as "the black candidate" to take away, frankly some of the message he offered in Iowa and New Hampshire? Are they using a southern strategy against him?

Michael Eric Dyson: Yes sir. It is the Nixon's strategy all over again, and Senator Obama has refused to play the race card. Senator Obama has refused to make this about race, even when he was being slapped and hit and shoved and kicked and pushed with race. He refused to give in to it. He refused to kowtow and bow down at the altar of race, and I might add rather courageously so, because the easiest thing for him to do would be to signify that it is about race and then therefore destroy the profound base the has, not only in black America but I think especially in broader communities. And so I think that the erosion of his support among white people in South Carolina, down to 10 percent, is an index of the success of the southern strategy of the Clintons and just how dishonest and disingenuous it has been. But Barack Obama himself, Senator Clinton has with her husband, I will say President Bill Clinton has most especially punched these code words in, has brilliantly used them, because as you know, black people who go around saying that Bill Clinton has been the friend of the Negro, missed the fact that a guy playing the saxophone on "The Arsenio Hall Show" and knowing his way around the hymns of black people in churches does not make him a politician who supported us. Look at signing the crime bill where the vicious three strikes and you're out law was enshrined legally. That is Bill Clinton. Look at the welfare reform, that's Bill Clinton. Look at this failure to support Lani Guinier. That's Bill Clinton. To use Sista Soulja to marginalize Jesse Jackson, and to show to white America that he was not concerned so much about urban situations with black people that he would give up on that interest, that's Bill Clinton. Look at

Joycelyn Elders, who simply said that a consideration of all alternatives to abstinence would be self-pleasuring that could tap down on HIV, and others got fired, that's Bill Clinton. So Bill Clinton has not been a friend of black people in terms of public policy. He has manipulated the racial sentiment that people feel toward him positively, black people, because he knows the folk ways and morays of black culture, but when it comes down to substance of politics Bill Clinton has manipulated as brilliantly as any other southern white politician, maliciously so, black sentiments. So black people have to get up off of this "we going to support the Clintons because of what we owe them." In politics, you do not owe anybody anymore than the support you give to them, and they in turn should give back to you as politicians a recognition that you support them. But black people hold on to this forever, in perpetuity, adinfanitum, and any other Latin word you can figure out to say forever; we're holding on. Bill Clinton has manipulated us, and I think it is unfortunate, and Barack Obama has stayed above the fray. And those who are working with him have stayed above the fray, but the impact of this…these are body blows. These are not just left hooks and the right crosses. This ain't the uppercut. When you are in a battle in boxing, this is body punching on the inside when the referee comes in, and by the time the referee comes in, you done hit the cat, rabbit punches three, four, five times on the body… body blow, body blow, body blow, and then the body falls. These are the unfortunate and undignified body blows that are being done by the Clintons in the clinch to really try to affect Mr. Obama. But again, he is brilliantly and bravely and courageously stayed above the fray. But let us not pretend we don't know what is going on.

Roland Martin: It is 7:22. We are talking with Dr. Michael Eric Dyson. We will return… got a couple more questions for him.

Doc, I got a question for you. You made a point about eroding white support. Obama really was appealing to people on a different level, and I wanted to bounce something off of you. Let us say he wins South Carolina. How does he get back on message? How does he return to a message that is appealing to a variety of people? I mean, let me bounce this off of you, he does something along these lines, because he told the American people, this is the return to the days of slash and burn politics. America does not want that or need that. America does not want or need to see the day when we have distortions, I guess outright lies, coming from the president because we have seen enough of that in the last two administrations. I can guarantee you this. If that kind of attitude returns, we won't see universal healthcare, we will not see any change on climate change, we will not see any action take down the critical issues because the hardened part which is on each side will dig in and we'll be left with a nation continually to buy the long side of red and blue, liberal and conservative, Republican and Democrat. America, do not fall for this. Don't accept this as a status quo. Don't believe for a second that this is change. This is what got us into the war in Iraq. This is how we lost the White House eight years ago. We had enough of that. Changing the poisoned waters of Washington means not returning to the politics of old but embracing a new reality which dictates that we can find the common ground on the issues that matter. Don't accept the politics of old. Stand up and say enough is enough. We can do better and with Obama and the White House, we will do better. Is that what he needs to lay out moving forward?

Michael Eric Dyson: Yes, take it down and send it to him right now. To his credit again, Senator Obama has taken the high road and has consistently wanted to only focus on the issues, but I think that is the way to do it, to tell the American people when he wins in South Carolina this Saturday, that he wants to return to the high ground, that he has staked out. There is nothing wrong with comparing and contrasting viewpoints among candidates for president of the United States, but let us not marginalize him as the black candidate. He is not trying to be the president of black America. He is trying to be a president of America. He has ideas that are worthy of consideration for the entire nation, and I think that along the lines you just suggested, that the bitter politics, the fracas that has been generated out of this fighting back and forth, will not lead to a transformation of America. It is not the politics of change. It is the same old stuff back in the '90s. We like '90s sitcoms, we must like '90s presidencies. Let us move forward to the new generation. A new era where Americans of all stripes and hues and genders and sexual orientations are able to come together around the candidacy for true change. And in that sense, Senator Obama positions himself away from, as you say, this bitter and poisoned well of passion and sentiment that have nothing to do with the fundamental issues that concern us. In this sense, Senator Edwards was right, the bickering cannot get us child care for our young people. The bickering can't get us healthcare for the 40 million and so who are neither employed, most of them, but most of them, all of them are not insured, and they use the emergency room and its healthcare maintenance. So we have got to deal with the issues economically and socially that appeal to most Americans. I think when white Americans and black Americans and Latino Americans, and Asian Americans begin to see again that Senator Obama does offer the hope of change and stays away from that vicious fray, he will rise again, and I think that he will have an excellent shot on Super Tuesday to really make a difference in the minds of the voters who will be going to polls.

Roland Martin: Last point doc with the reality from a Machiavellian standpoint, the tactics, the strategy used by the Clintons is working.

Michael Eric Dyson: Well, no doubt, but I think that then he has got to get counter Machiavellian, and you know, he got to go to the other Makaveli, Tupac Shakur, you know, who understood that what you have got to do is to express the truth as eloquently and as brilliantly and as passionately and as simply as you can and rely upon the instincts of your voters to support you. I think that what Barack Obama has done more than any recent politician is depend upon the good instincts of the American people. He has believed in them, and they in return have rewarded him by believing in him, and I think he has got to reclaim that kind of energy in going forward. At the same time, I think he can't be naïve and I think that his surrogates and other people who were around have to fight some of these battles in ways that do not leave him bloodied or bowed, but at the same time, as he continues to take the high road, he continues to hammer away at the ideas and the issues that America understands are importance. The economy, getting us out of Iraq, and also figuring out a way to leverage the domestic budget, so to speak, to defend the most vulnerable, and with the working class and the middle class. I think Barack Obama has those ideas and he is going to hold on in there. They are enough to get him victory if, I think he understands that in his own Machiavellian strategy, he has got to tell the truth about American democracy and its principles and practices, and by sticking that issue, he shows that he has the wherewithal, the integrity and the intelligence to make a difference even among people who are beyond his own racial category. And I think he has brilliantly done in the past, he will return to that right now.

Roland Martin: Ladies and gentleman, Dr. Michael Eric Dyson. Doc, thanks a bunch.

Michael Eric Dyson: Always good to talk to you Brother Martin. You are doing a good job brother.

Roland Martin: I appreciate… thank you sir, I appreciate it.

January 28, 2008

Voters Not Swayed by Racial Politics

EVEN AS VOTERS IN SOUTH CAROLINA headed to the polls Saturday to deliver a beat-down to Sen. Hillary Clinton for Sen. Barack Obama, former President Bill Clinton continued to stoke the racial fire, hoping an ember would ignite his wife's campaign and lead it to victory.

As reported on Jake Tapper's ABCNews.com blog, at a stop in Columbia, S.C., the former president was asked to respond to Obama's comment that it "took two people to beat him."

Instead of answering the question, he said, "Jesse Jackson won South Carolina in '84 and '88. Jackson ran a good campaign. And Obama ran a good campaign here."

Tapper said no one asked about Jackson. His name never came up. Yet Clinton had no problem invoking it. Isn't the reason obvious?

The ridiculously called first black president didn't mention his win in 1992 or that of Vice President Al Gore in 2000—or even then-Sen. John Edwards' win in 2004. He decided to bypass all of these gents and link Obama with Jackson, who is beloved in black America but stirs hatred among many whites.

I'm sure some of you are saying, "Oh, Roland. Stop reading race into everything!" But what we all have learned over the years is that race is a hot commodity, and it has been used effectively by all kinds of candidates to stir people up along racial lines.

Since Richard Nixon implemented the "Southern strategy" in 1968, which was intended to get Southern whites to side with the GOP because of their anger at the Democrats for passing civil rights legislation, it has been a staple of American politics, especially down South.

It has been used largely by the Republicans over the years, and Democrats always have blasted it as race-baiting. So the idea that a former president—a beloved Democrat, especially among African Americans—would do such a thing to help his wife was considered nonsense.

During CNN's coverage Saturday night of the South Carolina Democratic primary, commentator Carl Bernstein called it "unthinkable." But it really isn't.

Clinton has used race when it suited him over the years. (Check out Rep. Jesse Jackson Jr.'s book, *A More Perfect Union*, where it's covered on six pages.) And a top adviser to the campaign of Sen. Hillary Clinton admitted to Ron Fournier of The Associated Press in a report published Friday that it was the campaign's intent to turn Obama, who has avoided the race issue deftly, into "the black candidate." Based on the results in South Carolina, it backfired badly.

The jury is still out as to whether it hurts Obama in the nearly two-dozen state Feb. 5 contests, but what the voters in South Carolina made clear is that they won't reward candidates who play the race card.

And basking in the glow of a 28-point win, with more votes than Clinton and Edwards combined, Obama stressed his inclusive campaign during his victory speech: "What we've seen in these last weeks is that we're also up against forces that are not the fault of any one campaign but feed the habits that prevent us from being who we want to be as a nation.

"It's the politics that uses religion as a wedge and patriotism as a bludgeon. A politics that tells us that we have to think, act and even vote within the confines of the categories that supposedly define us. The assumption that young people are apathetic. The assumption that Republicans won't cross over. The assumption that the wealthy care nothing for the poor and that the poor don't vote. The assumption that African Americans can't support the white candidate; whites can't support the African American candidate; blacks and Latinos can't come together.

"But we are here tonight to say that this is not the America we believe in. I did not travel around this state over the last year and see a white South Carolina or a black South Carolina. I saw South Carolina. I saw crumbling schools that are stealing the future of black children and white children. I saw shuttered mills and homes for sale that once belonged to Americans from all walks of life, and men and women of every color and creed who serve together, and fight together, and bleed together under the same proud flag. I saw what America is, and I believe in what this country can be."

Sure, Obama received one-fourth of the white vote and won an overwhelming percentage of the black vote. But when you look at those white voters, he really scored well among those between the ages of 18 and 29. That is the generation who grew up with hip-hop, and they are less likely to be hung up about race.

They don't respond to racial appeals because they didn't know Jim Crow. They don't have any understanding of busing. If you say white flight, they'll look at you with a quizzical look. Bottom line: America has tired of playing the race game and is looking increasingly for people who see others for who they are, not their little niche. Obama isn't naive to believe racism will disappear if he's president. He told me that after his win in Iowa.

But at least Saturday, in the state where the first shot was fired nearly 150 years ago to kick off the Civil War, the voters of South Carolina told their fellow Southerner, Bill Clinton, and his wife, Sen. Clinton, that the tired political games of the past should remain there. Then, and only then, can we recognize one another as what we truly are: Americans.

February 1, 2008

Conservatives Had Better Learn to Like McCain, or They Risk Losing the White House

HE'S FIERCELY PRO-LIFE. When others were abandoning President George W. Bush over the war in Iraq, and later the controversial "surge" decision, Sen. John McCain was unwilling to break from the president.

Yet when you listen to conservatives, they have a hatred for McCain that is close to their absolute dislike of Sen. Hillary Clinton and her husband, former President Bill Clinton.

What gives?

Conservatives continue to be up in arms because McCain refuses to be a lackey and buy into a lot of their pet issues. First, they rip him on voting against Bush's tax cuts. Yet what all of them refuse to acknowledge is that the Congress under Bush— the Republican Congress—behaved like an out-of-control teenager with his parents' credit card and spent wildly. For McCain, it was simple: Tax cuts with no spending limits would lead to a fiscal crisis.

What happened? A surplus left by President Clinton was turned into a massive deficit by Bush and the GOP-led Congress. And today we sit on the verge of a financial crisis.

Then there was campaign finance. Sick and tired of big money controlling politicians, McCain teamed up with Sen. Russ Feingold of Wisconsin to pass a law that severely restricted the dollars in federal elections. This angered conservatives because they viewed the issue as a First Amendment cause, when in fact, they really were upset about the GOP losing a major advantage over the Democrats when it came to fundraising. With that window narrowed by the law, they didn't want to see that disappear. The U.S. Supreme Court struck down some parts of the law, but that still hasn't satisfied the money vultures on the right.

Lastly, immigration. In an effort to exercise leadership on a volatile issue, McCain chose not to be a demagogue and work out a compromise bill that would curtail the nation's unsecured borders and figure out a way to do something with the 12 million illegal immigrants in the nation. If you talk to the rabid conservative talk show hosts and their wild and crazed listeners, their only option is to throw them all out of the country. In former Massachusetts Gov. Mitt Romney, they have a very sympathetic ear.

But we all know the truth. That will never happen. *never.* You are not going to move 12 million people out of the U.S. You are not going to see multiple industries collapse. You are not going to see billions of dollars spent to round up families and deport them.

Let me be clear: It's not going to happen.

So instead of drooling at such prospects, McCain worked with Democrats and some Republicans to offer a solution, which included making illegal immigrants learn English and pay a fine. The solution also included targeting businesses that hire illegal immigrants and forcing immigrants to get in line to apply for citizenship.

Yet the anger in America was too great. Whites, blacks, some Hispanics, conservatives and yes, even liberals, couldn't stomach doing this first and not securing the borders.

During Wednesday's debate at the Reagan Library, McCain conceded that his law wasn't palatable, and something else must be done.

Folks, that's called a pragmatic leader trying to solve a difficult situation.

The Primaries

So now we're left with conservatives trying to do anything to stop McCain, with some even suggesting—especially evangelicals—that they might run a third-party candidate.

Word to the wise: Shut up, suck it up and deal with it.

If McCain wins the nomination, he is the best option the GOP has to stopping the candidacies of Sens. Hillary Clinton and Barack Obama.

History also serves as warning. Remember 1992? Fiscal conservatives—boy, where did they go with this current Republican administration?—were up in arms because President George H.W. Bush went back on his no taxes pledge. They railed against him for months, which led them right into the arms of billionaire Ross Perot.

With his assaults on an inefficient government and the trade policies of America, Perot captured the hearts and minds of many and threw his hat into the ring.

So instead of facing an unknown Democrat from a small Southern state in Bill Clinton, the incumbent Bush had to fend off a pit bull like Perot.

The result? Clinton won 43 percent of the vote; Bush 37.4 percent; and Perot garnered 18.9 percent. There is no doubt that Perot played a large role in denying Bush a second term.

Democrats had the same problem that year. They weren't happy about the somewhat conservative Clinton. Liberals and progressives didn't like him, but they had to accept him as their choice. Now, he's treated like the Ronald Reagan of the Democratic Party.

The last reason it's nonsensical to toss McCain aside is because the U.S. Supreme Court is one vote away from having a conservative majority. Do you actually think conservatives are dumb enough to destroy McCain, paving the way for a Democrat to potentially appoint three Supreme Court justices in the next four years?

Conservatives, take a chill pill. McCain isn't the Antichrist. He's an independent voice who has been willing to talk tough to you, even when you didn't like it. But he sides with conservatives more often than not.

If you continue on your present path, you may very well be looking at the Democrats enjoying what Bush enjoyed his first six years: Democrats controlling the legislative, judicial and executive branches.

Are you willing to live with that?

February 4, 2008

Forget an Obama-Clinton or Clinton-Obama Ticket

DEMOCRATS ACROSS THE COUNTRY ARE ABUZZ over the possibility of the "dream ticket," featuring Sens. Hillary Clinton and Barack Obama running for the White House in November.

In the words of one of "The Sopranos" characters, "Fuggetaboutit!"

Look, this might sound exciting and history-making to have a woman and an African American competing against the Republicans, but there are multiple reasons why this won't happen:

CLINTON WILL NOT BE OVERSHADOWED BY AN UNDERLING. Clinton is hugely popular in Democratic circles, but truth be told, that pales in comparison to the love and affection showered on Obama. This is a guy who brings people to tears just by speaking, and he attracts the disenfranchised and folks on the left and right. When you have the children of elected officials putting pressure on their parents (Sen. Claire McCaskill of Missouri is one example) to support this guy, you know he is touching people in a place others haven't in 40 years. The role of a vice president is to be supportive of a presidential candidate, not to be someone who overshadows the candidate.

OBAMA WOULD NOT WANT TO CARRY CLINTON BAGGAGE. He has offered a vision of change, and having to answer for the years of strife under the Clintons would be too much. It would make sense to have a fresh face serving as his vice president who doesn't engender anger among some in the Democratic Party and definitely the GOP. An Obama run would be about going after Republicans and independents, and Clinton being on the ticket would make that very difficult.

WAY TOO MUCH BAD BLOOD BETWEEN THESE TWO DURING THIS CAMPAIGN. A lot of folks say that George H.W. Bush rankled Ronald Reagan by declaring his economic plan "voodoo economics." That didn't keep Reagan from adding Bush to the ticket. But Bush was one of those loyal guys who would have done anything for the party ... and himself. I don't see that for Clinton and Obama. Sure, their attacks on one another are what you expect in a campaign, but it has gotten very personal. Obama says she is a return to the "politics of old," and that doesn't bring a smile to her face. The race-baiting Southern strategy used by former President Bill Clinton and the surrogates of Sen. Clinton have absolutely angered Obama's camp. There is too much blood on the floor, and you just don't forget that.

NO. 2 IS UNTHINKABLE FOR CLINTON. She went through the behind-the-scenes battles with Al Gore when he was her husband's vice president. She's not interested in second fiddle, and she doesn't want to have to fight to be on the stage. For her, it's all or nothing. She's also 60, and being VP to Obama means that if he wins two terms, she'll be 68 running for the highest office in the land. It's not outside the realm of possibility, but she'll have to confront the skeptics who are snipping at the heels of Sen. John McCain: He's too old.

OBAMA DOESN'T WANT TO BE AN LBJ. When Lyndon Baines Johnson was the vice president under President John F. Kennedy, he was ostracized and marginalized because of the influence of Robert F. Kennedy. With Bill Clinton serving as consigliore to a President Hillary Clinton, Obama would be on the outside looking in. He knows the likelihood of him doing anything of substance and having influence in a Clinton administration. When former Democratic candidate Sen. Joe Biden of Delaware was asked whether he wanted to be her VP, he said competing with Bill Clinton isn't his cup of tea. Some would say that serving as VP two terms under Clinton would give Obama administrative experience, and he would be 54 when he could run, but I just don't buy it.

Now, as a way out, I would expect to see these two on a ticket *only* if Clinton is the nominee and they run the numbers and determine that the best chance of winning would be with Obama. She wants to be president that badly and would discount the bad blood. Then, they would hope he accepts it.

I just don't see any of it happening. This might be seen as a dream ticket, but it is not a match made in heaven.

February 4, 2008

WVON-AM/Chicago: Dr. Cornel West on The Roland S. Martin Show

Maria Shriver: "So, I'm standing here today not, because I'm cousins with her, not because I'm best friends with her, not because I admire her or her. I'm standing here because I want to be here.

"And I wasn't on the schedule. I wasn't on the schedule and I thought to myself when I woke up this morning, I thought there is no place I should be, but right here today.

"And I want to give a little shout out to my daughter Catherine, who is a first time voter. And I was at a horse show with her, which is why I am attired like this and I have not brushed my hair and I did not do my make up. And I said to her at 7:30 this morning. I think I should be at UCLA.

"And she said to me, mommy, if you think you can help, if you think can change just one person, if you think you can make a difference, then go."

Roland Martin: Folks welcome back that was the first lady of California, Maria Shriver, yesterday at the UCLA Barack Obama president to a rally, joined on-stage by Michelle Obama, Oprah Winfrey, Caroline Kennedy. You also had the Executive Secretary and Treasurer for the AFL-CIO Maria Elena Durazo. She was also there. Of course Michelle walked out with Stevie Wonder. It was a major, major rally...

Roland Martin: What do you think, do you sense something going on? Do you sense something going on all across this country? As I said, over the weekend the *LA Times* endorsed Obama. The Albuquerque newspaper endorsed Obama. The wife of Robert F. Kennedy, Ethel Kennedy, endorsed Senator Obama over the weekend. And let me tell you why the Clinton campaign is very worried. After nearly every debate. after every debate, I always get an e-mail. I always get an e-mail from the Clinton campaign talking about she won the debate, how hands down she beat everybody would come to the debate. Thursday night, did not get an e-mail. Friday, did not get an e-mail. I am telling you, there is some serious concern among the Clinton campaign. They said early on, they have always said, they have always maintained, we are going to destroy him on Super Tuesday. We are going to win this campaign on Super Tuesday. But the polling data suggests that he is beating her in Alabama, in Colorado, it is within two points in Missouri. That he is competitive in Idaho. Although it is showing that, according to poll she's up 17 in Massachusetts, but several other polls do not indicate that. He is also targeting certain districts in New York. Again there is some serious concern among the Clinton campaign that again, this campaign will go beyond, beyond February 5th, and the states following February 5th, Maryland, he has a huge lead. Virginia, has a huge lead. Louisiana, has huge lead. So something is certainly happening in this campaign.

Sharon McGee: I think, Roland when we get back to this enormous endorsement by the First Lady of California. We cannot diminish that. Because you have to understand that the core of Clinton's support is white women. So when you have this woman come on stage with Oprah and Michelle Obama, it is like that slam dunk. It's unbelievable.

Roland Martin: Folks, joining us to the studio is someone who is familiar with this audience. We heard him, so many different times and he was certainly one of the supporters of Senator Barack Obama. Ladies and gentlemen, he needs no introduction Dr. Cornel West. Doc, how are you doing?

Cornel West: Brother, it's a blessing to be here. I want to salute for you throwing down so wonderfully on CNN. Man you've been superb, you've been excellent. I must say though, man, I was blessed to hear sister Sharon McGee in the morning. I might have to move to Chicago. Both style and substance. She got it going on now, brother.

Roland Martin: Well, I am certainly glad that you are here. You were speaking at St. Sabina yesterday.

Cornel West: Brother Pfleger, that's special brother right there.

Roland Martin: Yes, sitting right here in the studio.

Cornel West: Yes, Brother Pfleger, special brother and we praised the Lord yesterday. Brother kept the focus on the cross and connected it to struggle for justice, my brother.

Roland Martin: We talked about that struggle for justice, it was interesting yesterday. Oprah Winfrey also talked about that. She really nailed in terms of what the purpose of this whole movement was. She did not just here and say, "Oh, I am simply supporting this guy. He is just somebody who I like, somebody who you know, who has a great speech, a great message." She really linked in terms of the women's movement and the Civil Rights Movement. I want to play that. I want you to respond on what she had to say

Oprah Winfrey: *This is, I believe a unique moment in our collective history of women's rights and civil rights. Because so many people have struggled that we would have the right as women people, and the right as black people, to be considered as equals. And now look at this campaign. The two front-runners, a black man and a woman.*
What that says to me is we have won the struggle. We have won the

right to compete fairly and be considered as viable candidates. Because this election itself is a declaration of victory for women's rights and civil rights.

And now we are free. We are free for the first time to be able to take full advantage of all the rights and privileges of American citizenship.

Roland Martin: Doc, what do you think of that?

Cornel West: Well, one, I am just so glad to see sister Oprah stepping forward like that. You know, I have always said that her entrepreneurial genius is unparalleled. I've always been a little critical of my dear sister because I wanted to see more political courage and she's coming forth in a serious way. But I think she still has to make a distinction. We have to make a distinction between breakthrough and victory. That this is a breakthrough that we have sister Hillary. A breakthrough that we brother Obama. The victory is still further down the road. Because we know white supremacy and male supremacy are still operating in very powerful ways, covert and overt, in our society. And we won't be able to declare victory until we push that across the board for ordinary people, for everyday people. But the breakthrough is real and it is good to be in the same camp as sister Oprah. I am not used to that. You know what I mean. I love my dear sister and I am glad her success is having tremendous impact, especially young girls all around the world. But she spoke with power and courage at UCLA yesterday.

Roland Martin: But the thing that I think, who she represents and this is important, is that, a significant number of people who were disenfranchised, who have never, she made a point even yesterday. "How many of y'all would have thought you would be at a political rally?" And I think that's what really jumps out. The number of people who just say, "I am sick of politics. I do not want to be involved in it." But this is what happens when someone special comes along who touches those kind of people.

Cornel West: And there I think we just have to give a credit to brother Barack. Brother Obama actually has vision, charisma, brilliance; this unique capacity to mobilize people who have been outside of the system; not participating. Not just young, but significantly young people. And the fact that Oprah Winfrey and Maria Shriver and Caroline Kennedy and others had jumped on that bandwagon is a very positive thing. But I give the credit to brother Barack for that though.

Roland Martin: Well, I will tell you what, I am going to break in a second, while I tell you a story I was talking with the Clarence B. Jones. Dr. King's speechwriter.

Cornel West: He got a new book coming out you know.

Roland Martin: Yes, he does.

Cornel West: I read that book.

Roland Martin: And he said that a woman who worked for him a long time ago named Roberta, called him up she said, "Clarence who you supporting?" He said, "Well, I am leaning towards Senator Obama." This is about three weeks ago. He since endorsed Senator Obama. And he said that, "Roberta what are you going to do?" And he said, "Roberta is a hardcore confederate flag, decal on her truck, shotgun on the rack, always been in her life Republican." And she said, "Well, me and my girlfriends love Oprah. So since we can't vote for her, we are going to vote for Obama."

Cornel West: Wow.

Roland Martin: He said, "You can't get more Republican hardcore from South Carolina than this woman." He said, so the effect is certainly he is having on a significant number of people is there.

Cornel West: That's powerful. But footnote we have to add is that even with a vote for Obama, it still does not mean that sister is not dangerous!

Roland Martin: Especially with a shotgun rack!

Cornel West: We still got to pray for that sister. I am glad she is voting for Obama though, but she still got work to do, brother.

Roland Martin: Has this become in many ways bigger than the candidate himself?

Cornel West: There's no doubt about that, brother. What we are experiencing is the melting of this political ice age, where it has been fashionable to be indifferent to the suffering of most vulnerable. And in is such a melting, lo and behold the social misery of the late great, James Cleveland, called ordinary people, that their misery becomes more visible. And so the debates over, jobs with living wage, healthcare, childcare, quality education, corporate greed, wealth and inequality, ecological crisis, all of these now move to the center. We saw that in the debate on Thursday with sister Hillary and brother Barack. And what Barack actually then signifies and symbolizes is the end of the Southern strategy, the end of race-bating political realignment that has been successful for the Republican Party. The end of rendering invisible these disgraceful schools system and the unavailable child and healthcare and so forth. So in that sense it's very real now. I should say, I think in some ways I prefer the Curtis Mayfield song that he wrote for

Aretha over the En Vogue cover "Giving Him Something He Can Feel." Michael Jackson, I can say, can you feel it? But see when Aretha sings it, I feel it a little bit more than Michael singing it.

Roland Martin: What was interesting yesterday, Bill Clinton was in Los Angeles. And what I found to be interesting is that he sort of was on this apology tour. And *LA Times* describe the reaction of black churches as polite applause. I kept trying to explain this to the people at CNN. Black folks across the country have been greatly offended by his comments and, literally, I've gotten phone calls from Yellow Dog, Democrats saying, "If she wins the nomination ain't no way in hell I'm voting for her." That's how angry people have responded.

Cornel West: We don't forget and we ought not forget. He was out of control, no doubt about that. But also people forget that during the '90s you had the crime bill. You had mandatory sentences. Three strikes you are out. You had Rwanda, you had NAFTA, that devastated workers. You had a welfare bill that Reagan wouldn't sign, that he signed in order to triangulate, which is to say, win the next election. You see, that is opportunism. And black folk, we like opportunity. We can't stand opportunism. And when we see it, we're revolted, we hate it precisely because it's so rare that we have a moment that we can seize a genuine opportunity. That why it is so significant about brother Obama and that why I am here to do a full court press for my brother. That this is a genuine opportunity. There is no doubt about that.

Roland Martin: I want to play this sound bite here from Michelle Obama. Here is Michelle Obama yesterday at UCLA.

Michelle Obama: *Again, see this is a young man who grew up like regular folks. The product of a single parent household. His mother was 18, A 18-year-old white woman trying to raise a black kid in the '60's.*

Now she had to be a dreamer, and she was a little bit naïve, but because of that sometimes they lived on food stamps, but Barack, because of her dreaming got to see the world. See because that little girl from Kansas had the nerve to think that she could travel the world and study women's issues in places like Indonesia. So Barack got to see the world in ways that most Americans do not. Imagine the President of the United States who looks at other countries with the level of respect and understanding without fear.

Imagine a President of the United States who understands the impact that a great nation like ours can have to a small village, near Kisumu in Africa, not because he's gotten a policy briefing but because he has a grandmother who lives in that little village.

Cornel West: Yes, sister Michelle, she is eloquent. Remember Cicero defined eloquence as wisdom speaking. I would highly recommend folk to hear sister Michelle Obama at grand opera house in Wilmington, Delaware where she spent just two days ago. It was a whole hour. It was the most powerful thing you can hear. I mean alongside brother Barack speeches in Iowa and in South Carolina, Michelle right there with him.

Roland Martin: That is why they call her the closer, absolutely.

Cornel West: She was right there with him. South of Chicago got a whole lot of to be proud of.

February 5, 2008

WVON-AM/Chicago: Illinois Senate President
Emil Jones on The Roland S. Martin Show

Roland Martin: To the phone lines right now, State Senate President Emil Jones. Sir, good morning.

Emil Jones: Good morning. How are you, Roland?

Roland Martin: I am doing great. This was a day that you pushed and encouraged Senator Barack Obama to actually see...how does it make you feel for this Super Tuesday?

Emil Jones: It makes me feel good to see one from my own community, a young, bright, intelligent young man as ironic this is Black History Month and this is what the movement is all about. And he is an extraordinary individual and we should be out for him in record numbers. It is important that we vote, not only for him for president, but vote for his delegates because it is a balance of delegates. Go take the time. When you see the Obama delegates, vote for each and every one of them today and it is an important election. Today is like a tsunami. Folks are coming out to vote and they are excited about it. But I am really glad, Roland, to see you on the national scene on CNN to give some sort of balance to the reporting that comes out because it is all disgusting to me, some of these pundits and commentators, the way they try to slap things very subtly.

Roland Martin: Well, you know, and that is one of the things that I certainly watch out for. I know I tick some people off by jumping on them but I tell people all the time, my philosophy is very simple...that if they're going to fire me in the end, I better say what the hell I want to say while I'm there.

Emil Jones: That is right, no question about it. This is a very exciting election. We have some great, great local candidates. We got Will Burns in the 26th district, who is a protégée of Barack Obama, he should do it extraordinarily well. I trust that the people will vote for him. Out further south we got Stan Moore running for state representative, another fine young man in the 27th district. But Barack Obama is bringing the people to the polls. In all my years in politics, I have not seen so much excitement of voters wanting to be involved.

Roland Martin: Well, I will say this, Senate President Jones, when Senator Obama announced that he was running for the U.S. Senate, if I am correct, there were what, just two or three people standing next to him?

Emil Jones: Yes.

Roland Martin: Yes, so it was I think first of all, I know you were standing there and I believe was it Senator Meeks? I cannot quite remember.

Emil Jones: Well it was Senator Meeks and Congressman Davis, I know Congressman Jackson was there but he and I discussed that early on, the strategy for winning the senate seat, and there was the doubters as always. But we always knew he had the talent, he had the ability to attract voters from all across the state, a lot of my colleagues in the senate, downstaters, suburban…were in his corner supporting him in that election and he shocked the world more or less by the margin of his victory. He is a well likeable individual, very talented, very smart, and he has a great ability to bring folks who are against each other, together to work for the common good and that is what is going to take to be a great president during this period of time in our life.

Roland Martin: All right, Senate President Emil Jones. I appreciate it sir, thanks a lot.

Emil Jones: All right my friend.

Roland Martin: Thank you, you take care.

February 5, 2008

WVON-AM/Chicago: The Rev. Marcia Dyson on The Roland S. Martin Show

Roland Martin: Let's holler at our good friend Rev. Marcia Dyson. How you doing Reverend Dyson?

Marcia Dyson: I am doing great, how you doing this morning, Roland?

Roland Martin: I am doing great. I am doing great. Your girl is up 15, 17, 20 points in several states last week. Now it is neck-and-neck. You might be doing some serious praying today.

Marcia Dyson: Well, you know I am not doing any serious planning… but I am hoping.

Roland Martin: You know you are doing some serious praying. You know you are praying.

Marcia Dyson: It is time to make change and we all should plan that is why you got the people in the Democratic Party running for the presidency because we hope that they not only are planning but have made some plans. And I am just here to say that first I am glad that we are out and up in the outpour that Chicagoans and all of Illinois getting all excited about the process, especially when you have been reigned so long by a great dynasty called The Daleys in the most segregated city of Chicago that maybe that change could start right there in the city of Chicago. But then, it tips in, let us get it across the nation. You know Hillary Clinton is on target. People tried her, saying that she will be ready day one. Really, she was ready yesterday with the healthcare program that she really is calling for, truly a healthcare program that leaves no one out.

Roland Martin: You know what that is interesting. I was watching CNN this morning, Doc Reverend, and that Sanjay Gupta said that frankly, the plans of Clinton and Obama are 95 percent the same.

Marcia Dyson: Well, you know what if you talk about—are they really?

Roland Martin: No, he is an actual medical doctor, a partial observer.

Marcia Dyson: Yes I know Dr. Gupta, you know I watch television because I try to keep a check on you but even if that is so...

Roland Martin: Now you cannot keep a check on me now.

Marcia Dyson: ...It's a world of difference who is that 5% in the conversation that he is talking about? And the fact that she devised a plan over 14 years ago so that she is a visionary on that so everybody...

Roland Martin: Yes, but it didn't work, it didn't work 14 years ago. It did not work 14 years ago. It did not work 14 years ago, you know that.

Marcia Dyson: Pardon?

Roland Martin: It did not work 14 years ago.

Marcia Dyson: No, it did not work but if you allow the blueprints of the conversation to be stated which everybody demonized before wishing all the presidential candidates, not only our good Senator Obama but the rest of the candidates try to jump on and devise the plan because though it did not work it does not mean that it should not work is because we have narrow minded people who could not accept that kind of program, did not understand that kind of program, and allow that conversation to be on the table so she may not have been able to cook the goose but she sure did shoot it and bring it out of the field.

Roland Martin: I've got to ask you this question.

Marcia Dyson: Yes sir, yes sir.

Roland Martin: I've got to ask you this question. I was watching her on ABC "This Week with George Stephanopoulos" and he asked, and Senator Obama asked repeatedly during the debate was there going to be... was she going to garnish wages? How is she going to make it mandatory? On ABC with George Stephanopoulos, she said that garnishing wages was on the table.

Marcia Dyson: She said it might be.

Roland Martin: No, no, no, no. One second, one second. Doc, Doc, Doc...when somebody says it might be, that means it is on the table. So, what would you say to these people who are listening on WVON right now who say, "Wait a minute if under her healthcare plan, they might garnish wages to force people to pay for healthcare?" Do you think people are going to be excited about somebody garnishing their wages?

Marcia Dyson: No. No more about people who in the Democratic Party that are supposed to be solid would hear somebody say that they might not support somebody if their team does not win their nomination.

Roland Martin: No, no, no that does not, definitely nothing to do with the question.

Marcia Dyson: They may not be excited about the possibility there might be garnishing wages but what I would hope that it would do is to wake up people and say, "Look we need to have this." It is the conversation that I admit I have not had with the senator face-to-face about that. In fact, you would be glad to know that I lost my voice in South Carolina and have to be solid for a week...

Roland Martin: Yes, but you are defending it.

Marcia Dyson: But that is to fill up the conversation so we have to get. We are going to see the "might" in one person. Okay please look at the "might" all over, then we will know.

Roland Martin: But should not we be concerned?

Marcia Dyson: ...the consensus of the people who are working for her on the health plan project.

Roland Martin: But shouldn't we be concerned though, that Senator Clinton has a health plan that calls for mandatory opt-in.? [Overlapping voices]

And no, no, no, one second hold up Doc, her plan is mandatory. She said it in the debate but hold—wait a minute. But if she says that garnishing wages is one of the options on the table, should that not cause people to take a pause when it comes to whether or not we want to support that?

Marcia Dyson: Once she is president, that is what you absolutely do. [Overlapping voices]

Roland Martin: I do not want to get the bamboozle. I do not want to wait until she becomes president to get my wages garnished. [Overlapping voices].

Marcia Dyson: I really hate that word, but you know what, talk about being bamboozled. You know let me cut to the chase, everybody is heightened about this political process. We know what the candidates will and say that they can do because you really never know until you get it into the oven. I support Hillary Clinton because she has at least been in the kitchen, and not just talking about the White House. But what I do want to say to my African American community because I know that you have a great following listening there, especially my brothers and sisters who live in the city of Chicago knowing that this is one of the most racist and most segregated cities in the nation is that what we got to stop doing is you started off with *You Better Think* and that song *Change*. Think about the change that you have made Martin, Roland. I am alarmed about the zealousness of our people like even when people like Tavis Smiley who brought us the State of the Black Union is being demonized and vilified because he is telling us to be objective. I'm horrified.

Roland Martin: No, actually that is not just what Tavis saying. No, no, no, Tavis is being criticized because Tavis equated the support for Senator Obama as being all about emotion and African Americans were offended because he would suggest that, well, people are supporting Obama based upon emotion. I heard the—in fact I heard the initial commentary he gave. I was on the show the next day and that is why people were offended. It is as if African Americans are not making an informed decision, that is why Tavis has gotten ripped a new one.

Marcia Dyson: Well, I think that we should really make an informed decision.

Roland Martin: But we are.

Marcia Dyson: That when all of this is over, that one thing when, after Super Tuesday, that we have to think of is another 20 something of our states to go.

Roland Martin: Yes, we do.

Marcia Dyson: That our people, that we realize the first and great front that we have to have for those who are Democrats to have democratic front and stay solid with that opportunity for people to really go to the side. We are not going to be by emotion only. I am not even going to state what Tavis says. I believe our people are going to have an informed decision and I hope that discipline, that an informed decision and not an emotional one, which I would not say. But I am just saying this, read a little bit more. Let us not take cliff notes only and make that decision, okay?

Roland Martin: And I agree. And I would also say do not make the assumption that because something that President Clinton did that it will happen again under a President Hillary Clinton. Two different people, two different situations, two different White Houses and so again, so I would say it to Tavis Smiley or anybody else, if black folks were not emotional in supporting Senator Hillary Clinton, don't you dare make the same assumption that black people are emotional in supporting Senator Barack Obama. I appreciate it.

Marcia Dyson: I appreciate you.

Roland Martin: I got your blood pressure up, but you know I got to do it just to make sure you are on your toes.

Marcia Dyson: You said you would not make me talk again but that would not happen.

Roland Martin: Uh-huh, thanks a lot I appreciate it.

WVON-AM/Chicago: Actress Kerry Washington on The Roland S. Martin Show

Roland Martin: Right now, I want to go to one of the top actresses in all of Hollywood, but someone who is also politically astute. The Obama people say that, "Man, she has been strong on the campaign trail," and of course always, always a pleasure to have her here. Ladies and gentleman, Kerry Washington. Kerry, good morning.

Kerry Washington: Good morning.

Roland Martin: Always good talking to you. Just saw you last week in L.A. at the debate.

Kerry Washington: Yeah, I am loving this campaign trail thing. It is much more fun than any movie I have ever done.

Roland Martin: Now, you have been out there stepping for Obama, why? Why is he your candidate for president?

Kerry Washington: You know I will be honest with you. I had a really hard time choosing. You know because I am obviously a woman and I am obviously African American. I am from New York, so she was my senator. I voted for her in the Senate and I voted for Bill for president. And what I really had to ask myself was, "Was I willing to let go of the ideas of gender? Was I willing to let go of the ideas of race? Was I willing to let go of the idea of indebtedness?" Because I know a lot of people who feel like they are making this decision because they owe something to somebody, and I really have to go, I cannot vote for somebody because they are black or because they are a woman, or because of what they have given me in the past, because these are elected officials that they have given me something, it is because we put them there. So, they owe us something. When I put all of that aside, I just realized that, he, based on principles and values, he is the next best president of the United States. You know and I stopped worrying about man, woman, black, white, rich, poor. You know when I stopped Republican, Democrat. When I let go of all those things that divide us and polarize us, which is what he does. He moves past those things in to a place of values and principles. When I do that it is really clear to me that he is who we need right now to run this country.

Roland Martin: You know Kerry, you made an excellent point when you said, "who owes what." I keep telling people again. It is nothing against

Senator Clinton. It is nothing against former President Bill Clinton, but I do not buy this nonsense about, well, black people owe the Clintons. You know I say, "Wait a minute, I say that promissory note frankly was torn up going through impeachment and politics. It is not what you get from the eight years ago or 12 years ago or 16 years ago. It is what you are born to do for me in the future."

Kerry Washington: Yes, I mean I would be honest with you. I do not even approach the impeachment thing because I do not know what I would do if that went on, but I just feel like, it is our people, it is our leaders in powerful positions because we put them there and they owe *us* something. We do not owe them anything. And you know, I love the good things that happened during that administration. Great! But you know until somebody gives me my 40 acres and a mule, between you and me, I want to talk about promises, you know what I mean?

Roland Martin: Absolutely.

Kerry Washington: Let us make decisions based on today. I do not think, I can afford to go into this next administration based on a sense of owing somebody something. I try not to live my life that way and it is not about you know forsaking anybody. It is about saying, "Let us all come together." I like the Clintons, again I voted for Bill Clinton, you know for president. And I think Hillary is a great senator. I think she would make a great president one day. But today, right now, we need Barack Obama because we cannot go into a general election with somebody that galvanizes the right against them. We cannot go into a general election feeling like we are attached to the past or that we are carrying the past with us. Because the way that this country has been run up to this point, we are at a dangerous place and I think, when I look at what he has done in this campaign, Senator Barack Obama, he literally has not taken any money from lobbyists, from special interest groups, from big business and this is revolutionary, because it costs countless millions of dollars to run for president, hundreds of millions of dollars.

Roland Martin: Right.

Kerry Washington: And by him not taking money from these big business people, he is not going to be accountable to any of them when he gets into the White House. When he walks in that Oval Office, the only person he is going to owe a favor is the American people. He is going to responsible to us, not to the healthcare industry, not to the pharmaceutical company, not to the oil industry. And some of the other candidates are way too far down the line taking money from those people because they will be a little torn about who they are held responsible to.

Roland Martin: All right, okay folks. I told you all she loves this stuff, Kerry Washington. Hey, we appreciate it and I certainly—let us not make it your last time. We look forward to having you on as we move forward the campaign.

Kerry Washington: My pleasure and absolutely. I think we are in this to the long haul so let us talk as much as possible.

Roland Martin: All right thanks Kerry, I really appreciate it. Thanks a lot.

WVON-AM/Chicago: Iyanla Vanzant on The Roland S. Martin Show

Roland Martin: ...hook to the lines and on the line Dr. Iyanla Vanzant.

Iyanla Vanzant: Good morning, how are you?

Roland Martin: Doing great. Today is campaign day all across the nation. Some 24 states are in play and getting a sense from you, you have endorsed Senator Hillary Clinton. Why is she the choice?

Iyanla Vanzant: Well, I am voting my conscience you know. I wish I could give you this wonderful rhetorical speech but I really cannot. I prayed about it and I asked for direction and guidance. I asked for what I needed in this country. I think I represent many, many people. My history represents many people and when I look at Senator Clinton does not mean I do not absolutely love and adore Senator Obama, I absolutely do. My conscience said a woman for a change. A woman for a change, a woman for a change, a woman with history, experience, and a record to bring change in the way this country rolls because this is an all boys network, and I just think this is the time for us to build a new kind of relationship, not only with foreign governments but also within our country and for me I believe that Senator Clinton has what it takes to build those kinds of relationships. That does not mean that anyone else does not have it but when I look at the time. How he came to me, Roland, was the right thing at the wrong time with the wrong thing.

Roland Martin: Now as we look forward and I am going to break it about 45 seconds so we will probably get this comment in. As you talk about the all boys network. What was very interesting is Senator Clinton will say would change being a woman president but of course because of ratio, the dynamics in America, Obama cannot reply the changes having an African American president, as well. And so, now what do you make with all this talk about a Clinton-Obama ticket or an Obama-Clinton ticket, which frankly I have seen in .com is not going to happen. That is a high dream. And the state of the Clinton campaign, Lanny Davis wrote on his memo, Terry McAuliffe was out there. They were sort of tossing us out there. The Obama people saying forget that. We are not even entertaining the notion of that kind of ticket.

Iyanla Vanzant: Right. I do not thing they should. I think that each candidate, stay focus on their vision and that vision will unfold as it needs to for the good of this country. I just think the whole process is exciting. That we have one person who you hardly ever hear from a woman and one person that we hardly ever see, a black man when we look at society...

Roland Martin: Actually, well actually I used a little bit different. I was—I try to qualify because we did of course we did have an African American woman running '72 and [overlapping voices].

Iyanla Vanzant: Shirley Chisholm?

Roland Martin: Right, so I always say that [overlapping voices].

Iyanla Vanzant: ...and we had no [overlapping voices] in the '80s.

Roland Martin: But what I always say when people say that a woman running we have a black man running, I would say no, we have a white woman running and a black woman running just to be—just to be you know.

Iyanla Vanzant: Absolutely. Absolutely correct. [overlapping voices] than running together, they are running at the same time. So, that makes all the excitement.

Roland Martin: All right, all right now, have you already voted?

Iyanla Vanzant: I am in D.C.

Roland Martin: Oh so you got to wait until next week.

Iyanla Vanzant: Yes.

Roland Martin: ...next week. Well, that is going to be an interesting [overlapping voices] there.

Iyanla Vanzant: ...particularly the young people those first time voters, 18 and up, get out and vote. We need your voice. We need your presence. We need your energy. Get out and vote and of course I would say support Senator Hillary Clinton.

Roland Martin: All right thanks a bunch, I appreciate it.

Iyanla Vanzant: Thank you my love, bye, bye.

Roland Martin: Thank you.

WVON-AM/Chicago: Maxine Waters on The Santita Jackson Show with Roland S. Martin

Santita Jackson: I got a lot of people who want to talk about this election, and I want to bring on... let me bring on Congresswoman Maxine Waters out of California. Out of Los Angeles, who is going to tell us what is going on out there. Congresswoman Maxine Waters how are you?

Maxine Waters: I am fine, how are you Ms. Jackson?

Santita Jackson: I am doing fine Congresswoman Waters. Talk to me, what are the trends in California? We are seeing the polls it seems like some polls say it is too close to call. Some polls give Senator Obama the edge, some other polls give Senator Clinton the edge. What is it looking like?

Maxine Waters: Well, Santita... I think that what is happening now has confounded the most knowledgeable pundit in politics. What you have is too close to call. You have the fact that the Hillary advantage has been reduced and that Mr. Obama's numbers have risen and nobody knows what is going to happen.

Santita Jackson: How did that happen, did you think South Carolina helped Senator Obama that much? Did it disadvantage Senator Clinton that much? What happened? I mean are Hispanics coalesced behind Senator Obama?

Maxine Waters: I do not know what the cause of it is. I do believe that Mr. Obama has been working organizationally longer, harder and smarter. And that he has captured the attention of each of the congressional districts having people on the ground for a long time. And I think

175

that he has searched, and that search has reduced her advantage and I do not think it is about issues as much as it is about a kind of energy that has been created by him in his campaign.

Santita Jackson: Now, as you see them, what are the compelling issues in this primary season moving into the general election season?

Maxine Waters: Well, I think the compelling issues are those that have been alluded to. The economy, comprehensive universal healthcare, the Leave-No-Child-Behind policies of the Bush administration that need to be corrected. Because education is a serious issue that must be dealt within this country. I think the housing crisis and the subprime mess that we are in because this administration was not paying attention and the oversight agencies have allowed predatory lending to be the order of the day. I think that all of the issues of the African American community, mandatory minimum sentencing and the fact that a disproportionate number of African Americans are being locked up for small amounts of crack cocaine while those who have in their possession and are selling larger amounts to get a slap on the wrist. I think that voting rights, all of these issues are extremely important and they did get some discussion on the debate. But one of the campaigns is about inspiration and hope, and the other campaign is really about more concrete proposals. And the concrete proposals are not getting enough attention because the news media is not forcing the attention on the concrete proposals. They are rather trying to find the convergence of confrontation and this is what they have been doing with this race. Trying to create controversy, so as to have more journalists interested and involved with.

Santita Jackson: Let me ask you this, ultimately why then did you, is that why you have been settled upon Senator Clinton as your choice? Because you held up for quite some time.

Maxine Waters: I look at the two campaigns basically the way that I recently just described them to you. I weighed what they were saying, listened to them in the debates, read everything that they had written, and I too am more of a policy wonk. I want concrete proposals and I want some answers to some of these issues. While I have a real appreciation for the fact that inspiration and hope is always needed, we did not just start dealing with inspiring people raising their levels of expectation. We have been living with the mantra, "keep hope alive" for a number of years that was initiated by someone that we know very well, Reverend Jackson. It is time for concrete proposals, and I simply understand and know in the most profound way that the universal healthcare proposal that has been set forth by Hilary Clinton is absolutely a sound proposal that is so very much needed. I am focused on the fact that African Americans are dying from preventable diseases. Everywhere we look in our communities across this country, people are having their limbs amputated from diabetes. Diabetes is ravishing our communities, cardiovascular diseases. Cancer, black woman die from breast cancer, late detection, no access to the healthcare systems that we have. Only healthcare being received in emergency room. The heart attacks among younger and younger people. And so I think that healthcare is a vital issue that must be dealt with. She has been involved with trying to bring about universal healthcare for a long time, and she now understands and knows how to deal with the special interest. She has been working on it for all of these years. She got slapped down by the special interest and the insurance companies when her husband was in office and now she's has got it, she knows it. And I do not think that any of the other candidate had a handle on it. That emergence is extremely important. If we get our health together we can get our lives in order. We can deal with confronting the ills of this society. But if you cannot move around, if you cannot get out of bed, if you do not have healthcare, you cannot begin to take control of your life, and so that emergence is extremely important to me. She has concrete proposals to deal with universal healthcare for all, every American. Not some but all of them. So I started with you know, who's got the proposals, who is talking real information? Again, I appreciate the hope and inspiration. But it is time to move in to implementation.

Santita Jackson: You know what, that having been said, we got Roland who is going to be rolling through our shows today... you know Roland Martin does mornings live here WVON?

Maxine Waters: Sure.

Santita Jackson: But Roland also is on CNN and he is at the CNN headquarters up in New York. Roland Martin.

Roland Martin: Yes, Santita.

Santita Jackson: Hey Roland, you got some questions for Congresswoman Maxine Waters.

Maxine Waters: Thank you, yes Roland.

Roland Martin: Congresswoman Waters, I watched ABC "This Week with George Stephanopoulos" and when he asked Senator Clinton specifically whether or not she would include as a part of her health plan, garnishing of wages. She answered the question, but she is essentially saying that is on the table. That is one of the criticisms by Senator Barack Obama that we have not heard, how do you mandate it, and so will you talk about her health plan. I heard CNN's Dr. Sanjay Gupta say pretty that much Obama and Clinton are 95 percent there. So how do you deal with the issue of garnishing waves as a possibility in order to mandate it? How is that more superior than Senator Obama's plan?

Maxine Waters: Well, I think he should be on the table for a discussion. One of the things that bothers me is, we have too many people earning $75,000 a year, who simply would not buy any health insurance. She has in her plan subsidies to help people who cannot afford healthcare but we've got to create some responsibility. We cannot have people who can afford to purchase healthcare, who are not purchasing it and showing up at the emergency room. So that should be on the table for a discussion.

Roland Martin: Now, I heard you talk about inspiration and hope, but isn't that a bit disingenuous in that the media's talked about that, when in fact Senator Obama has laid out a significant number of policy positions that are very specific, yet for people to suggest that it was just about inspiration and hope, that is not accurate in terms of what he has done in this campaign.

Maxine Waters: Well, actually what he has done is he has led with a generic message of inspiration and hope. As a matter of fact, he has not consistently advanced his proposals. That is why they are less known, he talks generically about change, he talks generically about inspiration, he talks generically about bringing the country together. He talked about bringing together Republicans and Democrats, and having

Republicans in his administration as well as Democrats. No he has not consistently and often enough talked about concrete proposals about how he intends to create this big thing called change. What does it mean? What is the definition of change? No, he has not.

Santita Jackson: Well, let me ask you both this. Let me direct this to you, Congresswoman Maxine Waters. There is a lot of talk about an Obama-Clinton, Clinton-Obama ticket and think, I suspect it is because largely there is not a lot of ideological difference between the two. Do you think it is at all feasible after this contentious campaign is over that they might share a ticket? Congresswoman Waters?

Maxine Waters: They are both very capable, obviously, she brings certain things to the table and he brings certain things. And I think, when most people think about it, and out of the pain of having to make the decision, they say, look they both have qualities that we like, wouldn't it be great... wouldn't it be the dream ticket if the two of them came together and that was advanced to them at a Los Angeles debate and they kind of toyed with it. We know usually how those decisions are made but I think because it keeps surfacing and people are talking about it more and more, it just may end up with serious consideration.

Roland Martin: But Congressman Waters, the people who are actually advancing these are the Clinton folks. I received... Terry McAuliffe was advancing it on New York 1, Lanny Davis was advancing in a column, he said, the only way Obama would be on the ticket if he is the VP, so it raises the question, I mean, I talked to the Obama people, none of their people are advancing this notion of a Clinton-

Obama ticket. So, why all of a sudden are the Clinton folks talking about this? What is the point behind it?

Maxine Waters: I do not know that the Clinton folks are. The first time I really heard it was at the debate in Los Angeles where it was raised by Wolf Blitzer, and international audience. So I do not know that there is any one group talking about more than others. I think when you have it raised by Wolf Blitzer in CNN with an international audience then it perks up the interest of a lot of people and maybe a lot of people are talking about it.

Roland Martin: That makes sense, because I know, like I said Terry McAuliffe was talking about it and Lanny Davis of course who is a big time Clinton supporter was talking about it. I have gotten several other e-mails from Clinton supporters saying the same when the Obama folks said, "Look that is not what we are talking about. Our goal is not to be on some ticket." They said, "Our goal is to win the nomination."

Maxine Waters: I am probably like most people, I really heard it first with CNN and that is the debate in Los Angeles and that seems to me that a lot of other conversation has been sparked by that international exposure of it. That is where I first got it.

Santita Jackson: Let me ask this question, because this has been on my mind since I read the comment. It is moving forward because what concerns me, Congresswoman Waters and Roland Martin, is creating an atmosphere that would be healthy enough for us to walk out of Denver and win in November. That having been said, Oprah Winfrey said something that I think speaks to where we are historically, "This is I believe a unique moment in our collective history of women's and civil rights. Now look at this campaign the two front-runners are a black man and woman. What that says to me is we have won the struggle and we have the right to compete." What do you think of that, have we won the struggle or are we still in the midst of it, Congresswoman Waters?

Maxine Waters: Well, I think to say that we have won the struggle is kind of a broad all encompassing description of how she was feeling. And I think that a lot of people are feeling advancement, feeling new possibilities. I do not know if we could wrap it all up and sign off and say we have won. But it is certainly is progress to have a woman and an African American competing, and down to the last two in the Democratic Party primary politics. It is a good thing, and I think that her statement really does describe the fact that a lot of people are feeling very positive about it. I do not know if it means we have won the struggle, but I think she really is turned on at this point and think that it is a great thing. And many people do.

Santita Jackson: Roland, you got the final question, we got less than a minute.

Roland Martin: Congressman Waters, you are supporting Senator Clinton what will happen, what would be your view if your congressional district when the votes are tallied, if it comes out that they supported Obama more than Clinton? If you constituents speak what would that actually say to you in terms of what your district is saying versus who you are supporting?

Maxine Waters: Well, if my district votes for Obama over Clinton that is fine. My recommendation is but a recommendation, I do not order people... they want to know what I think and what I feel... as a leader I share that with them, the final decisions are theirs... there are times when my district does not always agree with me, as you know I have a very diverse district. The majority of my district is Latino, one-third almost of my district is white, many people do not know what my district did... and sometimes they agree with me... disagreed with me on my opinions. What I feel with police abuse and a lot of decisions, I have a section of my district who does not agree with me. So we are not always in step... as this views are created from time to time.

Roland Martin: As a superdelegate, if your district votes for him, will you as a superdelegate support what your constituents say?

Maxine Waters: That all depends on what question you are asking. If he is the nominee than I will support him. Is that what you are asking?

Roland Martin: No. I am asking if your congressional district votes for Obama or for Clinton, if it goes down to a superdelegate decision at the convention... would you vote along with your constituents or who you endorsed?

Maxine Waters: Well, if you are asking me if I'll switch because there appears to be a difference at this point, and if they come out basically even from California. No, I am not going to arbitrarily switch my vote. If we get in to a bargaining situation at the convention and we have an opportunity to talk with both sides, and if we see certain things happening. I reserve the right to bargain... but I do not advance my decision with you on the radio today.

Santita Jackson: And that Roland, is the answer and I thank you...

Roland Martin: Got you...

Santita Jackson: Roland Martin I thank you. Congresswoman Maxine because that having been said, that is the nature of politics at the end of the day many people have put their heart...

February 5, 2008

WVON-AM/Chicago: Spike Lee on The Santita Jackson Show with Roland S. Martin

Santita Jackson: And right now, we have got one of my favorite people in the world indeed, an icon. An icon in the American cultural life and our political lives as well, filmmaker, Spike Lee. How are you Spike Lee, welcome to the show.

Spike Lee: Well, feel great calling from New York City, home of the world champions New York Giants.

Santita Jackson: Hey, hey, hey. They had me screaming in the fourth quarter. Oh, my gosh! I fell asleep until the fourth quarter. It was great.

Spike Lee: It was a great game, but that is over and you know, that was really a game, but this is real life here, Super Tuesday and people got to get out and vote, and I am voting for Barack Obama, your homeboy.

Santita Jackson: All right, my homeboy, and Spike Lee, we are joined of course by Roland Martin who precedes me on the morning drive show here, but he is manning the center down at CNN up in New York today, Roland, how are you?

Roland Martin: Doing great. Spike, how are you doing?

The Primaries

Spike Lee: Roland, man you had me dying on CNN. What's the sister's name, the Republican, what's her name?

Roland Martin: Amy Holmes.

Spike Lee: Sometimes I usually want to jump across that table and choke that sister!

Santita Jackson: Shame on you Spike. You see she is better than that.

Roland Martin: She is okay... Spike, I will tell them...

Spike Lee: Man, she, her and Condoleezza Rice should get together or something. They...I know how to think.

Santita Jackson: How did you arrive with the conclusion to support to endorse, I mean, in a hearty way, Senator Barack Obama?

Spike Lee: Well, here is the thing. The biggest mistake I think our white brothers and sisters make is they think that we as African Americans is one monolithic group. That we all think alike, look alike, do everything alike, and so, I am for Obama because he is the best person for the job, so why automatically we vote for somebody that looks like...that means we are voting for him because he is black. That is an insult to the intelligence and intellect of the black voter. They don't say about the whites you know, whoever wants to vote for? So Obama, I feel is the best person, you know, I am really dismayed... what is really turn me off with Hillary Clinton is her husband.

Santita Jackson: What about him?

Spike Lee:　　　All this first black, African. First of all, no one has ever explained to me what are the attributes he possessed him being the first black president.

Santita Jackson: But Spike, wait a minute. Why is it only now that this narrative has changed? To make this quite frankly, I have been in the quandary for years since I heard that. Why is it only now?

Spike Lee:　　　It changed because the dynamics changed. Here's the thing; he prided himself. He wore that like a badge of honor. But when a black man came out of nowhere and run up against his wife, all that stuff was put aside. So when Obama comes in and kicks Hillary in the butt in South Carolina, what does he do? All well, Jesse Jackson won South Carolina. You know, so what does that mean? Again, that Obama just did that because blacks only voted for him because he's black? I mean, all this whole thing about Dr. King, and she says that "I'm going control my husband." If she is in control of Bill Clinton that means that she approved all that stuff that he has been saying about Obama.Iit is the classic good cop, bad cop scenario.

Roland Martin: Hey Spike, you make an interesting point, because one of the things, it was very interesting during that week, a lot of people CNN and other networks were saying, "Well, I am not quite sure it's race-based because Bill Clinton is beloved." And I said, "No guys, this is a classic Southern strategy and what has happened is it backfired. Bill Clinton was in Los Angeles over the weekend, going to black churches, all of a sudden, they recognized that African Americans are saying, "You know what, we do not like it." and now, I have got people who said, who are yellow dog Democrats who said, "If she gets the nomination, I am not voting for her." They recognized this is a problem.

The Primaries

Spike Lee: Yes, you know, we are getting smarter. You can fool us eight or nine times, but the tenth time, we're not going for the okey doke. We are smarter than this. I was watching South Carolina very closely. Roll out David Dinkins. Roll out Charlie Rangel. Have Bob Johnson say the crazy stuff about Obama. Have Andy Young say some crazy stuff about Obama. It's not working. These (folks) have always been on the Clinton gravy train, soppin' up the gravy with biscuits. Their influence is negligent. You know, it's not working. We are not going for that.

Roland Martin: Well, I will say... Santita I will say he was pretty interesting, thus far, but what we are seeing is, in like for instance... remember the State Senator from South Carolina who said that if Obama wins the nomination, he is going to destroy the Democratic Party. Guess what? Obama won his district 8 to 1. Every black member of Congress that has endorsed, Senator Hillary Clinton, Obama has won their districts, 2, 3, 4, 5, 16 to 1, and people are watching today what happens in Brooklyn, what happens in Harlem, what happens in many of these states.

Spike Lee: Right.

Roland Martin: And so to speak, very interesting to see what happens.

Santita Jackson: But you know, elected officials have never led change. It is always been people who have done that.

Roland Martin: True.

Santita Jackson: We saw these 20... 24 years ago when Reverend Jackson ran, we are seeing this again as Senator Obama runs, and so I want Spike

Lee to give us an affirmative word as to why we should vote for Senator Obama, and in general, why we should get out and vote today on Super Tuesday?

Spike Lee: Number one, I think that he's trying to bring people together. For far too long, since our so-called forefathers came here, took the land from Native Americans, enslaved our ancestors for 400 years, this country is been about division. Obama is trying to get us closer together. Hillary Clinton is very divisive. You got a white woman who don't like her butt. This country is going to hell in a hand basket. We are in a recession. Look where we are in the world. We have lost our moral authority. We are in a war that has no end, but McCain, the Republican candidate probably says "I do not care we are going to be there for 100 years." I mean, to me it is obvious. If you care about this country, you love this country, what your choice should be.

Roland Martin: Spoken from Spike Lee folks. Somebody who has always been shy and reticent about expressing his viewpoints.

Santita Jackson: But thank god for him, because indeed, Spike Lee has used his art to elevate our minds, to get us about... to get us about...

Spike Lee: Can I say one thing?

Santita Jackson: Of course, Spike.

Spike Lee: I want to know when we as a people are going to reprimand our fellow African Americans who are saying some crazy stuff about Obama? I love Andy Young. He was there with Dr. King's Civil Rights Movement, but it seems there has to be an age limit, because once these guys get outside of a certain age, he said Clinton had more black women than Obama. Those crazy statements! What Bob Johnson said about Obama before introducing the town meeting, that was insane.

Roland Martin: Sidney Poitier and all others, and talk about Leno, he is doing the neighborhood. I mean, look, I have debated Bob on Michael Baisden's show and he said, "Well, I was talking by his community organizing days." I'm like, "Bob, no you weren't. You know you were talking about something else. Stop it."

Santita Jackson: Well you know, I will tell you this. This is my position of all of that. I think that all of these remarks are incredible and often times a lot of regrettable, awful things are said in the heat of battle and that doesn't excuse it but it does happen. That having been said, what I want us to do is as we agree, let us... as we disagree, let us be agreeable because I don't want it to happen in 2008 what happened in 1968, what happened...

Spike Lee: But can I ask you a question?

Santita Jackson: Well, sure... and Spike, and what happened in 1980, because I saw with my eyes wide open, Ted Kennedy, bless his heart, tear the party apart. We walked out of New York just as divided between Kennedy and Carter, and Reagan was able to walk up the middle. In 1968, there was a division between the Kennedy forces and the Humphrey forces and Eugene McCarthy forces, and Nixon was able to walk right up the middle. And that is what really, really concerns me beyond...

Spike Lee: Can I ask you a question?

Santita Jackson: Of course.

Spike Lee: Do you think a Republican can get elected after eight years of Bush?

Santita Jackson: Absolutely... absolutely, because you know what? They said the same thing in 1968. They said the same thing in 1980, and Reagan was able to walk up the middle. Nixon was able to walk up the middle. Nixon did not win in a landslide in '68. He won in a landslide in '72, and Reagan, this so-called...

Spike Lee: Well, this last year's election was stolen anyway.

Santita Jackson: Well, I mean in 2000 and 2004.

Roland Martin: Well, but you know with Spike, the point that you are making, I must be honest. I have heard that from a lot of different people, and I think... and that is why I call it... and I have said it on CNN, I have said it on WVON, that is why I called on Howard Dean, chairman of the Democratic National Committee, to stop sitting on his butt. The point is you want to win in November and when you have candidates who alienate the most important base of the Democratic Party, black voters, you are going to have a problem.

Santita Jackson: There is no question.

Roland Martin: You are going to have a problem.

Santita Jackson: There is no question, but this is not you, and that having been said, while you...

Roland Martin: All right, absolutely.

The Primaries

Santita Jackson: No, no... and that having been said while we have a candidate we like and love, let us apply the same principle to those people we don't like and love, because this has been an ongoing strategy for decades.

Spike Lee: I know, but... what if you heard anybody... say any crazy things about Hillary Clinton on behalf of Obama camp?

Santita Jackson: Look, I was right there.

Spike Lee: Name one.

Santita Jackson: Wait... let me tell you something Spike. I was right there when Clinton walked in the room and gave us Sister Soujlah, and no one said anything, even though that was a blatant, People look at it as an attack upon Reverend Jackson, but it was an attack upon black people, and letting folks know how he was going to handle black folks for four or eight years. My point is simply this: Let us elevate the conversation. Those things have been said, Bob Johnson has made an apology. You can accept it, you cannot accept it. I think we need to elevate the tone, because you know what? The world needs a sane American president.

Spike Lee: I am with you on that.

Santita Jackson: I mean, we have got to elevate the tone. I don't want to dwell on what all of these regrettable remarks because they are not helping us, because if we... let me tell you this, I will reaffirm this Spike, I reaffirm this Roland. If we let this sore fester in our community, we will have a Republican in the White House in January 2009, I promise you that.

Spike Lee: I understand.

Roland Martin: Well, spike, you got a comment?

Spike Lee: Can I just say… can I just say one thing?

Roland Martin: Yeah.

Spike Lee: Do you think that these outbursts that we have talked about this last minute or so, you think they are orchestrated or they just said this on top of their head?

Santita Jackson: Let me take you back…

Spike Lee: I say Clinton has gone through his Rolodex and called all these black folks and called in his chips.

Santita Jackson: Now, let me tell you something. You know what? I tell you. I can go back to 1992. Paul Begala, George Stephanopoulos, and James Carville at the event where the Sister Souljah moment was made. Of course, these, this is the way, welcome to the big league sweetie. This is how the game is played. This stuff is orchestrated. People have their alliances, their political alliances. We've seen this before. This is how it is played. Where Senator Obama can win is by keeping the tone elevated and running his race and not getting down here caught in the muck in the mire. That is how he is going to win. He started losing points when he got down here caught in the muck in the mire, getting off of his point. If he stays elevated, which is where everybody needs him and every candidate needs to be, he will win. If he comes down, and if we allow the conversation to be degenerated, we will all lose.

The Primaries

Roland Martin: Well, I will tell you what Spike...

Spike Lee: I agree with you.

Roland Martin: Spike, I believe... I flat out believe that they were orchestrated. In fact, I was told point blank on a conference call with some of their biggest fundraisers, President Bill Clinton said to them, I know I am ticking African Americans off, but keep moving forward without strategy. We knew that is the part of the strategy and I could tell you this here, they are playing with fire because the point is not whether or not they are going to lose black votes. That is not the point. The question is, will it suppress turnout. They are playing a very dangerous game if they get the nomination. It is also why I believe the Clinton folks are trying to float out the possibility of a Clinton-Obama ticket as a way to sort of say "Hey, black folks. You might be upset, but hey, if we get it, we will put him on a ticket," which I do not think for a second they'll actually do. So Spike, I think you are right on the money with your observation.

Santita Jackson: Well, let us be clear. Clinton never won with the majority of white votes. He always won with the majority of black votes, a majority of Hispanic votes, and white women. He never won with the majority of white votes.

Spike Lee: Well, can I ask you now?

Santita Jackson: Sure.

Spike Lee: Okay. But do we have to get this guy because what he did, that mean, we told him that he did a couple of things like black vote. You know, eight years ago, that means for eternity? We are indebted to Hillary Clinton?

Roland Martin: Absolutely not.

Santita Jackson: Spike... but that is not what I am saying...

Roland Martin: Great point... great... [overlap]

Santita Jackson: No, no... but that... that having been said.

Spike Lee: ...type of thinking, that a lot of black people think like that!

Santita Jackson: But wait a minute, like I said to you at the top of the interview Spike...

Spike Lee: "Ooh, Bill Clinton he's good for us. He was a good president.

Santita Jackson: No, but that having been said Spike...

Spike Lee: No, no... but let me tell you both, something at the top of this interview. I said I am mystified like Randall Robinson wrote in his book, by the whole black president phenomenon. I have been mystified by that. But that having been said, let us stay on the point of this campaign.

Roland Martin: Of course. [overlap]

Spike Lee: Yeah. I mean we're on point, but we can still talk about this.

Santita Jackson: I think we have got to talk about it all Spike, but let me tell you something. If we do not begin to correct this conversation and make it positive and elevate, elevate the tone, we are going to have a problem in the fall. We are going to have a problem.

The Primaries

Roland Martin: Hey Spike... Spike, this campaign...

Spike Lee: I think we had a great elevated a conversation, I mean...

Santita Jackson: You got to do it.

Spike Lee: We are talking about all these things that have acted and you know, how people votes or sways, and I think that your audience is enjoying this because maybe... they might not be sophisticated to know how these tricks are being run on them.

Santita Jackson: And you know I want Spike to come back to the Santita Jackson Show, because this is what we talk about on this show everyday, because I let people know about the tricks.

Roland Martin: We will do it.

Santita Jackson: I love you Spike Lee.

Roland Martin: Hey Spike.

Spike Lee: The okey doke!

Santita Jackson: The okey doke. I got it.

Roland Martin: Hey Spike, we appreciate it man. Thanks a lot.

Santita Jackson: Keep it up man. I love you on CNN. Keep them people at deep check.

Roland Martin: I will do. Talk to you Spike. Peace!

February 8, 2008

Democratic Superdelegates Should Not Decide Race

MILLIONS OF VOTERS FROM IOWA TO NEW HAMPSHIRE to Alabama to Missouri have gone to the polls or caucuses since January to choose between Sens. Hillary Clinton and Barack Obama for the Democratic nominee for president. And with the race so close, it looks as if for the first time, the primaries in May and June will have a huge say in who the nominee will be.

Yet it increasingly appears that 796 powerful Democrats could very well be the deciding factor in determining who goes up against Sen. John McCain in the November election.

Unlike the Republicans, the Democrats don't believe in winner-take-all primaries and caucuses. For them, it's proportional. That means if you win certain areas, you walk away with delegates. That's why Clinton won California and took home a large number of delegates, but Obama got his own chunk for winning various congressional districts.

But it's those pesky superdelegates who are looming large over the Democratic National Convention because neither Clinton nor Obama appears likely to grab the 2,025 delegates needed to secure the nomination. So that means the superdelegates, comprising roughly 20 percent of all Democratic delegates, will break the logjam.

While Democrats such as party Chairman Howard Dean are fretting about this razor-thin difference between Obama and Clinton, I frankly think it shows that Democrats have two folks locked in a fierce battle, and the voters are making tough choices. They don't have a dog in this hunt other than whom they want to see in the White House. You don't have voters cutting backroom deals in exchange for their votes, and in exchange for their votes, they aren't asking candidates for the moon.

Oh, so not the case for party leaders.

These superdelegates—a combination of members of Congress, former members of Congress, governors, mayors, former presidents, former vice presidents and other key Democrats—can do as they wish. They are bound by no rules or precedent, just whatever tickles their fancies or ignites their souls.

The Primaries

The Democratic Party instituted this weird system—I think it sounds more like the Politburo during the days of the Soviet Union—in order to maintain control over their voting process. They didn't want to see a fractured party and have the drama play out on TV, so they created a system that would give party leaders control over the system. A lot of folks likely thought this was a fail-safe system, never to be used, but just like those nuclear code sequences, they are there if you need them.

It appears the Dems are very close to choosing the nuclear option. And just like there is no winner in a nuclear war, there will be no winner if the superdelegates cut a deal and choose the Democratic nominee.

Such a sequence would be a slap in the face to the voters. Democrats should feel comfortable that they rose up early or late to go out to the polls in the heat, cold or rain to make their voices heard. Instead, in one swoop, all of the months of studying, listening and arguing will be for naught.

Because we have this archaic system, a word of wisdom to these superdelegates: Don't go against the wishes of the voters. This campaign is too important for your egos to get in the way.

Instead of cutting their own deals, all of the superdelegates should study how their constituents voted and use that as a barometer. Sen. Barbara Boxer of California said she would vote for the candidate who won the popular vote in her state. That means Sen. Clinton will pick that one up.

In an interview on my station—WVON in Chicago—I asked Rep. Maxine Waters, who endorsed Sen. Hillary Clinton, on Super Tuesday whether she would vote for Obama if her congressional district backed him.

She first said she wouldn't discuss the issue on the radio; then said that a lot of her constituents often disagree with her decisions; and then said she would consider negotiating for certain things with the candidates before deciding. Waters was a bit testy with my question (go to my blog on Essence.com and listen to the full interview) but was noncommittal over what she would do.

In my humble opinion, governors should cast votes for the candidates who won their states; former members of Congress should vote along the same lines as their former constituents; and all other party leaders should base their votes on who won the most states. That's the best way to showcase broad-based support.

These scenarios are clearly up for discussion and debate. But in an unfair—and undemocratic—system, there has to be some sanity. And allowing superdelegates to do as they wish isn't good for the Democratic Party, and it surely isn't right for America.

February 11, 2008, Essence.com Blog

Why Obama Should Skip Tavis Smiley's State of the Black Union

SEN. BARACK OBAMA TOOK A LOT OF HEAT last year from participants in Tavis Smiley's State of the Black Union annual confab, which was held in Virginia. To be fair, he was a little busy that day...announcing he was running for president!

Some of the folks there were beside themselves, and frankly, were childish about it, even saying that he should have put off his presidential announcement to be there.

Now, almost a year later, he is faced with a similar dilemma.

Tavis has announced that he will hold his State of the Black Union annual talkfest on Feb. 23 in New Orleans, La. This is a huge event attended by thousands each year; broadcast on C-SPAN; and attracts some of the nation's top black activists, politicians and intellectuals.

During his commentary Thursday on the "Tom Joyner Morning Show," the most listened to black radio show, Tavis said he's invited the three top candidates, Republican frontrunner, Sen. John McCain of Arizona, and Sens. Hillary Clinton and Barack Obama. He said only one has accepted, and he will wait until tomorrow for the other two to decide.

He didn't say which one decided to attend, but on Friday, Clinton announced that she was attending.

In his commentary, Smiley said he was going to snap on those who don't attend on Tuesday's show, demanding that they own up to black issues and zero in on social justice issues as outlined in the book he edited, *The Covenant with Black America.*

The Primaries

Here is my analysis of the situation, and hopefully it will put this presidential campaign and the delicate task of navigating the waters of black politics in perspective.

1. CLINTON MUST ATTEND. She led Obama in all of 2007 among black voters by huge margins. But that trend has shifted-dramatically. At best, she's polling at 25 percent among African Americans. Her acceptance is critical because she needs to capture 30 percent to 40 percent of the black to really stop Obama.

The perceived racial slights toward Obama by Clinton campaign surrogates, as well as her husband, former President Bill Clinton, has done significant damage in the black community. His attempts to explain the comments haven't mollified African Americans. Her appearance at the event can help her restore her standing among a vital Democratic constituency, which she will need to turn out en masse if she wins the nomination.

Also, her campaign doesn't have the cash Obama has. She needs any free media. And if Obama shows up, that means all the national media will be there, and the stage is set for her. Tavis said on the air that he would push for the candidates to debate the issues. She's called for more; Obama has only accepted two.

Smart politics on her part, and if I were advising her, no doubt I would tell her to attend.

2. OBAMA MUST LOOK FORWARD, NOT IN THE PAST. The Louisiana primary, which he won handily, was on Saturday. Why go back to Louisiana for an event on Feb. 23? That is not to dismiss the needs of people along the Gulf Coast. But the only way he can truly help them is if he wins the nomination and the White House.

Obama needs to be solely focused on Texas and Ohio. Those two mega-states offer a huge bounty of delegates, and he needs to win a large state to move ahead of Clinton. She polls strongly in both states, and they are a huge part of her winning strategy; so much of her time will be spent there in the coming weeks.

All his time must be on the ground. In Texas, he must blanket South Texas because of the Hispanic influence. He didn't do well among Hispanics in California, and he must change that.

There is some hope (no pun intended). When former Dallas Mayor Ron Kirk ran in 2002 for the U.S. Senate, he took 74 percent of South Texas. Yes, a Hispanic was running for governor, but that bodes well for Obama. In Ohio, he must do well among blue collar Democrats. Clinton has owned these low-to middle-income voters, and Obama must score well among them.

If Tavis wanted to have an impact, he should have held his event before Louisiana or before the Mississippi primary. As the saying goes, bad planning on your part doesn't constitute a sense of urgency on mine.

3. HE CAN'T BE DEFINED AGAIN AS THE BLACK CANDIDATE. Some will say he must avoid black folks to be more palatable to whites and Hispanics. I disagree. But you can't deny the reality that he's running for president of the United States and not president of Black America. The week of the South Carolina was all about race, and he knows that is not a winning discussion because of this nation's history. His campaign successfully beat back that issue since South Carolina, winning nearly all-white states like Utah, Idaho, Montana, Minnesota, Delaware, Connecticut, and Nebraska.

Obama is looking to have mass appeal, and showing up in New Orleans at a State of the Black Union event doesn't help him at all in a close race.

4. SEND MICHELLE OBAMA. What is the purpose of surrogates if you can't make it somewhere? His wife is perfectly suited for this event, and that frees him up to go elsewhere. Plus, he's his top surrogate, and having a female counter your female opponent isn't a bad matchup.

Ask any campaign manager and they will tell you that when it comes to politics, especially in a close race, every minute matters. Candidates are on the phone lines campaigning, trying to raise money, and secure endorsements.

Spending the day with Tavis and his panelists is vital for Clinton. For Obama, time spent courting Latinos in Texas is more important.

African Americans are asking a lot of Obama; the best chance blacks have ever had of one of their own capturing the White House. I often hear folks say they want to know if he is going to back "their" issues. It is no different than how white women are feeling about Clinton. These are indeed historic firsts.

By the way, when people say that black issues are being ignored in the campaign, they are wrong.

PHOTOGRAPHIC
REFLECTIONS

The Best Political Team on Television gathers for a photo in New York, October 2007. *Edward M. Pio Roda/CNN*

The beginning of my hour-long interview with then-Sen. Barack Obama in his U.S. Senate office in Washington, DC on June 14, 2007, for the TV One special, In Conversation: The Senator Barack Obama Interview. It later won the 2008 NAACP Image Award for Best Interview, beating out ABC's Good Morning America, CNN and BET. *Fritz Blakey/TV One*

I finally get on the air at CNN on the night Sen. Obama wins the Iowa Caucuses, along with legendary journalist Carl Bernstein, Jan. 3, 2008. *Edward M. Pio Roda/CNN*

Gloria Borger and me, along with Anderson Cooper, in the Air Force One Pavilion, at the CNN Republican presidential debate at the Ronald Reagan Presidential Library in Simi Valley, California, January 30, 2008. *Edward M. Pio Roda/CNN*

All smiles with director Steven Spielberg prior to the CNN Democratic presidential debate between Sens. Barack Obama and Hillary Clinton at the Kodak Theatre in Los Angeles on January 31, 2008.

Making a point next to *Time's* Mark Halperin at the CNN/Time America Votes 2008 afternoon special in 1 Time Warner in New York on Super Tuesday, February 5, 2008. *Edward M. Pio Roda/CNN*

One of many on-air appearances outside the Lorraine Motel in Memphis, Tennessee, now the National Civil Rights Museum, on April 4, 2008, the 40th anniversary of the assassination of the Rev. Dr. Martin Luther King Jr. *Lisa Buser/CNN*

My interview with Michelle Obama in the Trump Hotel in Chicago on Aug. 21, 2008, for the TV One special, In Conversation: The Michelle Obama Interview. That interview won the 2009 NAACP Image Award for Best Interview, beating out CNN, the Oprah Winfrey Show and BET. *Parrish Lewis/TV One*

Rockin' to the house band at the Democratic National Convention at the Pepsi Center in Denver, Colorado, on August 25, 2008. Who wouldn't dance when songs by Earth, Wind and Fire, and Aretha Franklin, are on! I tried to get Christian Broadcast Network and CNN contributor David Brody to jam along with me. *Edward M. Pio Roda/CNN*

Having a little fun on our daily CNN Radio/CNN.com show with Charles Barkley, along with my co-host Lisa Desjardins of CNN Radio, at the CNN Grilll on August 25, 2008, at the Democratic National Convention in Denver, Colorado. *Mark Hill/CNN*

Kickin' it with Jamie Foxx at the CNN Grill in Denver. *Mathieu Young/CNN*

Interviewing Hill Harper of CSI:NY, and Harvard Law School classmate of then-Sen. Barack Obama, on August 27, 2008, in Denver. *Mark Hill/CNN*

Making a point on the air with CNN contributors Hilary Rosen and Dana Milbank, and "American Morning" anchor John Roberts. *Mark Hill/CNN*

Then-Sen. Hillary Clinton speaks at the Democratic National Convention on Aug. 26, 2008. *Roland S. Martin*

The stage is set for then-Sen. Barack Obama to accept the democratic nomination before 80,000 people at Invesco Field in Denver. *Roland S. Martin*

More than 80,000 await Obama's acceptance speech. *Roland S. Martin*

Crowd cheers as Sen. Barack Obama takes the stage. *Roland S. Martin*

Wolf Blitzer, Anderson Cooper, Campbell Brown, Gloria Borger, John King, and I, analyze the acceptance of Sen. Barack Obama at Invesco Field. *Edward M. Pio Roda/CNN*

CNN on-air and production team gather for team photo at Invesco Field in Denver on Aug. 28, 2008. *Edward M. Pio Roda/CNN*

Me and my partner in crime, Donna Brazile, at the Republican National Convention in Minneapolis, Minn., on Sept. 1, 2008. *Edward M. Pio Roda/CNN*

Me and my longtime friends, Donna Williams and her husband, Michael, chairman of the Texas Railroad Commission and a Republican U.S. Senate candidate from the Lone Star state. *Roland S. Martin*

Interviewing DNC Chairman Howard Dean, along with Lisa Desjardins, at the CNN Grill in St. Paul, Minn. *Jeremy Freeman/CNN*

Arch rivals all smiles. Texas Sen. Kay Bailey Hutchison, a graduate of the University of Texas, and me, a graduate of Texas A&M, flash the Hook 'Em Horns and Gig 'Em signs, respectively, at the CNN Grill in St. Paul, Minn. Credit: *Edward M. Pio Roda/CNN*

Me and Donna Brazile getting down to the music at the CNN Grill. (The video of us dancing in CNN Grill in Denver was a huge YouTube hit.) *Jeremy Freeman/CNN*

Having a little fun with CNN editorial producer Stephanie Kotuby at the RNC. *Roland S. Martin*

CNN coverage of the 2008 U.S. Presidential Election Viewing Party at Time Square in New York City, New York. Crowds of people watch the final results for the 2008 Presidency. *David Holloway*

Tears begin to well at 11 p.m. EST on November 4, 2008, as CNN calls the 2008 presidential election, proclaiming Sen. Barack Obama as the president-elect of the United States. *Edward M. Pio Roda/CNN (left) Robert Felk/CNN (right)*

With Bill Bennett looking, I share a historical perspective on what it means to see the first African American elected president of the United States. *Edward M. Pio Roda/CNN*

Watching President-elect Barack Obama give his acceptance speech along with CNN Contributor Amy Holmes. *Edward M. Pio Roda/CNN*

Wolf Blizter, Anderson Cooper, Soledad O'Brien, David Gergen and myself on the roof of the Newseum on Jan. 17, 2009, the beginning of CNN's coverage of the 2009 Inauguration of President Barack Obama in Washington, D.C. *Edward M. Pio Roda/CNN*

Sharing a laugh with Larry King, Douglas Brinkley, and Jeff Johnson. *Edward M. Pio Roda/CNN*

Braving the cold with Soledad O'Brien in the Mall in Washington on Jan. 19, 2009. *Roland S. Martin*

More than 2 million gather on Jan. 20, 2009, in Washington, D.C. as they watch President Barack Obama sworn in as the 44th President of the United States. *Roland S. Martin*

Michelle Obama waits in the cold for her husband, President Barack Obama, to walk out onto the U.S. Capitol. *Roland S. Martin*

A truly emotional hug as Congressman John Lewis, who was almost beaten to death on Bloody Sunday, (March 7, 1965), in Selma, Ala., a march to get blacks the right to vote. Lewis shares an embrace with the first black president of the United States. Lewis is also the last living speaker who addressed the crowd on Aug. 28, 1963, the day Dr. Martin Luther King Jr. gave his famous "I Have A Dream" speech on the steps of the Lincoln Memorial. *Roland S. Martin*

The First Family listens to a speaker on Inauguration Day. *Roland S. Martin*

Aretha Franklin sings "My Country, 'Tis Of Thee" at the inauguration. *Roland S. Martin*

Vice President Joe Biden is sworn in his wife, Jill, looks on. *Roland S. Martin*

President Barack Obama sworn in by Supreme Court Justice John Roberts. *Roland S. Martin*

Barack Hussein Obama II is sworn in as the 44th president of the United States. *Roland S. Martin*

President Barack Obama gives his inauguration speech. *Roland S. Martin*

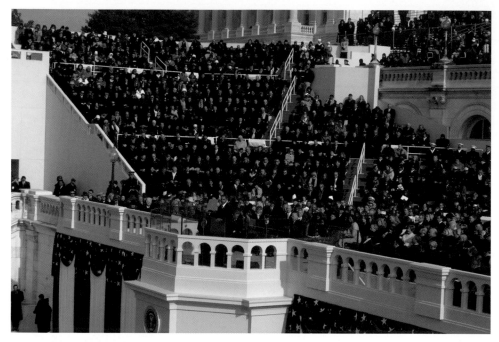

President Barack Obama gives his inauguration speech. *Roland S. Martin*

Rev. Joseph Lowery, a veteran of the Civil Rights Movement, gives a stirring benediction at the inauguration of President Barack Obama. *Roland S. Martin*

The Joint Center for Political and Economic Studies, the nation's most prestigious think tank devoted to African American issues, released a survey showing that the top issues to blacks are the war in Iraq; healthcare; jobs and the economy; and education.

Sounds to me like the candidates have spent a lot of time on those issues, although they could always do more.

As an aside, when I asked my radio listeners on WVON in Chicago if Obama should skip the event, we got 29 calls in two hours, and only two said he should go. And this is a crowd that is normally in agreement with Smiley.

February 12, 2008, Essence.com Blog

Hillary: Obama Won Louisiana Because of Black Folks; Disses Small States He Also Won

WHEN JOHN EDWARDS GOT BLOWN OUT of Nevada by Sens. Barack Obama and Hillary Clinton, he didn't offer a bunch of excuses.

All he said was, "I got my butt kicked in Nevada."

Since Clinton loves to praise Edwards, why don't she take a page out of his book and admit that over the weekend, Obama kicked her butt?

Clinton and her campaign staff have feverishly tried to dismiss Obama's wins in Washington State, Nebraska, Maine, and the Virgin Islands as small states that will otherwise go Republican in the fall. As it relates to Louisiana, she suggested that the black vote made his win a possibility.

The problem with this is that is flawed in several areas. First, Clinton campaigned hard in Washington, where she had both female U.S. senators backing her. In Maine, she was supposed to win. And in Louisiana, CNN exit polls show that 50 percent of all voters were white, and 44 percent were Black. Large percentage? Yes. But more white votes.

As a result, Clinton has made her task hard. She is likely to lose D.C., Maryland and Virginia, meaning she must win Texas, Ohio and Pennsylvania.

My suggestion for her new campaign manager, Maggie Williams: tell the candidate to spend more time campaigning in small states, rather than ignoring them by focusing on the larger ones. Does she want to be the Democratic nominee of the Big States or all of America?

NAACP's Bond Late to the Game Regarding Democratic Delegate Battle

NAACP CHAIRMAN JULIAN BOND'S decision to weigh in on the Democratic Party's conundrum when it comes to seating delegates from Michigan and Florida has created a firestorm of discussion on blogs and talk shows, and frankly, I'm still unclear as to what his intent was.

Sure, he and others have the freedom to weigh in on the issue. But why be a Julian-come-lately now, when the nation's oldest and largest civil rights organization said nothing initially when the rules were made by the Democratic National Committee?

The DNC was clear: Only four states—Iowa, New Hampshire, South Carolina and Nevada—would vote before Feb. 5. The first two didn't like the competition, but after hearing criticism that ethnic and geographic voices were not playing a part in determining the nominee, the party moved up Nevada—because of the Hispanic population there and the fact that it's a Western state—and South Carolina—because of its black population and the fact that it's a Southern state.

DNC officials dropped the hammer and said if other states moved up, they would be punished severely. But the legislatures in Florida and Michigan, along with their governors, figured they could strong-arm the party to bend to their will, so they voted, approved and then signed into law bills to move up their primaries.

Anyone with a brain could see that if the DNC went through with their threat, voters there would be disenfranchised. Had the NAACP and other groups gone after the state legislators then, we wouldn't be in this position now. And with Sens. Barack Obama and Hillary Clinton so tight in the race for delegates, the decision not to fight the actions in Michigan and Florida is causing all kinds of problems.

The Primaries

Obama's position has been that the states broke the rules, all the candidates agreed not to campaign there, and the DNC should enforce the rules to which all sides agreed. But Clinton is leading the charge to seat the delegates, especially because she "won" both states, even though she often was quoted as saying the results won't mean a thing because those primaries will not count.

But because she didn't knock Obama out of the race on Super Tuesday and has since lost eight caucuses and primaries, she desperately needs those delegates, and her camp told *The New York Times* they will do everything they can to get them seated.

This brings us back to Bond, a veteran of the Civil Rights Movement, who has pretty much run the group since the messy departure of Bruce Gordon as president and CEO this time last year.

In his Feb. 8 letter, Bond said he was worried that voters in both states "could ultimately have their votes completely discounted if they are not assigned delegate representation for the Democratic National Convention."

When the story was picked up by *The Associated Press*, it was reported that he wanted the states to be given to Clinton and then seated in her favor. NAACP officials told me that was not the case. They said he was not advocating on behalf of one candidate or another.

In an e-mail to me, Bond explained his reasoning behind the letter: "When these rules were set it was suspected at the time that they would be discriminatory for states with large African American populations. It seemed a harsh rule to disenfranchise millions of our voters just to appease the thousands of white voters in Iowa and New Hampshire," he said.

"Party rules never stated that candidates had to take their names off of the ballot as was the case in Michigan. This was something that the Iowa and New Hampshire state parties imposed on the candidates in a bidding war to show their allegiance to the first-in the-nation "white" primaries.

"Both Iowa and New Hampshire strongly *opposed* the addition of South Carolina and Nevada as early primary states. They fought the Black and Hispanic Caucus tooth and nail to stop this addition of states with Black and Brown populations having a greater say in the nomination process. They lost and in retaliation made the candidates sign a pledge to them—not the DNC—to not campaign there and not have their names on the ballot. Hillary Clinton, Dennis Kucinich and Chris Dodd refused to sign this pledge and left their names on the ballot. Clinton did not go into Florida until after the polls closed keeping her pledge. The Obama campaign miscalculated on this issue and should have stood with Michigan and Florida given their strong African American populations.

"Had Obama won these states I am sure many people would be supporting this change in the rules."

As someone who has opposed the leverage of Iowa and New Hampshire, I'm in agreement that they should not always be first. Yet that has nothing to do with today, and Bond knows it.

What is unclear is why he waited so long (he also didn't notify the NAACP's 64-member board of the letter) and why, according to my NAACP sources, he wrote the letter with help from Mary Frances Berry, former head of the U.S. Commission on Civil Rights, as well as Wade Henderson, CEO of the Leadership Conference on Civil Rights.

The letter was drafted hurriedly on Friday, as evidenced by the three misspelled words in it. It's not clear why there was such a sense of urgency to get it out, but the fact that it came to light on Tuesday night, when Obama was steamrolling Clinton in Virginia, Maryland and the District of Columbia, has some conspiracy-minded bloggers making all kinds of assertions.

I have called and e-mailed Berry and Henderson for their responses, but none of my calls or e-mails has been returned.

The NAACP had an opportunity to speak for disenfranchised voters before this mess was created. That's when they should have weighed in. Their actions now look suspicious, and Bond has no one to blame but himself as the de facto leader of what once was a relevant organization.

February 20, 2008, Essence.com Blog

No Spin Zone: Clinton Camp Knows They Got Beaten Badly

ELECTION NIGHT IS ALWAYS THE TIME FOR AIDES from all political camps to spin the election results as best as they can.

Normally, our e-mail boxes are flooded with e-mails from the team of Sen. Hillary Clinton.

Last night, nothing.

No, really. *nothing.* No statements. No spin. Eerily quiet.

Earlier, the Obama campaign said the Wisconsin primary would be a "no excuses" night for Clinton. They were right.

Her camp didn't blame it on Wisconsin being a red state. A small state. A caucus state. A black state.

At the end of the day, the Clinton camp had to accept the reality that their candidate got beaten to the pulp, and people have more respect for you when you take a butt kicking and not try to explain it away.

February 21, 2008, Essence.com Blog

Michelle Obama's Patriotism Questioned

IN THE AGE OF THE INTERNET, any comment can all of a sudden become an international crisis as bloggers, talk show hosts and others seize on it and becomes larger than it is.

That's what Michelle Obama is going through over a comment she made in Milwaukee on Monday that has gotten the super-patriotic in America all riled up.

"For the first time in my adult life, I am really proud of my country," Obama said. "Not just because Barack is doing well, but I think people are hungry for change."

That comment about being really proud for the first time as an adult took off like wildfire, aided by Cindy McCain, the wife of Republican presidential contender John

McCain, who said later that day, "I have, and always will be, proud of my country."

The Obama camp didn't really do much about the comment for the first 48 hours, but by Wednesday, had to get Michelle to further explain what she meant.

"What I was clearly talking about was that I'm proud in how Americans are engaging in the political process," she told WJAR-TV. "For the first time in my lifetime, I'm seeing people rolling up their sleeves in a way that I haven't seen and really trying to figure this out—and that's the source of pride that I was talking about."

Was it a big deal? Nope. But remember, in the post-Sept. 11 world, patriotism has gone overboard with hyper folks waiting to declare anyone who isn't as strong on the issue as them out of step with American thought. And as a potential first lady, a possible first African American First Lady, the wife of the guy who they all keep saying is a Muslim—even though he isn't—Michelle's comments will be studied and analyzed more so than those of Cindy McCain.

First, I heard the comment and got it right away. But the Obama campaign team is going to have to do a much better job in being aware of the perception of certain comments and not shrug them off.

Remember the comments Sen. Barack Obama made about Ronald Reagan during the week of the Nevada caucus? Team Obama didn't see the big deal. Then they had to spend three to four days having to deal with the backlash, and that took time away from the message.

But an interesting twist to the Michelle Obama patriotism story were the comments of Fox talk show host Bill O'Reilly.

On his radio show while discussing the controversy, he said: "I don't want to go on a lynching party against Michelle Obama unless there's evidence, hard facts, that say this is how the woman really feels. If that's how she really feels—that America is a bad country or a flawed nation, whatever—then that's legit. We'll track it down."

Was Bill slamming Michelle? Nope. In fact, he was saying that he didn't see all the fuss. My problem is why does he have to use the word lynching?

We all know the history of lynching in America, and when use it in that context. But I just think folks need to be sensitive to such words. And that includes Bill O'Reilly.

It was just last month that the Golf Channel suspended anchor Kelly Tilghman for two weeks for saying during a live broadcast that what younger golfers should do to Tiger Woods is "lynch him in a back alley."

Tiger said Kelly is a friend and meant no harm, but it's about the choice of words that we use. I'm always cognizant of such things when I'm on the air because they can be interpreted by people in different ways.

Yet using a word like lynching should cause someone to say, wait a minute, maybe I ought not say that before opening my big mouth.

I'm sure Bill will get all defensive and slam the PC police, but denying the history of lynching and what it means is nothing to scoff at or blow off.

February 22, 2008

For Clinton to Win, She Must Focus, Focus, Focus

ELEVEN DAYS. THAT'S HOW LONG SEN. HILLARY CLINTON has left either to extend this Democratic presidential campaign and fight for the nomination or to see her longtime ambition disappear, possibly forever.

Her husband has made it clear already that the junior senator from New York must beat the junior senator from Illinois in Texas and Ohio, or this campaign is over.

That's why Clinton should ignore the faulty advice of her chief strategist, Mark Penn; tell her communications director, Howard Wolfson, to stop peddling the plagiarism charges against Sen. Barack Obama; and go full-throttle on the economy.

You got it. Return to the 1992 mantra of James Carville and Paul Begala: It's the economy, stupid.

There has been one constant about the presidential campaign of Sen. Barack Obama. Ask anyone. It has boiled down to the best bumper sticker you can find: Change.

Simple. Direct. To the point.

Clinton? She has had more messages than wardrobe changes at a Beyonce concert: "Ready Day One." "I have 35 years of experience." "Solutions, not speeches."

Part of the reason America has no clue about the real Hillary Clinton is we keep getting so many different versions of who she is.

In order for Clinton to right this ship, she should make this campaign about one issue, and that is the state of the American economy.

Texas ranks third, behind California and Florida, when it comes to home foreclosures. People are flat-out going crazy because subprime loans are causing their interest rates to skyrocket. During Thursday night's debate, Clinton hit on that subject hard. But guess what will get all the attention? Her being booed for the Xerox comment about Obama's speeches. Was it cute? Sure, even if it ticked off the folks in the room. But a good line isn't reason enough for an undecided voter to choose her over Obama. It's just a good line that likely was fed to her by one of her highly paid and clearly ineffective campaign operatives.

Clinton and Obama spent more time Thursday night in the CNN/Univison debate talking about Cuba, rather than having an in-depth discussion about the skyrocketing cost of tuition, which has really hit public universities, such as the University of Texas. More kids are dropping out before they finish college. Because of the financial crisis on Wall Street, the No. 1 college loan fund, Sallie Mae, announced a few weeks ago that it will cut back on college loans. For black and Hispanic children, a Pew study found that not being able to go to college will keep them poor. Who will make up more voters in the Democratic primary in Texas? Blacks and Hispanics. Folks, that's a pocketbook issue.

Clinton has lost 11 straight races, if you include the votes of Democrats who are abroad, because her campaign has been schizophrenic, unwieldy and unable to recognize the force of power she's running against. Her job is to not fight against his speeches. That's an uphill battle. In fact, don't even mention his speeches, Sen. Clinton. Take your eyes off what he's saying and doing, and put it on the people.

Why did so many folks like her closing line in Thursday's debate? Because it had nothing to do with her; it had to do with the American people.

Throughout this campaign, she has emphasized how she's going to solve all of our problems. Obama? He constantly invokes "we." That resonates.

Thursday night, she said: "Whatever happens, we're going to be fine. You know, we have strong support from our families and our friends. I just hope that we'll be able to say the same thing about the American people, and that's what this election should be about."

Yep, "the American people."

As Clinton goes around Texas and Ohio, she should return to the strategy she employed in New Hampshire: Stop trying to compete with Obama in rallies, and convene town hall meetings. Take questions. Allow your inner policy wonk to take over.

She did well in the debates last year because she didn't bother showing her soft side. Instead, she made clear that she wanted to be the smartest person in the room. For those who haven't warmed up to Clinton by now, it's too late. This is when her strength must be emphasized over any perceived weakness.

No one can guarantee what is going to happen during the next 11 days. But one thing is for sure: If Clinton chooses to operate the same way she has done during the past month, the only speech she'll be giving March 5 is one announcing that she is suspending her campaign.

Many have said Obama has led a charmed life. But they forget he got whipped summarily by Rep. Bobby Rush in Chicago. Clinton? This is only her third campaign. She's never lost. She's never tasted defeat personally in an election.

That all could change in two weeks if she doesn't lock and load on the economy.

It's all on you, Sen. Clinton. So what are you prepared to do?

March 4, 2008, Essence.com Blog

Caucuses Are Packed in Texas

FOLKS ARE E-MAILING ME FROM CAUCUS SITES.

My brother is in Pearland, Texas. He said there was no parking at the school. So they had to park in the shopping center. He said 200 folks were standing outside. Now he says they are not letting anyone in because they have exceeded the fire code, and are trying to figure out what to do.

My wife is in Dallas County and she said, "that the lines are a quarter of a mile down the street where she is, and they are doubled up on each side. People are walking from parking lots in a shopping center a quarter of a mile away and people are walking from the freeway to the school."

My parents are at a polling place in Houston. My dad said, "People are all over the store. The lines are long around here. This place is exploding. It's unbelievable. And people are steady coming in. It's is a humongous line."

My other sister and her husband are in College Station, Texas and she said it was "crazy turnout" and they "had to move folks into the hallways because the room was too crowded." He said the precinct captain said in the last election there were four people. Today, 200 people.

March 5, 2008, Essence.com Blog

Democrats Move on to Battle Another Day

SEN. HILLARY CLINTON'S CAMPAIGN asserted that she had to win Texas and Ohio to remain in the race for the Democratic presidential nomination.

She got exactly what she needed.

In a big night for Clinton, she beat Obama in Ohio, Texas as well as Rhode Island. After winning 11 consecutive races, Obama only scored a victory in Vermont, thus throwing the race back into a hotly contested one.

The Obama campaign maintains that its delegate lead is virtually the same as it was prior to the vote yesterday. That's true. But like it or not, the major momentum that Obama had going into the March 4 elections has evaporated, and now he has to re-calibrate his message.

For Clinton, she was very successful in targeting Obama with some sharp jabs, forcing him the last 72 hours of the campaign to respond to her, rather than get his message out to the public.

Expect her to keep it up and stay even more aggressive against Obama, trying to keep him off balance.

What he needs to do is improve his media operation. Obama doesn't have a pit bull; someone who will have a big bark-and bite! to face down Clinton.

They are playing for keeps. The Obama campaign ran in the final days as if they were playing not to lose.

That's a bad decision.

His people shouldn't feel confident. They should redouble their efforts. That whip should be cracking harder and harder and harder.

He should ride higher and harder.

There is no doubt that he can break her will and spirit by winning Mississippi, Wyoming and Pennsylvania. Forget winning on points. He needs to knock her out. She cannot be hobbled. Her knees cannot buckled. She must be *knocked out* to get the point.

Also, what are his plans for April 4, the 40th anniversary of King's assassination?

His focus should be on *jobs, jobs, and more jobs*. That's why King was in Memphis, helping those sanitation workers. The economy is the problem today, that's what King was fighting for. And I would have the head of the Teamsters and SEIU right there as well with him as a show of unity.

March 7, 2008

Now it's Obama's Turn to Make the Adjustments

ASK ANY BOXING TRAINER AND HE'LL TELL YOU that you can walk into the ring with a well-designed plan to beat your opponent, but as the fight progresses, you might have to alter your plan.

After losing 11 straight races to Sen. Barack Obama, Sen. Hillary Clinton was faced with a tough choice: continue on the same path and keep losing or shake up her fight plan to keep battling another day.

She accepted the "resignation" of her campaign manager, Patti Solis Doyle; brought in Maggie Williams; paid more attention to her campaign finances, especially online fundraising; and went after Obama with a different line of attack, which some have described as negative.

Frankly, the "3 A.M." ad that questioned his qualifications as commander in chief—without overtly saying it—should be seen only as negative, based on the tone and tenor of this campaign. But it will pale in comparison to the ads we will see in the fall. That, folks, is just smart politics.

So she won three out of four states, staved off defeat, and now has a little pep in her step heading into the Wyoming caucus, Mississippi primary and the big contest on April 22, the Pennsylvania primary. More importantly, she has forced Obama to question his campaign plan and put the onus on him to go to his corner to get instructions from his trainer in order to win the next round.

Obama faces a tougher task because of his denunciation of the politics of old, which has sort of tied his hands. He is expected to be Mr. Positive on the campaign trail and not go negative against Clinton. Yet there are ways in which he can define Clinton better that not only will not be seen as negative but also will reposition him better leading into the final contests.

For one, the Clinton campaign successfully has sold the media on the idea that the next important contest is Pennsylvania. The day after her wins Tuesday, nearly every show was talking about what needs to happen April 22, as if the Wyoming and Mississippi races were afterthoughts.

Obama must hit Clinton hard on being a "big D" Democrat who doesn't really care about the "little d" democrats. Remember how she essentially brushed aside Obama's wins in Utah, Idaho, Washington state and other places as nothing but red states they have no way of capturing in the fall? Her argument is that Democrats must win the big states: California, New York, Ohio, etc. This plays to her advantage because she won them. (Sorry, I don't include Michigan and Florida, and you already know why.) This falls in line with her "50-plus-1" strategy: Just win the same states as Al Gore in 2000 and John Kerry in 2004, and then you flip Ohio or Florida to win the White House.

But Obama's thinking is more in line with Democratic National Committee Chairman Howard Dean: Create a 50-state strategy to establish Democratic dominance on the federal level—more of a supermajority—but also on the state level. By changing the discourse and suggesting that she will only care about Dems in large states, he will be able to speak to the hearts and minds of those small states, and more importantly, he will rally those superdelegates who felt put off by Clinton's dismissive comments.

A key argument for Obama to make is that redistricting is two years away, and Democrats need control of governorships and state legislatures. Only through targeting those places will that become a reality.

Second, jump right in her face on the foreign policy front. She claims she was integrally involved in the release of Kosovo refugees and the Irish peace talks. Fine. So demand the following: If you were so involved in foreign policy, why did the Clinton administration fail in Rwanda and have a horrible plan for Somalia? There were clear international failures during the eight years of President Bill Clinton, and she needs to be forced to say what she did and didn't do. Obama has used the cherry-picking argument but has been weak in selling it. Nail it to try to nail her.

Finally, Professor Obama has to return. One of the reasons he did so well in the Los Angeles debate is that he chose to go head-to-head with her on policy. Everyone said that's her strength, but he held his own. He needs to make a more convincing argument when it comes to the economy. The economic plans they have are not overwhelmingly different. What he has to do is come out from behind the podium and make it plain. Speak to voters in Mississippi about the tragedy of the Gulf Coast; tell voters there and in Wyoming why he will help their kids go to college; present his urban and rural economic renewal programs to the voters in Pennsylvania. Don't concede any ground to her on these points.

Is this fight over? Absolutely not. But Obama can't afford to look at his lead among pledged delegates and think he will maintain that and go to Denver with the superdelegates' support. In Las Vegas, every boxer is told to win it in the ring and not depend on the judges.

This is now a 15-round heavyweight match instead of 12 rounds. Clinton has no choice but to brawl. It worked Tuesday, so why stop doing it?

Obama? He is sort of the boxer who is technically proficient and wants to showcase those skills. But you can't dance all night. Sometimes you've got to slug it out in the middle of the ring. That doesn't mean being nasty or trashing your opponent. But it does mean fighting hard until the bell rings in the final round and never letting your guard down.

Obama, you let your guard down before Tuesday. Don't do it again, or you just might get knocked out of the nomination.

March 11, 2008, 1:55 P.M.

Ferraro Says if Obama Wasn't Black, He Would Have No Chance

A LOT OF ATHLETES HAVE MADE A NUMBER OF DUMB COMMENTS, and among those were the racial assertions made by Isiah Thomas and Dennis Rodman in 1987 about Larry Bird.

In an effort to discredit the Boston Celtics star, Thomas and Rodman said that if Bird was black, he would be just an average basketball player. Both of them were roundly slapped around, because whether you couldn't stand the Boston Celtics—count me in!—Bird had game, and anybody who played against him knew that he was one of the game's best. That's why he's a pro basketball Hall of Famer and a member of the NBA's top 50 ever cast of players.

The Thomas-Rodman-Bird flap came to mind when I heard about the recent comments made by former Democratic vice presidential candidate Geraldine Ferraro.

The 72-year-old former congresswoman has spent a lot of time running her mouth this campaign season, and now she has unleashed another barrage of comments, fanning the flames of the hot button issues of race and gender.

In an interview with the *Torrance Daily Breeze*, Ferraro said that if Sen. Barack Obama wasn't black, there's no chance in hell he would be leading the Democratic race for president.

"If Obama was a white man, he would not be in this position," she continued. "And if he was a woman (of any color) he would not be in this position. He happens to be very lucky to be who he is. And the country is caught up in the concept."

This is the second time Ferraro has tried to drive her nonsensical gender agenda into our minds, and it's time that we say enough to all the back and forth over race and gender.

Look, America has a racist and sexist history. Women have been treated horribly in this nation, having to fight for respect, whether it's the right to vote or equal wages for equal work. And we know the horrors of slavery, and the laws that subjected African Americans to second-class status during the decades of Jim Crow.

So, women and African Americans have been treated horribly, so can we cut the crap over who suffered more?

A white woman like Ferraro, who has gone through a lot of hell over her 72 years, knows what it's like to be a woman in a power position. But I'm sure there are many black male politicians who know what it's like to be a black man trying to climb the political ladder. She has no understanding of that—nor of a black woman running for high office—so how does she know how "easy" it is?

So Geraldine, give it a rest.

Let the rest of us see two talented politicians who have earned their way to this position, and not have to deal your efforts to pit women against men and black against white.

March 12, 2008, Essence.com Blog

Ferraro Resigns From Clinton Campaign

AFTER TWO DAYS OF BEING UNDER ASSAULT for her race-based attacks on Sen. Barack Obama, former vice presidential candidate Geraldine Ferraro was forced to resign from her position as a member of Sen. Hillary Clinton's finance committee. She did so in a letter to Clinton, writing:

"Dear Hillary— I am stepping down from your finance committee so I can speak for myself and you can continue to speak for yourself about what is at stake in this campaign.

"The Obama campaign is attacking me to hurt you.

"I won't let that happen.

"Thank you for everything you have done and continue to do to make this a better world for my children and grandchildren.

"You have my deep admiration and respect.

"Gerry"

It was a tough day as the Clinton campaign was under assault on all fronts by Ferraro's repeated-and various-accounts of what she said and meant to say.

Three hours before she resigned, I talked to one of the members of the Congressional Black Caucus supporting Clinton who told the campaign, "Either you come out shutting this thing down or we will."

They are asking for a formal apology from Ferraro and for her to clarify her comments.

The member of Congress said Clinton "is taking this on the chin" and we need to shut this down and move on because its "gone too far."

The Member of Congress said you should see a response "sooner rather than later."

Other black supporters of Clinton were also angered at Ferraro's campaign and didn't hold back in letting campaign officials they were angered by her comments.

Tonight, Clinton speaks in Washington, D.C. at a presidential forum sponsored by the National Newspaper Publishers Association, the most influential group of black publishers. We'll see how she responds to this latest racial gaffe in her talk to them.

March 13, 2008
Florida, Michigan Don't Deserve A Do-over

FOR THE LAST TWO WEEKS WE HAVE WATCHED nearly every political hack from Michigan and Florida hit the airwaves to tell us that voters in those states deserve to have their votes counted, and new elections should be called for—and paid for—by the Democratic National Committee.

One word they all keep tossing around is disenfranchisement. Because of this nation's sordid history on the issue of denying African Americans the right to vote, those calling for a re-vote know the true power of the word, and just uttering it sort of backs the opposition up.

But folks, I'm sorry. Knowing full well how the two political hacks—also called governors—of Michigan and Florida deliberately chose to ignore the Democratic Party rules and try to leapfrog the other states, I just don't have any compassion for the both of them.

Just listening to Jennifer Granholm of Michigan and Charlie Crist of Florida whine, complain and throw hissy fits on national TV is just too much.

They keep blaming Howard Dean, chairman of the DNC, for this debacle. But he's not to blame. They could have vetoed the bill, or told their state legislatures to stop the grandstanding and get on with the people's business. But they chose otherwise.

Yes, I do feel sorry for the voters in those two states because their votes should have mattered. It would have been great had they counted. But it was the elected officials in both states that chose to go down this terrible path. Had they just remained where they were, their delegates may have made the difference in this close presidential race between Sens. Barack Obama and Hillary Clinton.

But they didn't. They flat out ignored the rules voted on unanimously by the Democratic Party. Officials from both states knew before voting—and signing the bill into law—that the DNC was going to sanction them. Yet their arrogance overrode their common sense.

Now it's March, and less than a dozen states remain, and Michigan and Florida are demanding that the DNC, superdelegates, even the campaigns, do something to allow them to vote again. And by the way, come up with a way to foot the $20 million to $30 million it will cost for a full-fledged election.

If it were my call, I would tell them, "See ya in four years."

Sure, that's pretty harsh, but 48 other states followed the rules. There is no doubt some of those states thought this would be over by Super Tuesday on Feb. 5 and wanted their state to have a say in who the nominee would be, but they chose to be patient and wait their turn.

Michigan and Florida didn't.

Senators and members of Congress from multiple states were clamoring to get in on the action. But with the DNC's threat looming large, they got with the program.

Michigan and Florida didn't.

So we are all supposed to feel sorry for Sens. Carl Levin of Michigan and Bill Nelson of Florida because they want this issue addressed by the DNC, but were they pleading with their governors to not sign the law changing the dates? Nope!

The compassion just isn't there for the arrogant folks from Michigan and Florida.

If this is all about seating delegates, fine. Split their numbers down the middle and give half to Clinton and the other half to Obama. There. We just saved $30 million.

But the DNC should protect the integrity of their rules process. If they acquiesce, how many states will pull the same trick in four years? The precedent would have been set and anyone else could make the same argument: please, please, give us another chance, even though we brought this on ourselves.

No. Enough. Let's end this madness and tell Florida and Michigan that they had their shot. They blew it. It's time to move on and let the people who know how to play by the rules get on with this process. They made their bed. Now sleep in it.

And the people in Michigan and Florida should throw out the bums who stiffed them. Somebody must pay for the sins of these two states, and they should look to the politicians who keep running their mouths on TV demanding a re-vote.

March 17, 2008, Essence.com Blog

Conservative Talkers Want to Keep Obama-Wright Feud Going

SORRY I HAVEN'T BEEN ABLE TO POST ANYTHING on this topic today. I have been absolutely swamped doing radio and TV interviews over the continuing saga over comments made from the pulpit by the Rev. Jeremiah Wright, the retiring senior pastor of Trinity United Church of Christ in Chicago.

One of the reasons this story continues to go on and on is primarily because the conservative media-those rabid right wingers on TV and radio-so desperately want this to continue.

Why?

Because they know their candidate, Sen. John McCain, is lukewarm among the party faithful, and they desperately need to take down the Democratic frontrunnner, Sen. Barack Obama.

Some media folks have said that this all started with a report by Brian Ross on ABC. True, the broadcasting of racially charged comments were first reported by ABC, but the person who has been riding shotgun on this for more than a year is Sean Hannity, who hosts a nationally syndicated radio show and is the co-host of "Hannity & Colmes" on Fox News Channel.

Ever since his super-charged debate with Wright last year, Hannity has had his eyes locked on Obama, blasting him for every little comment.

So when the tapes of Wright preaching came to light, Hannity was like a kid in a candy store.

Now, the Obama campaign should have clearly known that this was going to be a problem. Last year, the drama was about Trinity's Black Value System. Hannity was foaming at the mouth on this one, even though he and other conservative talkers have decried the so-called lack of morals and values in black America. Here is a church that advances a value system and these nut jobs lose it.

But knowing full well that Wright has always been a tough talker in the pulpit, the Obama campaign—or Wright himself—should have not been put on his African American pastoral committee. This has nothing to do with not loving or supporting your pastor. This is called the reality of politics. You lessen any potential fallout and minimize the damage.

Not doing so has cost the Obama camp immensely. Last Monday, he was down 12 points in the polls in Pennsylvania. He wins Mississippi, the flap involving Geraldine Ferraro comes out, then this at the end of the week, and now he's down 16 points. Don't think for a second that those white voters in rural Pennsylvania weren't paying attention.

But this is also about largely white America being clueless about what happens in black America. There is nothing that Wright has said that I have not heard tons of times in black churches. In fact, I've heard wild comments made by white pastors!

In fact, Sen. John McCain has had to deal with some of his faith supporters making controversial statements and being confronted by them. Pastors John Hagee and Rod Parsley have been on the firing line, but certainly not to the degree as Wright.

But folks, the real deal is that none of this means a hill of beans if you are about to lose your home. It means nothing to the 14,000 folks at Bear Stearns who are likely to lose their job after they were sold after seeing the company stock price go from $70 to $2 in a week. And it will do nothing for the thousands of war veterans returning from Iraq who don't have a job.

This is all hype and drama that sells papers and gets folks to watch TV.

Let's just call it what it is.

March 18, 2008
WVON-AM/Chicago: Rep. John Lewis on The Roland S. Martin Show

Male Speaker: *Like other predominantly black churches across the country, Trinity embodies the black community in its entirety—the doctor and the welfare mom, the model student and the former gang banger. Like other black churches, Trinity services are full of raucous laughter and sometimes body humor. They are full of dancing and clapping and screaming and shouting that may seem jarring to the untrained ear. The church contains in full the kindness and cruelty, the fierce intelligence, and the shocking ignorance, the struggles and successes, the love and yes, the bitterness and biases that make up the black experience in America.*

Roland Martin: Welcome back, 7:41, 19 before eight. You are listening to "The Talk of Chicago," 1690/WVON. I am Roland Martin, the place where we do not allow right wing hate to coexist. That is the way we roll. While you are in the phone line right now I want to go to a special guest, Congressman John Lewis from Georgia. Congressman, good morning.

The Primaries

John Lewis: Good morning, how are you this morning?

Roland Martin: I am doing great Congressman. We chatted briefly yesterday on Michael Baisden show.

John Lewis: Well, it was good to chat with you and I am happy and delighted to be on your show. Thank you for your great work.

Roland Martin: Not a problem, sir. You heard many speeches over the year. You were present there on August 28, 1963. Give us your assessment of the speech yesterday by Senator Barack Obama.

John Lewis: Oh the speech that Senator Barack Obama gave yesterday was one of the greatest. It was so meaningful. It was so complete. It was inspiring, it was informative, it was very sensitive and well prepared and well delivered. I told someone yesterday that it reminds me of the speech that Lyndon Johnson gave in 1964 at Howard University on race and the one he gave on March 15, 1965 in response to Bloody Sunday in Selma, Alabama. But it also must be compared with the speech that President Kennedy gave on June 11, 1963 in response to the crisis in Birmingham and the crisis in the South.

Roland Martin: What are the things that jumped out obviously after such a speech and everybody wants to frame it as such? You had the critics of Senator Obama, mainly conservative critics, a radio talk show host, a television talk show host who say—well, he did not go far enough, "He should have disowned Reverend Wright. He should have disowned his church." When you hear those kind of comments what is your response?

John Lewis: It just made me so sad that people cannot see through over their criticisms, their hate, and—what else do you want the man to do—to fit in the middle of Michigan Avenue or a Pitt Street in Atlanta, fit in Pennsylvania Avenue in Washington, and just give it up? I do not know what else he could—he said everything that needed to be said. These people will never support Barack Obama.

Roland Martin: Well, that is one of the points made on CNN and, sir, I would certainly hope that—you know I do not know if the shows are calling you, but I would certainly hope that you would definitely appear on CNN and CBC and the Fox and use your voice as well because, I mean, you bring a unique perspective, and I think it is important to have people with conviction to be able to go toe-to-toe with the messengers of hate, if you will, and express with clarity exactly what happened yesterday.

John Lewis: I think Barack Obama yesterday through that speech had educated and   sensitized a nation. He led the nation in a conversation on race and, whatever happens, this man, this one African American brother took that stage and transformed that podium in Philadelphia into a modern day pulpit.

Roland Martin: A lot of folks were saying, why did Congressman John Lewis switch? Were you even more proud of your decision, sir, to follow the will of the voters in your district after yesterday?

John Lewis: I was more than proud. I knew I did the right thing and I was convinced yesterday more than ever before that I have done the right thing by switching to Barack Obama. He spoke from the soul and that he has got out of his heart. He was so sincere. He was appealing across racial lines and you know he did not have to do what he did, he did not have to say what he said but he did it and he was so human, not just as a African American but he made it plain and clear that he was a composite of all humanity.

Roland Martin: What is next? I mean he is going to give a major speech today on Iraq. Obviously, you already have Fox News trying to say were there other sermons out there. He has addressed this issue. What would you advise him to do moving forward when you have the crabs who want to pull him back down to the bottom of the barrel?

John Lewis: I think he should keep moving ahead, not looking back, just moving ahead, take this message to the American people, to the voters of Pennsylvania and to those other states that have not yet had an opportunity to cast their votes. I think he is going to be okay.

Roland Martin: Right, I have seen a lot of folks who say—well, I hear his candidacy is doomed. I read a piece on political.com where the Republican strategists are saying, "Oh this is great. We are going to use this, use this big time come the fall." I personally believe that he showed yesterday that he was more presidential than he has ever been because it takes courage and dignity to be able to deliver that type of speech, to challenge America at its core to give a racial timeline of how race has impacted both folks who are white and black as well.

John Lewis: Well, you know picking up *the New York Times* this morning and the lead editor described it as a fulfilling courage. It was courageous and that is what we need now more than ever before, raw courage and Barack Obama demonstrated yesterday raw courage. We need a leader, we need a symbol, we need a president who will show and demonstrate that courage.

Roland Martin: Well, I could not put it better myself, sir. I certainly appreciate the conversation. John Lewis, thank you very much for joining us, sir.

John Lewis: Well, thank you, sir. Have a great day.

March 20, 2008, Essence.com Blog

The Truth Behind the Rev. Jeremiah Wright's 9/11 Sermon

AS THIS WHOLE SORDID EPISODE has played out over the last week regarding the sermons of the Rev. Jeremiah Wright, I wanted to understand what he *actually* said in this speech. I've been saying all week on CNN that context is important, and I just wanted to know what the heck is going on.

I actually listened to the sermon Rev. Wright gave after September 11 titled, "The Day of Jerusalem's Fall." It was delivered on Sept. 16, 2001.

One of the most controversial statements in this sermon was when he mentioned "chickens coming home to roost." He was actually quoting Edward Peck, former U.S. Ambassador to Iraq and deputy director of President Reagan's terrorism task force, who was speaking on Fox News. That's what he told the congregation. He was quoting Peck as saying that America's foreign policy has put the nation in peril.

"We took this country by terror away from the Sioux, the Apache...the Comanche, the Arapaho, the Navajo. Terrorism.

"We took Africans away from their country to build our way of ease and kept them enslaved and living in fear. Terrorism.

"We bombed Grenada and killed innocent civilians, babies, non-miliatry personnel.

"We bombed the black civilian community of Panama with stealth bombers and killed unarmed teenagers and toddlers, pregnant mothers and hard-working fathers.

"We bombed Kadafi's home, and killed his child. Blessed are they who bash your children's head against the rock.

"We bombed Iraq. we killed unarmed civilians trying to make a living. We bombed a plant in Sudan to pay back for the attack on our embassy, killed hundreds of hard-working people, mothers and fathers who left home to go that day not knowing that they'd never get back home.

"We bombed Hiroshima. We bombed Nagasaki, and we nuked far more than the thousands in New York and the Pentagon and we never batted an eye.

"Kids playing in the playground. Mothers picking up children after school. Civilians, not soldiers, people just trying to make it day by day.

"We have supported state terrorism against the Palestinians and black South Africans, and now we are indignant because the stuff that we have done overseas is now brought right back into our own front yards. America's chickens are coming home to roost.

"Violence begets violence. Hatred begets hatred. And terrorism begets terrorism. A white ambassador said that y'all, not a black militant. Not a reverend who preaches about racism. An ambassador whose eyes are wide open and who is trying to get us to wake up and move away from this dangerous precipice upon which we are now poised. The ambassador said the people we have wounded don't have the military capability we have. but they do have individuals who are willing to die and take thousands with them. And we need to come to grips with that."

He went on to describe seeing the photos of the aftermath of 9/11 because he was in Newark, N.J. when the planes struck. After turning on the TV and seeing the second plane slam into one of the Twin Towers, he spoke passionately about what if you never got a chance to say hello to your family again.

"What is the state of your family?" he asked.

And then he told his congregation that he loved them and asked the church to tell each other they loved themselves.

His sermon thesis:

1. THIS IS A TIME FOR SELF-EXAMINATION of ourselves and our families.

2. THIS IS A TIME FOR SOCIAL TRANSFORMATION (then he went on to say they won't put me on PBS or national cable for what I'm about to say. Talk about prophetic!) "We have got to change the way we have been doing things as a society," he said.

Wright then said we can't stop messing over people and thinking they can't touch us. He then said we may need to declare war on racism, injustice and greed, instead of war on other countries.

"Maybe we need to declare war on AIDS. In five minutes the Congress found $40 billion to rebuild New York and the families that died in sudden death, do you think we can find the money to make medicine available for people who are dying a slow death? Maybe we need to declare war on the nation's healthcare system that leaves the nation's poor with no health coverage? Maybe we need to declare war on the mishandled educational system and provide quality education for everybody, every citizen, based on their ability to learn, not their ability to pay. This is a time for social transformation."

3. THIS IS TIME TO TELL GOD thank you for all that he has provided and that he gave him and others another chance to do His will.

By the way, nowhere in this sermon did he said "God damn America." I'm not sure which sermon that came from.

This doesn't explain anything away, nor does it absolve Wright of using the N-word, but what it does do is add an accurate perspective to this conversation.

The point that I have always made as a journalist is that our job is to seek the truth, and not the partial truth.

I am also listening to the other sermons delivered by Rev. Wright that have been the subject of controversy.

And let me be clear: Where I believe he was wrong and not justified in what he said based upon the facts, I will say so. But where the facts support his argument, that will also be said.

So stay tuned.

March 21, 2008, Essence.com Blog

The Full Story Behind Wright's "God Damn America" Sermon

I JUST FINISHED LISTENING to the nearly 40-minute sermon Rev. Jeremiah Wright gave on April 13, 2003, titled, "Confusing God and Government."

For those of us watching and listening to the media in the last week, it is better known as the "God Damn America" sermon.

Wright's scriptural focus was Luke 19:37-44 (reading from the New Revised Standard Version).

In this sermon, Wright spoke about the military rule during biblical days, led by Pontius Pilate. It was clear, through his language, such as "occupying military brigade" that he was making an analogy to the war in Iraq.

"War does not make for peace," he said. "Fighting for peace is like raping for virginity.

"War does not make for peace. War only makes for escalating violence and a mindset to pay the enemy back by any means necessary," he said.

He then gets to the thesis of his sermon, saying, "y'all looking to the government for only what God can give. A lot of people confuse God with their government."

Wright criticizes the Bush administration and it supporters for using Godly language to justify the war in Iraq. He equates using God in America as condoning the war in Iraq to the same perspective of Islamic fundamentalists.

"We can see clearly the confusion in the mind of a few Muslims, and please notice I did not say all Muslims, I said a few Muslims, who see Allah as condoning killing and killing any and all who don't believe what they don't believe. They call it jihad. We can see clearly the confusion in their minds, but we cannot see clearly what it is that we do. We call it crusade when we turn right around and say that our God condones the killing of innocent civilians as a necessary means to an end. We say that God understand collateral damage. We say that God knows how to forgive friendly fire.

"We say that God will bless the shock and awe as we take over unilaterally another country, calling it a coalition because we've got three guys from Australia, going against the United Nations, going against the majority of Christians, Muslims and Jews throughout the world, making a pre-emptive strike in the name of God. We cannot see how what we are doing is the same thing is the same thing that Al-Qaeda is doing under a different color flag—calling on the name of a different God to sanction and approve our murder and our mayhem."

He continues on his thesis of equating government with our God, saying that God sent the early settlers to America to take the country from Native Americans; ordained slavery; and that "we believe that God approves of 6 percent of the people on the face of this earth controlling all of the wealth on the face of this earth while the other 94 percent live in poverty and squalor while we give millions of tax breaks to the white rich."

He also criticizes the "lily white" G-7 nations for controlling the world's capital. Then Wright speaks to:

1. GOVERNMENTS LIE. "This government lied about their belief that all men were created equal. The truth is they believed that all white men were created equal. The truth is they did not even believe that white women were created equal, in creation nor civilization. The government had to pass an amendment to the Constitution to get white women the vote. Then the government had to pass an equal rights amendment to get equal protection under the law for women. The government still thinks a woman has no rights over her own body, and between Uncle Clarence (Thomas), who sexually harassed Anita Hill, and a closeted Klan court, that is a throwback to the 19th century, handpicked by Daddy Bush, Ronald Reagan, Gerald Ford, between Clarence and that stacked court, they are about to undo *Roe v. Wade*, just like they are about to undo affirmative action. The government lied in its founding documents and the government is still lying today. Governments lie."

"The government lied about Pearl Harbor. They knew the Japanese were going to attack. Governments lie. The government lied about the Gulf of Tonkin. They wanted that resolution to get us in the Vietnam War. Governments lie. The government lied about Nelson Mandela and our CIA helped put him in prison and keep him there for 27 years. The South African government lied on Nelson Mandela. Governments lie.

"The government lied about the Tuskegee experiment. They purposely infected African American men with syphilis. Governments lie. The government lied about bombing Cambodia and Richard Nixon stood in front of the camera, 'Let me make myself perfectly clear...' Governments lie. The government lied about the drugs for arms Contra scheme orchestrated by Oliver North, and then the government pardoned all the perpetrators so they could get better jobs in the government. Governments lie.

"The government lied about inventing the HIV virus as a means of genocide against people of color. Governments lie. The government lied about a connection between Al Qaeda and Saddam Hussein and a connection between 9.11.01 and Operation Iraqi Freedom. Governments lie.

"The government lied about weapons of mass destruction in Iraq being a threat to the United States peace. And guess what else? If they don't find them some weapons of mass destruction, they gonna do just like the LAPD, and plant the some weapons of mass destruction. Governments lie.

2. GOVERNMENTS CHANGE. He said long before the United States colonized the world, so did Egypt.

"All colonizers are not white. Turn to your neighbors and say that oppressors come in all colors."

He then went back to the Bible and spoke about the changing of kings in Babylonia.

"Prior to Abraham Lincoln, the government in this country said it was legal to hold African in slavery in perpetuity...when Lincoln got in office, the government changed. Prior to the passing of the 13th, 14th and 15th amendments to the Constitution, government defined African as slaves, as property. Property, people with no rights to be respected by any whites anywhere. The Supreme Court of the government, same court, granddaddy of the court that stole the 2000 election. Supreme Court said in its *Dred Scott* decision in the 1850s, no African anywhere in this country has any rights that any white person has to respect at any place, any time. That was the government's official position backed up by the Supreme Court—that's the judiciary; backed up by the executive branch—that's the president; backed up by the legislative branch and enforced by the military of the government. But I stop by to tell you tonight that government's change.

"Prior to Harry Truman's government, the military was segregated. But governments change.

"Prior to the Civil Rights and equal accommodation laws of the government in this country, there was backed segregation by the country, legal discrimination by the government, prohibited blacks from voting by the government, you had to eat and sit in separate places by the government, you had sit in different places from white folks because the government said so, and you had to buried in a separate cemetery. It was apartheid, American style, from the cradle to the grave, all because the government backed it up.

"But guess what? Governments change. Under Bill Clinton, we got a messed up welfare to work bill, but under Clinton blacks had an intelligent friend in the Oval Office. Oh, but governments change.

"The election was stolen. We went from an intelligent friend to a dumb Dixiecrat. A rich Republican who has never held a job in his life; is against affirmative action (and) against education—I guess he is; against healthcare, against benefits for his own military, and gives tax breaks to the wealthiest contributors to his campaign. Governments change. Sometimes for the good, and sometimes for the bad."

"Where governments change, God does not change. God is the same yesterday, today and forever more. That's what his name I Am means. He does not change.

God was against slavery on yesterday, and God, who does not change, is still against slavery today. God was a God of love yesterday, and God who does not change, is still a God of love today. God was a God of justice on yesterday, and God who does not change, is still a God of justice today.

"God does not change."

3. HE THEN SPEAKS OF THE GOVERNMENT IN HIS BIBLE TEXT AND SAID THE ROMANS FAILED. Then he said the British government failed even after it colonized the world. He said the Russian government failed. The Japanese government failed. The German government failed.

"And the United States of America government, when it came to treating her citizens of Indian descent, she failed. She put them on reservations.

The Primaries

"When it came to treating her citizens of Japanese descent fairly, she failed. She put them in interment prison camps.

"When it came to putting the citizens of African descent fairly, America failed. She put them in chains. The government put them on slave quarters. Put them on auction blocks. Put them in cotton fields. Put them in inferior schools. Put them in substandard housing. Put them scientific experiments. Put them in the lower paying jobs. Put them outside the equal protection of the law. Kept them out of their racist bastions of higher education, and locked them into positions of hopelessness and helplessness.

"The government gives them the drugs, builds bigger prisons, passes a three strike law and then wants us to sing "God Bless America." Naw, naw, naw. Not God Bless America. God Damn America! That's in the Bible. For killing innocent people. God Damn America for treating us citizens as less than human. God Damn America as long as she tries to act like she is God and she is Supreme.

"The United States government has failed the vast majority of her citizens of African descent. Think about this. Think about this. For every one Oprah, a billionaire, you've got 5 million blacks that are out of work. For every one Colin Powell, a millionaire, you've got 10 million blacks who cannot read. For every one Condi-Skeezer Rice, you've got 1 million in prison. For every one Tiger Woods, who needs to get beat at the Masters, with his Cablanasian hips, playing on a course that discriminates against women, God has this way of brining you up short when you get too big for your Cablanasian britches. For every one Tiger Woods, we've got 10,000 black kids who will never see a golf course. The United States government has failed the vast majority of her citizens of African descent."

"Tell your neighbor he's (going to) help us one last time. Turn back and say forgive him for the God Damn, that's in the Bible though. Blessings and curses is in the Bible. It's in the Bible."

"Where government fails, God never fails. When God says it, it's done. God never fails. When God wills it, you better get out the way, 'cause God never fails. When God fixes it, oh believe me it's fixed. God never fails. Somebody right now, you think you can't make it, but I want you to know that you are more than a conqueror through Christ. You can do all things through Christ who strengthens you."

He then went on to talk about the salvation of Christians through the death of Jesus Christ. The sermon ended with a song proclaiming, "God never fails."

March 21, 2008
The Politics of Race and Faith

THE REVELATION OF CONTROVERSIAL COMMENTS made by the longtime pastor of Sen. Barack Obama—and the equally hot aftermath from the general public that led to the junior senator from Illinois delivering a strong speech/sermon on race in America—has opened anew the explosive connection between three of the most volatile issues today.

If a poll were taken, there is no doubt that race, faith and politics would be the most emotional, passionate and divisive topics. Why? Because all three are so deeply personal. What one person sees as a negative, another would determine as a strength.

Republicans strongly believe that they are superior and right on the direction of the nation compared to Democrats. African Americans are protective of their culture and ways of living, while whites routinely ask why we can't just be one nation with no labels. Catholics contend they are members of the one and only true church, while Baptists will say that being dipped in water after making a personal decision to give your life to Christ is the true way of salvation for the believer.

As a Christian, I've seen church members go toe-to-toe when discussing either of these issues, and I can remember some late-night debates in college that would have made the toes of Lincoln and Douglas curl.

So why did the comments of the Rev. Jeremiah Wright strike such a core, and how did it lead to Obama giving a speech on race? That was the question posed to me in a number of e-mails, and like Obama stated in his speech, it's really America's lack of understanding—no, refusal to accept—how the different races live and act.

The Kerner Commission stated in 1968 that we were living in two Americas—one black and one white. When we examine the TV shows we watch, those in the top

10 for whites are vastly different from those for blacks. Musical tastes vary; so do cultural norms. We all kid that during March Madness, the courts are loaded with mostly African American ballplayers, yet when the College World Series happens in May, you will see mostly whites on the baseball diamond.

But we are also separate when it comes to worship. The Rev. Dr. Martin Luther King Jr. said the most segregated hour of the week is 10 A.M. Sunday. And it still is. For Christians, we may celebrate the same Jesus, but how we do so and with whom is very different.

I fundamentally believe that whites, blacks—and yes, Hispanics and Asians— reacted differently when hearing the snippets of Wright's preaching. Not solely because of content but also style. For African Americans who are accustomed to a certain style of preaching—and a lot of Southern whites—the thundering voice that drops to a whisper and the weaving of social issues with the theological are common.

Even former Arkansas Gov. Mike Huckabee—while not embracing Wright— agreed with that point.

Yet our view of America is also different. Justified? No. Just different.

While many white Americans will look at Memorial Day or Veterans Day as an opportunity to celebrate our armed forces, African Americans do the same, but African Americans also will think historically of seeing and reading about black troops hanged from trees, still in their uniforms. They will think of soldiers returning home to America after World War II being forced to sit in the back of the train while German Nazis got to sit up front.

When Wright was castigated for being anti-American for saying "God damn America!"—which was not delivered in his speech about 9/11—I couldn't help but think about that famous speech Dr. King gave at Riverside Church April 4, 1967, when he blasted America's involvement in the Vietnam War. King was disowned by many of his supporters, was denounced as a traitor to the nation, and his speaking fees dried up.

See, even the man who many conservatives quote today with fervor was treated as an outcast in his own country.

Our shared experiences today may not be so raw and overt as America's racial past, but we can't forget how our past defines us today.

Are these excuses? Nope. Just a dose of reality.

I watched Joe Scarborough on MSNBC say, while qualifying that these weren't his views, that a blue-collar man in Youngstown, Ohio, didn't want to hear about race from a black man who went to Harvard and his black wife who went to Princeton.

He's probably right. But what Joe failed to mention is that same black man came from a home in which the mom had to go on welfare just to feed her family. That same black woman lived in a two-bedroom home and saw her parents bust their butts to make ends meet and scrape together every penny to send their children to the nation's finest schools.

Isn't that the dream of every white blue-collar parent and every black blue-collar parent? So why should such success be seen as anger toward someone else?

When we sit down, break bread together and truly listen and learn from one another, our worldviews change.

For the past few months, I've seen that experience up close and personal at my church in Chicago.

The Rev. James Meeks, founder and senior pastor of Salem Baptist Church—a predominantly black congregation—has been engaged in worship with a predominantly white megachurch, Willow Creek, led by its founder and senior pastor, Bill Hybels.

The pastors of the state's two largest churches have been engaged in the swapping of youth members and choirs, have preached at one another's church, and have made it their mission to break down the racial and economic walls that exist between Christians.

It has been rocky at times. To see the faces of African Americans watch the worship service of Willow Creek members has been a bit jarring, from the style of preaching to the music. But there is a common denominator: Jesus.

There is no doubt that a lot of Americans are angry and confused by Obama staying at Trinity United Church of Christ and not disowning his pastor. Folks, that's just not what churchgoers do. I don't recall people asking members of Jerry Falwell's church or Pat Robertson's church to leave in droves. They knew their leaders were fallible and made mistakes. Should they be criticized for hateful and divisive comments? Absolutely. Disowned? I never would say that.

This is an opportunity we have. Those of us in the media, as Obama said, can continue to run the same clips, but is that providing healing to America? No.

What we can do is begin to show where communities are coming together, talking openly and honestly about their frustrations and pain. Will we get angry and upset because the other person isn't getting what we are trying to say fully? Of course! But until we decide to look in that mirror and confront our deep-seated fears of the other because of their race, religion and political affiliation, we'll remain a fractured nation.

The Bible says don't put new wine in old wineskins. So let's stop using the resentments of the past and holding them against the people of today and the future.

So, what are *you* prepared to do?

March 28, 2008

Listen to the Candidates, Not Their Associates

IT'S BEEN AN INTERESTING WEEK watching folks analyze the outcry over the Rev. Jeremiah Wright's controversial comments, especially when they try to link them to Sen. Barack Obama.

Obama's supporters say it's wrong to associate his views with those of his pastor at Chicago's Trinity United Church of Christ.

His opponents say that surely his views are linked with Wright's, including the pastor's praise of Nation of Islam Minister Louis Farrakhan.

Conservative talker Sean Hannity—who incidentally many have accused of having associations with white supremacist Hal Turner, which he denies—was foaming at the mouth. He called Wright a racist and an anti-Semite and then said we all should assume Obama is also a racist and an anti-Semite.

Talk about a stretch. Frankly, it's just not plausible to suggest that you always share the same feelings or views as someone you know.

In remarks to a Pittsburgh newspaper, Sen. Hillary Clinton responded to a question about the Wright controversy by saying, "You don't choose your family, but you choose what church you want to attend."

True. Very true. But there's also some reality that politicians pick and choose whom they want to be associated with.

Clinton pressed Obama during a debate this year to repudiate and denounce Farrakhan's unsolicited praise of him at an event the Nation of Islam leader organized for his group in Chicago. The moderator, NBC's Tim Russert, brought up comments made by Farrakhan 24 years ago in his question to Obama.

Fine, so what do we make of then-President Bill Clinton publicly endorsing the 1995 Million Man March? Who called for that march? Louis Farrakhan. Who was the lead organizer? Louis Farrakhan. Who was the keynote speaker? Louis Farrakhan.

After he was out of the White House, President Clinton also endorsed the Million Man March. Who called for that march? Louis Farrakhan. Who was the lead organizer? Louis Farrakhan. Who was the keynote speaker? Louis Farrakhan.

Did Sen. Clinton privately or publicly rebuke her husband for supporting a man whom she has determined to be hateful and divisive?

Pennsylvania Gov. Ed Rendell, a leading supporter of Hillary Clinton's, once stood on stage with Farrakhan in 1997—at an event *The New York Times* said was "called to promote racial reconciliation after several recent high-profile crimes"— and praised him for his commitment to ending violence in the black community. Rendell was the mayor of Philadelphia at the time. According to the April 15, 1997, story in the *Times*, Farrakhan praised Rendell before 3,000 people at the anti-violence rally for "his courage and strength to rise above emotion and differences that might be between us or our communities." According to the *Times*, Rendell, who is Jewish, commended the Nation of Islam for its emphasis on family values and self-sufficiency. Must Clinton repudiate and denounce Rendell's past comments and association with Farrakhan?

Former Republican Rep. Jack Kemp is a huge supporter of Sen. John McCain's, and he also has a Farrakhan story. In 1996, when Kemp was the vice presidential running mate of Sen. Bob Dole, he told reporters that he wanted to meet with Farrakhan and praised his organization's focus on economic empowerment, family values and its pull-yourselves-up-by-the-bootstrap message—right in line with the GOP talking points. Kemp said he wanted to speak at the Million Man March. Boy, was he torn apart by Jewish critics and many in his own party. Kemp summarily criticized Farrakhan's comments about Jews and whites, but he didn't take his words back. By the way, Hannity pressed every African American supporter about Farrakhan, but he never got in Kemp's face about his comments. I wonder why? Must McCain repudiate and denounce Kemp's past comments and association with Farrakhan?

When it comes to homosexuality, no Clinton or Obama supporter should think of criticizing the other campaign's black ministerial supporters because that means most of their own would have to be disassociated from their campaigns.

On CNN's "The Situation Room," Paul Begala mentioned "hateful" things said about gays by the Rev. James Meeks, founder and senior pastor of Salem Baptist Church of Chicago and an Obama supporter. Meeks has made no bones about his firm opposition to homosexuality (and abortion), which is one of the reasons he's very close to many of the nation's white conservative pastors. (I know him well; I'm a member of Salem.)

And then there was the hoopla over gospel singer Donnie McClurkin when the Obama campaign recruited him to take part in a gospel concert tour around South Carolina. McClurkin has preached that homosexuals can be converted to heterosexuals. That set off a firestorm.

But Clinton also has issues with anti-gay pastoral supporters. The Rev. Harold Mayberry, pastor of the First African Methodist Church in Oakland, Calif., has voiced for years his opposition to homosexuality. In fact, some have said he has compared homosexuality to thievery. When Mayberry came out in support of Clinton, her campaign touted his endorsement, sans any mention of his anti-gay rants.

She also has received a $1,000 contribution from Bishop Eddie L. Long of the mega-church New Birth Missionary Baptist Church in Lithonia, Ga., who previously led a march in Atlanta against gay marriage.

Of course, when it comes to McCain, it's not a story when his ministerial supporters are anti-gay. It would be news if any of them actually supported homosexuality.

THE BOTTOM LINE: Everyone has an association that is open for scrutiny. Our real focus should be on the candidates and their views on the issues because one of them will stand before the nation and take the oath of office and swear to uphold and protect the Constitution of the United States.

April 4, 2008, Essence.com Blog

Reflections on the 40ᵗʰ Anniversary of Dr. King's Assassination and Why Obama Should Have Been There

MEMPHIS-FOR MANY, THE WEEK leading up to the 40th anniversary of the assassination of the Rev. Dr. Martin Luther King Jr. was a walk down the memory lane.

Hordes of reporters talked to ministers, civil rights leaders, sanitation workers and others about what it was like to march with Dr. King, and the events surrounding his last hours were like.

But for Martin Luther King III, he stayed on message: remembering April 4 was about recommitment to the causes his father fought for.

That point seemed to be in conflict during the five days I was in Memphis. I guess because remembering all of King's work is pretty easy compared to forging your own path.

During the last year of his life, King was focused on two primary issues: poverty and the war in Vietnam.

According to the latest CNN/Opinion Research poll, the top two issues today are the economy and the war in Iraq. Different times, but the issues remain the same.

As I talked throughout the day on CNN on Friday—with barely a voice due to allergies—I wanted our focus to remain on present day, and not get caught in the trap of the past. As a student of history, I appreciate the past because it sets us up for the present. But when we stay there, that's when we have problems.

There were so many people to commemorate the day, including Clarence B. Jones, King's personal attorney; Pastor Paula White; the Revs. Al Sharpton and

The Primaries

Jesse Jackson Sr.; Rev. C.T. Vivian, one of the bravest men during the Civil Rights Movement; Rev. Benjamin Hooks; Rev. Wyatt Tee Walker; and of course, presidential candidates, Sens. Hillary Clinton and John McCain.

Absent was Sen. Barack Obama.

And let me share a few words on that.

As I stood in the space that used to occupy Room 307 of the Lorraine Motel—now a part of the National Civil Rights Museum—and I looked across the crowd that stood in the rain and wind Friday, I tried to reconcile Obama not being there, and instead, staying in Indiana. My thoughts went back to my post about the Tavis Smiley affair, and the reality is that both are different.

I thought Obama should have been in Memphis because the nation's attention was focused on that day, and not Indiana, where he was. Had Obama been there he could have used the opportunity to further present himself in the image of King, someone who wasn't willing to shy away from the tough fights and stay focused on his work in the pulpit. To have Obama stand on that balcony would have meant that they may have killed the dreamer, but a potential Obama presidency represented the continuing of that dream. Had Obama been there he could have used the moment to make plain to America that King was not just a black man fighting for black rights, but someone who ended up freeing white Americans from their own racial prisons and forced them to truly embrace the U.S. Constitution they so dearly loved. Had Obama been there he could have met with the 18 black sanitation workers who are still on the job in Memphis because they don't have any city pensions. Yes, those men must still work because the racism in 1968 continues to affect their lives in 2008.

I've seen the talking points distributed by his campaign, suggesting that he was in Indiana because King's vision resonated across the nation. True, very true. But images have power, and the image of Obama on that balcony, speaking to the nation, would have meant more than him speaking in Indiana.

This, folks, was a missed opportunity by Obama.

April 4, 2008
Presidential Polls Don't Truly Speak to Race or Gender Issues

WHEN A NEW POLL COMES OUT, those of us in the media, especially on television, get excited and giddy over what the numbers may mean to the overall electorate.

As any good pollster will tell you, polls offer a snapshot into the minds of the voters on a given day. Of course, that view could change the next day for a multitude of reasons.

My BlackBerry and Treo were buzzing Thursday over the release of polling data showing that America is ready to elect a black president by overwhelming numbers. And those polled say we're readier to do so than we are to elect a woman.

According to a CNN/Essence Magazine/Opinion Research Corp. poll released Thursday, 76 percent of those polled say America is ready for a black president. Sixty-three percent say we're ready for a female president.

Feminist Gloria Steinem must be screaming, "See, I told you so!" But there are some other realities that we must confront before we accept the notion that gender is a greater barrier than race.

First, white men are 43 for 43 when it comes to the presidency. That's one heckuva ratio, and regardless of the excitement generated by Sens. Barack Obama and Hillary Clinton, if either gets the Democratic nomination, there is no way of guaranteeing that record won't continue to be perfect in a fall campaign against Sen. John McCain.

Second, no white women or African Americans ever have been this close. (I say white women because when we speak of women, African American women normally are not included; they typically are placed in the racial category.) In fact, only Elizabeth Dole on the GOP side has done anything of substance in a presidential nomination battle. Rep. Shirley Chisholm, an African American, ran in 1972, and former Sen. Carol Moseley Braun, also African American, was in the race briefly in 2004. (Rep. Geraldine Ferraro didn't run for president. She was selected as a vice presidential nominee.)

For African American men, the Rev. Jesse Jackson Sr. ran in 1984 and 1988, and prior to Obama, no African American did better than Jackson did. Former Virginia Gov. L. Douglas Wilder was briefly in the race in 1992, and the Rev. Al Sharpton ran in 2004. But neither did anything to truly impact the race.

So, does this mean that although Obama is an African American man, he must have a leg up against Clinton, a white woman?

I just don't accept that conclusion. Why? Just look at the real-time data of how the nation has elected white women and African Americans to high office.

Since Reconstruction, there only have been three black U.S. senators: Edward Brooke of Massachusetts and Braun and Obama, both of Illinois. Excluding Braun, there have been 34 female U.S. senators.

Since Reconstruction, only two African Americans have been elected governor in America: Wilder of Virginia and Deval Patrick in Massachusetts. There have been 27 women elected governor since Reconstruction.

As they say, the proof is in the pudding, and it's clear that if there is a greater barrier to office, it has been race, not gender.

This is not to engage in a contest of who has had the greater pain. But it's using real data for us to have a substantive discussion about what is at play here.

The polling data should be seen for what it is: Americans are growing more comfortable with the notion of African Americans and white women being in positions to go places where others previously have failed to go. When it comes to breaking barriers, it takes someone to walk across the hot coals in order to fulfill destiny.

All the women and minorities before them have paved the way for Clinton and Obama to be where they are. This race offers a blueprint for those in the future to seek higher office because they will be able to study what they did—well and badly—and create their own game plans.

So, we know it's guaranteed that the Democrats will achieve history with their selection of Obama or Clinton. We'll just have to see whether America's changing opinions on race and gender for the presidency will be reflected at the ballot box Nov. 4.

April 11, 2008

Democrats Finally Getting Religion on Religion

SWEET JESUS!

What has gotten into the Democratic Party when it comes to issues of faith?

On Sunday, CNN will broadcast the "Compassion Forum", an event hosted by CNN's Campbell Brown and *Newsweek* Editor Jon Meacham. It will explore issues of faith and morality with Democratic presidential candidates Sens. Barack Obama and Hillary Clinton.

This is the second time the top Democratic candidates will deal with issues of faith. On June 4, CNN's Soledad O'Brien moderated a forum that featured Obama, Clinton and former Sen. John Edwards. That forum's panel included religious leaders invited by the Rev. Jim Wallis, the head of the Sojourners Social Justice Ministry.

These forums should not be casually overlooked and blown off because they represent a significant shift in attitude from previous Democratic presidential campaigns. Democrats, in the words of Sen. Joseph Biden after the Sojourners forum, acted more like agnostics—others would say atheists—when it came to issues of faith.

For nearly 30 years, Republicans successfully used wedge issues, such as abortion and homosexuality, to rally their base to those social causes and elect candidates who were willing to go to the mat when they came up. Their outreach efforts were strong, consistent, and they delivered time and time again. And as long as Democrats were willing to ignore the ever-increasing concerns of people who tied their faith with public policy, the GOP would continue to clean up at the ballot box.

Yet the outreach efforts by Clinton and Obama should serve as an example to all Democratic officeholders that ignoring voters who feel strongly about their faith, and also public policy, will continue to lead to losses.

Sunday's forum, which will be held at Messiah College in Grantham, Pa., will allow each candidate to speak for 40 minutes on various moral issues, including poverty, global AIDS, climate change and human rights.

These are all vital issues that we should want to hear our presidential candidates discuss at length, and it's time that our debates and discussions with the candidates went beyond the war in Iraq, illegal immigration and terrorism.

While on the surface it looks good for Democrats to embrace those in the faith world, there are some serious potential land mines they are going to have to confront.

I always have maintained that people of faith who are conservative need to move beyond the issues of abortion and homosexuality and broaden what are deemed faith issues. But the Democratic Party is going to have to do the opposite—that is have some serious discussions as to how it's going to confront social issues and not ignore abortion and homosexuality.

For instance, I got an e-mail last week from several gay party activists who are disturbed that the Rev. James Meeks—founder and pastor of Salem Baptist Church, the second-largest church in Illinois—has endorsed Obama. Why? Because Meeks opposes abortion and homosexuality. I know him well because I am a member of his church.

In January, gay supporters of Obama were aghast that his campaign would allow gospel singer Donnie McClurkin to participate in a gospel tour around South Carolina because he has discussed being a former homosexual who converted to being a heterosexual. This is no different from gay activists being less than thrilled to see Sen. Hillary Clinton touting the endorsement of the Rev. Harold Mayberry, a Bay Area pastor who opposes gay marriage.

And when several gay bloggers heard that President Bush's spiritual adviser, the Rev. Kirbyjon Caldwell, pastor of Windsor Village United Methodist Church in Houston—the largest UMC congregation in the country—was backing Obama, they also cited his opposition to homosexuality, forcing the campaign to say he in no way would be campaigning on behalf of the candidate. Thus far, they have remained true to that, not making Caldwell available on behalf of the campaign since that endorsement came down three months ago.

In talking with officials from the Obama and Clinton campaigns, I jokingly said that if they both were trying to use only the black pastors who would pass muster by their gay and abortion rights supporters, they might be able to find two in the whole country!

If the Democratic Party is serious about fostering a relationship with the faith community, it is going to have to come to grips with the fact that there are Democrats of faith who are anti-abortion and against gay marriage but who are in agreement on other social issues, such as the response to the rapid rise of HIV/AIDS and eradicating poverty.

Abortion and gay rights activists clearly are not going to back down from advancing their agendas, but they can be assured that people of faith are not going to be silent for the sake of a political party.

What is clear is that in the political realm, there must be an understanding of the secular and theological worlds. And there are clear examples when folks who operate in the secular world want to apply their standards to those in the theological world and vice versa.

Is there room for people with opposing views on various issues to support either Obama or Clinton? Absolutely. But if the campaigns are hellbent on silencing their faith supporters because of such a disagreement, they risk alienating them, thus depriving the party of a broader constituency to take back the White House.

In other words, ignore the churchgoing folks and you don't stand a prayer of winning.

April 14, 2008, Essence.com Blog
Presidential Campaign Has Turned Into a Battle Over the Dictionary

IS THIS A PRESIDENTIAL CAMPAIGN or an English challenge?

All we keep hearing these days is who said what and what the meaning is.

Sen. Barack Obama is getting slammed for saying that voters in Pennsylvania are "bitter" over the state of the economy. Sen. John McCain had to apologize for a radio talk show host calling Obama a Chicago political "hack." Then Obama was called on to apologize for a liberal talker calling McCain a "warmonger."

Can we please cut the crap with the words and actually have all three candidates deal with real issues?

If you are broke, who gives a damn if someone says you are angry or bitter or mad? Broke is broke.

What was an exciting season has turned so childish that folks are now arguing over every little word uttered.

Remember what they said on the playground: sticks and stones may break my bones, but words will never hurt me?

It's time to grow up.

April 15, 2008, Essence.com Blog

It's Time for Bob Johnson to Shut Up

BET FOUNDER BOB JOHNSON proves again how he's an ignorant ass man.

In an interview with the *Charlotte Observer*, "Bumbling Bonehead Billionaire" Bob said that Geraldine Ferraro was right when she said Sen. Barack Obama is winning because he's black.

This is what he told the paper: "What I believe Geraldine Ferraro meant (is) if you take a freshman senator from Illinois called "Jerry Smith" and he says I'm going to run for president, would he start off with 90 percent of the black vote? And the answer is, probably not.

"Would he also start out with the excitement of starting out as something completely different? Probably not. He would just be a freshmen senator ...

"Geraldine Ferraro said it right. The problem is Geraldine Ferraro is white. This campaign has such a hair trigger on anything racial. It is almost impossible for anybody to say anything."

So, forget the fact that Obama raised $200 million. Forget that Clinton was beating him by 30 percentage points among African Americans until whites voted for him in Iowa.

It's all because he's black.

This is the BS that blacks have to contend with every day.

Years ago when I was a reporter at the *Fort Worth Star-Telegram*, I had a white reporter tell me, "Oh, you're getting job queries because you're black." Now, forget that he never belonged to any journalism groups, didn't network with editors nationwide, didn't send his clips out. I got offers just because I'm black. How about the fact that I worked my butt off?

See, this is code for diminishing black accomplishment.

By the way, Doug Wilder ran in 1992; Sharpton and former Sen. Carol Moseley Braun. They were all African American who were more known than Obama. Did they win? Nope!

Bob Johnson knows the truth. It's so easy to fall on race. That's just his way of dismissing Obama winning. Don't credit him coming up with a strategy that was appealing to the uninspired. Don't credit him reaching the young. It's all because he's black.

Utter nonsense.

Bob needs to focus on his sorry basketball team and repent from the degradation of black women he contributed to with the lurid videos on BET.

April 15, 2008

Understanding Why You Don't Call a Black Man a Boy

WHEN I READ ABOUT REP. GEOFF DAVIS (R-KY), using the word "boy" in reference to Sen. Barack Obama, I immediately thought of a routine—and subsequent book— by comedian Cedric the Entertainer.

While watching the movie "The Original Kings of Comedy," Ced had me rolling in the aisle as he was talking about being a "grown-ass man," and that eventually became the title of his best-selling book, *Grown-A$$ Man.*

For those who think African Americans are too sensitive about this issue and it's just a well-meaning person making a mistake, I understand that. But others must understand the history of African Americans and what it always has meant to black men for people to call them boys.

One, it's the ultimate sign of disrespect and is often more offensive than calling them the N-word. For years, black men were dismissed summarily and treated with disregard. It was as if their stature was diminished when someone white called them boys. I've heard black men describe the hurt and pain of growing up and having someone white call them boys in front of their own children.

Again, I know some are reading this and saying, "Why can't we all just get along and forget all this race stuff?"

That would be great, but our history is truly our history, and there are things left over that, when said, immediately conjure up those feelings of old.

Do you remember the images from the sanitation strike that the Rev. Dr. Martin Luther King Jr. was leading in Memphis, Tenn., in 1968? The most striking visual was that of the male protestors wearing signs saying, "I am a man!"

There was a reason they were wearing those signs.

You may have caught the Showtime movie "10,000 Black Men Named George," which tells the story of labor leader A. Philip Randolph, who organized the black porters of the Pullman Rail Car Company during the 1920s and '30s, known as the Brotherhood of Sleeping Car Porters. The name is derived from the fact that white passengers never bothered to learn the names of the porters and dismissively would call them all George, which was seen during those days as a racial slur.

Remember earlier this year when former President Bill Clinton referred to Obama as a "kid"? That evoked a similar reaction by some because it was seen as being dismissive of a sitting U.S. senator who also is a grown man with a wife and two daughters. Where I come from, we call that a man, not a boy or kid.

I have my own story when it comes to being called a boy. I was working at the *Austin American-Statesman* newspaper in Texas. An older white male colleague was talking to me, and in the conversation, he referenced me as a boy. I knew he meant no harm, but don't think for a second that it didn't cross my mind. He also stiffened up, realized what he said and quickly replied, "Now, you know I didn't mean to disparage you by calling you a boy?"

In this presidential campaign, we have had many instances when individuals have made references that were perceived as sexist or racist. Some have been called overt; others have been called covert.

I've heard men blow off comments about Sen. Hillary Clinton that are clearly sexist, and we do well to recognize that. I have a wife, sisters and nieces, and I sure don't want them treated with disrespect, so not objecting to sexism toward Clinton means that attitude will remain, and it may affect the women in my life one day.

Heck, Obama's comments about rural folks in Pennsylvania and the visceral reaction by some shows that even when it comes to guns and religion, some folks see that as an attack on who they are and where they come from.

When people suggest that we all shouldn't be so sensitive, I get what they are saying, but I also know that's always easy to say when you aren't the one who is being targeted.

Watching what you say is not being politically correct; it's realizing that words do matter and they have meaning.

This brouhaha over the comments by the Kentucky congressman won't blow up into a major story, and we likely will forget them. But let's treat all of this as a history lesson on race and gender and as a window into a world that many of us either don't know about, ignore or have long forgotten about.

April 17, 2008, Essence.com Blog
Last Night's Debate Was A Waste of My Time

I WAS A BIT MIFFED AT MYSELF for not setting my Tivo to record the Democratic presidential debate on ABC; I was doing *CNN's Election Center* and had to race home.

But when it was all over, and I saw the last half and then read the first half, I realized that I would have been wasting hard drive space. In fact, my wife was recording *American Idol* and recording *Criminal Minds*. I should have left well enough alone.

My radio callers this morning were up in arms at the debate, believing that questioners Charlie Gibson and George Stephanolopous were dead set against Sen. Barack Obama.

Frankly, that didn't concern me.

What I took issue with was so much focus on Rev. Wright, "bitter" comments, Bosnia, affirmative action, and other stuff that really didn't amount to much.

For instance, Obama got asked about not wearing a flag pin. Was Clinton wearing one? Nope. Was Stephanolopous wearing one? Nope. Was Gibson wearing one? Nope!

So, if no one was on stage wearing one, how big of a deal is it?!

A caller today from North Carolina had a great response: If you take off your wedding ring, does that mean you forgot you were married? That was pretty good!

But one of the most pressing issues in the nation-gas prices—was tossed out by Gibson near the end, saying there wasn't much time left to discuss.

"MR. GIBSON: We're running short on time. Let me just give some quick questions here, and let me give you a minute each to answer. What are you going to do about gas prices? It's getting to $4 a gallon. It is killing truckers."

Don't you think that question should have been higher up in the debate?

And why keep asking about them choosing one another as vice president? What is asked and answered? Both candidates, Speaker of the House Nancy Pelosi, and a bunch of other Democrats have weighed in on this, so do we have waste more time on it? They will not be running together, so can we move on?

Also, the only time HIV/AIDS came up was when Obama mentioned it regarding his church. With HIV/AIDS continuing to ravage inner city communities, it would have been nice to hear what Clinton and Obama had to say on the issue.

With Sallie Mae saying they are going to be more restrictive in giving student loans, I want to know what Clinton and Obama will do as president to provide resources for our kids to go to school. There were passing references, but nothing substantive.

But hey, when you have Rev. Wright and Bosnia, why bother with real issues?

April 18, 2008

An "Average" American Never Will Be President

CAN WE ALL JUST STOP THE SILLY NONSENSE over who is an elitist and whether an "average" American will occupy the White House?

Listening to the punditry today, you would think folks who revel in the comedy of Larry The Cable Guy or Katt Williams really would have a shot at the White House. It's totally absurd.

So, Sen. Barack Obama is all of a sudden an elitist because he went to Columbia and Harvard universities? And Sen. Hillary Clinton is an elitist because she went to Yale University? Do you actually think Sen. John McCain isn't an elitist? He went to an exclusive college—the United States Naval Academy—and that is one of the hardest places to get into. (You can't even apply unless a member of Congress recommends you.)

Karl Rove, who tries to portray himself as the common man but is just another rich Republican, has called both Democratic candidates elitists. Well, his former boss, President George W. Bush, went to Yale. So did Bush's dad, former President George H.W. Bush, and his granddaddy, former Sen. Prescott Bush. All three Bushes also were members of the super-elite organization Skull and Bones. George W. later went to Harvard.

He walked into the governor's mansion and the presidency on the strength of his name and his dad's money and connections. Sounds like an elitist to me!

But no, we're supposed to be fooled by the cowboy boots, folksy charm and him removing brush at his Crawford, Texas, ranch. (Don't forget the family compound in Kennebunkport, Maine, where all the "regular" folks hang out.)

Surely you recall when Bush nominated Harriet Miers for the Supreme Court? Those same conservative voices decrying the elitist Democrats were blasting her because she went to little old Southern Methodist University, that unremarkable—their view—university in Dallas. (By the way, that will be the home of the George W. Bush Presidential Library.)

You can bet a pitcher of beer that had she graduated from Harvard, Yale or Princeton universities, she wouldn't have been referred to derisively as too plain and not educated enough by the elitists in the Republican Party.

And let's stay with the Supreme Court for a moment. Where did its members go to school?

- Chief Justice John G. Roberts Jr.: Undergrad and law school: Harvard.
- Justice John Paul Stevens: Undergrad: University of Chicago. Law school:

Northwestern University.

- Justice Antonin Scalia: Undergrad: Georgetown University and the University of Fribourg, Switzerland. Law school: Harvard.
- Justice Anthony M. Kennedy: Undergrad: Stanford University and the London School of Economics. Law school: Harvard.
- Justice David Hackett Souter: Undergrad: Harvard; Magdalen College, Oxford; Oxford University. Law school: Harvard.
- Justice Clarence Thomas: Undergrad: Holy Cross College. Law school: Yale.
- Justice Ruth Bader Ginsburg: Undergrad: Cornell University. Law school: Harvard (attended); finished at Columbia.
- Justice Stephen G. Breyer: Undergrad: Stanford; Magdalen College, Oxford. Law school: Harvard.
- Justice Samuel Anthony Alito Jr.: Undegrad: Princeton. Law school: Yale.

That's pretty much an elite list of schools.

We have deluded ourselves into thinking the person elected to the White House is really and truly like the rest of us.

All three candidates don't know what it's like to face the daunting health care challenges millions of Americans are confronted with daily. Each is a member of the U.S. Senate, and they have the best health care money can buy for life; we pay for it! While your pension plan is shot to hell, their plan never will be under-funded. The members will see to that, courtesy of taxpayer dollars.

Forget how many times Obama bowls gutter balls, Clinton tosses back shots of whiskey, and McCain talks about how he's a regular guy. Each, courtesy of their $150,000-plus annual salaries, makes far more than the average American.

And when it comes to wealth, Clinton gets to enjoy the $100 million she and her husband raked in since they left the White House. (Even their hefty book advances dwarf regular authors.)

McCain's wife, Cindy, runs one of Anheuser-Busch's largest beer distributors and is worth more than $100 million. They never will be living paycheck to paycheck.

Obama is the poorest of the three, but he did earn more than a million bucks courtesy of his best-selling books, *The Audacity of Hope* and *Dreams from My Father*, after delivering the keynote speech at the Democratic National Convention in 2004. How many average Americans wouldn't mind having a million dollars in their savings accounts?

Bottom line: The narrative about our presidential candidates being just regular folks is a tired myth that gets repeated every day. And their efforts to show that they are "just like us" are really pathetic.

You don't have to go duck hunting, be seen buying milk at the grocery for your family, or having a beer at the local bar to show that you're "one of us." Just do what rich and highly educated folks do when they are in politics: Advance policies that at least will allow me to keep a few more dollars in my pocket so I'm able to afford a home.

One more thing: Don't buy fully into the nonsense tossed out by some of the loudest voices on television, radio and in print, who decry these "elitists" and trumpet that they are for the blue-collar, middle-class workers in Middle America.

Many of them pull down multimillion-dollar salaries and run into these same candidates on Martha's Vineyard and in the Hamptons when they all vacation. They, too, will pull every favor they have to get their children in the posh private schools and Ivy League institutions.

Yes, we even have elitists in the media.

Who would've thunk it?

April 19, 2008, Essence.com Blog

Ronald Reagan, Haters and the Obama Brush Off

MAYBE SEN. BARACK OBAMA has more in common with former President Ronald Reagan that we've previously acknowledged.

Remember during the week of the Nevada caucus he caught a lot of flack about his views on Reagan? Well, the issue of the Obama brush off this week reminds me of The Great Communicator.

But I must admit, as each day passes, it becomes even clearer how there are just different worlds various Americans live in.

After Obama brushed off his shoulders the day after the ABC debate, some folks made it clear that they are not up-to-date with the times.

First, MSNBC's Joe Scarborough.

The former Republican congressman, who thinks America is still living in the land of "Ozzie and Harriett" and loves to go on and on about how he is an Average Joe, was left scratching his head after seeing what Obama did on stage in North Carolina.

As Teresa Wiltz pointed out in a story in Saturday's *Washington Post*, he remarked: "We looked at each other and said, 'What's he doing?'"

Even some of Obama's white aides said the same thing, according to my sources in the campaign.

Now, I don't think this was a situation where the white folks were clueless and the black folks saw it as a hidden-some might say code-move designed for them to only know.

This is truly a generational thing.

I'll bet you $100 that a bunch of young white kids and adults steeped in hip-hop knew exactly what he was doing. Bottom line: the cool folks got it and the, well, less than cool folks had no clue.

"Not smart" was how the *Washington Post is* Richard Cohen called the brush off when he was on "Morning Joe with Scarborough."

Folks, I can tell you now that Cohen will never qualify for the cool crowd. (By the way, he found time for MSNBC, but when I tried to get him to come on my radio show a couple weeks ago, he told my producer that he simply never has time for such things, and he would have had to get up earlier to do Average Joe than do my show. Richie, come do my show, you might increase your cool factor!).

So here is a lesson in what Obama was doing.

The folks who are older than me grew up on the phrase, "Sticks and stones may break my bones but words will never hurt me."

Today? We say, "Shake the haters off."

Wiltz describes that as coming from a Jay-Z song, which says, "If you feelin' like a pimp . . . go and brush your shoulders off. . . . Get that dirt off your shoulder."

Although the Obama camp says the junior senator from Illinois has a few Jay-Z tunes on his iPod, I think there is a better song to illustrate the point, Big El's "Shake the Haters."

Whenever I get a crazy caller on my radio show who is complaining, I just crack out "Shake the Haters" and let 'er rip!

Basically, what it means is that whatever negative criticism comes your way-hate—then you just blow it off, or brush it off, and keep on steppin'. Oh, I'm sorry, that's keep moving forward for not the not so cool folks.

Comedian Katt Williams sees it another way. In his foul-mouthed but hilarious HBO comedy special, he says that only those people who are doing something good have to contend with haters. In fact, he said that if there were any haters in the audience, they could gladly hate on him because that means he was well on his way to greatness (Go to YouTube to see it. Way too many N-words and cursing for me to post on a family web site!).

Reagan? Oh yea, he was really good at shaking the haters off.

I recall that the 40th president of the United States was nicknamed "Teflon Ron" because he always had a sunny disposition and never seemed to let things bother him. Plus, when his administration was involved in some foul and illegal stuff-remember Iran Contra?—Reagan always came out smelling like a rose.

Who can forget the video of Reagan walking to the presidential plane or helicopter, and ABC's Sam Donaldson shouting a question, and the president would just cup his hands to his ear to say he couldn't hear. He didn't care a lick. Stuff just slid off Reagan.

He would get ripped in the press, and ol' Ronnie would just keep on smiling, basically saying, "Man, forget y'all. I'm the president. You're not. Deal with it."

Reagan was a cool cat. He was never seen sweating. Didn't snap. He would just smile and keep on stepping (That's "moving on to the next thing" for the not so cool folks).

That's exactly what Obama did the other day. He took a few jabs, smiled while doing it, and brushed off the haters.

Who would have thought that the cool bruh from Chitown would be acting more like that smooth player from Cali, Ronnie Reagan? (For the less-than-cool folks, I'll have to explain another day what's a smooth player!)

April 25, 2008

Look to NASCAR To Understand Democratic Presidential Race

IF NASCAR GOVERNED THE 2008 RACE for the Democratic nomination, this would be called "The Chase." In NASCAR, that is the period when the regular season is over and the winner of the season-ending cup championship is named based on who won the most points in "The Chase."

For Sens. Barack Obama and Hillary Clinton, they easily dispatched the likes of John Edwards, Joe Biden, Dennis Kucinich, Bill Richardson, Christopher Dodd and the others. Now it's down to both of them, and much like NASCAR's final 10 "Chase" races, Obama and Clinton are duking it out in the final 10 primary contests to see who will get the nomination.

In NASCAR, the points are reset during "The Chase," but that doesn't happen in politics. Clinton is down by a small—but large—margin. Why small? Because it's about a 1 percent difference. Why large? Because she would have to win at least 60 percent of the votes in all remaining primaries to close the gap between her and Obama in pledged delegates, and that's not going to happen.

Now what I'm befuddled by in the wake of Clinton's huge win in Pennsylvania—a victory that gave her the ability to raise $10 million in the first 24 hours afterward—is the media narrative that either candidate can't close the other out.

Frankly, it's pretty silly.

On one hand, you have Sen. Hillary Clinton, who began this campaign as the inevitable nominee. She's well-known as the former first lady; married to former President Bill Clinton; has spent 16 years on the national stage; served seven years representing New York in the U.S. Senate; and has put together an impressive campaign machine, even with all the bumps.

271

Obama? He has captured the nation's attention with his speeches and themes of hope and change; has spent eight years in the Illinois Senate and three years in the U.S. Senate; has raised in excess of $200 million; is driving plenty of new voters to the polls; and also has an impressive campaign machine, even with their inexperience showing.

But the real reason Clinton and Obama haven't been able to give one another the fatal blow and end this thing is that they are just too darn good. And they are riding shotgun over strong constituencies.

For Clinton, her base is made up of white women, elderly voters and blue-collar white voters.

For Obama, his base is made of African Americans, young voters and high-earning voters.

If you look at the exit polling of all the races from the beginning of the campaign, both individuals have been able to consistently maintain their lock on their constituencies, thereby making it harder for the other one to break loose and pull away to the finish line.

And don't look for them to do so now. Clinton and Obama will remain in a tight race going down the backstretch because they can count on the people who have brought them to where they are now. It's somewhat silly for my media brothers and sisters to act as if something magical is going to happen: Clinton will begin to take core Obama voters from him, or he will take core Clinton voters from her. Nope. Sorry. Ain't gonna happen.

So I suggest, folks, you just sit back and let this thing play out. The notion that Obama, who is leading, is somehow going to step back and allow Clinton to secure the nomination while he graciously accepts the vice presidential nod is nutty. And why would Clinton just turn her engine off when she still has a shot at overtaking Obama by persuading enough superdelegates to come to her side?

In NASCAR, you never let your foot off the pedal until you see that checkered flag waving. For the Democrats, until someone hits 2,025 delegates, you can bet these two will fight it and not leave anything in the tank.

Isn't that really a good thing?

April 28, 2008, Essence.com Blog

How Wright Won—and Lost—in 72 Hours

"WHY DON'T REV. JEREMIAH WRIGHT just sit down and be quiet? Don't he know he's hurting Sen. Barack Obama?"

If I had a nickle for every time someone has asked, e-mailed or texted me that in the last three days, I could retire.

And trust me, I get it.

Wright has had a negative impact on Obama's presidential aspirations because of the constant playing of snippets of his sermons. And many believe that his interview with Bill Moyers on PBS; his speech at the Detroit NAACP; and the appearance at the National Press Club on Monday morning is all about him.

Yes, that is all true.

But what would you do? If your 36 years in ministry was degraded, would you go and hide?

If right-wing radio and TV hacks like Sean Hannity, Lars Larson and others called you a bigot and anti-Semitic, and others who don't even realize that you served in the Marines and the Navy for six years, castigated you daily as being un-American, would you defend yourself?

Of course you would!

But there is a fine line that you must walk. And depending on how you do could determine how you are viewed and whether the presidential aspirations of Obama are severely damaged.

How HE WON

The interview with Moyers, along with the Detroit NAACP speech, were perfect opportunities for Wright.

He came across as thoughtful, smart, theologically sound, and more importantly—human—than he has in the last month. He has been unfairly portrayed as a raging lunatic, courtesy of the YouTube clips, and that's not him.

It's so much easier in a one-on-one setting to have your views heard.

Even his speech on Sunday was pretty good.

At moments funny and hilarious, Wright shone a light on our differences, and how we need to overcome them.

There is nothing wrong with having different music and worship styles. It's when we try to impose one as being superior or favored over the other. That was an excellent point he made.

I got a lot of e-mails from folks who said they saw him differently based on this, and that's always a good thing.

Even this morning's papers spoke to his message of change. He got great reviews from a variety of sources.

How he lost

I never thought appearing before the National Press Club was a good idea. I even told my radio audience a week ago that he should cancel.

One, it's not his element, and with there being questions, you never know which direction they are coming from.

Wright's opening statement was a good one, but it went all downhill from there.

The issue wasn't always just his answers. It was also how he answered them. He was too flippant, comfortable, cocky and arrogant in some of his answers. Where he should have expounded, he allowed a quip to simply end a statement. Where he should have been thoughtful, his histrionics and facial expressions led the way.

I'm sure someone will say that style over substance is silly. I concur. But Wright's style was a part of the substance, and he let it get in the way.

The one danger in being a smart ass person is that you come across as a smart ass. Wright was that way today.

Finally, he stepped on his own story! The headlines showed that his Sunday speech was well-received. Why let that moment not settle and folks get to savor it?

Now we're left with a different taste in our mouth.

Folks, perceptions matter. How people think of you, regardless of what you say, does matter.

Wright had a moment to rise above the "playing the dozens" statements and the "when they talk about your mama" rants. He could have presented himself as the learned man that he is. But he allowed the silly stuff to cloud his message.

Either his media handlers were incompetent, or he ignored them. That, folks, is a recipe for disaster.

As for Obama? Wright even more dismissed him as a politician today, and that's not good. He did his member no favor with his actions today, and Obama is going to have to bear down even more so to move beyond Wright.

If you disagree, fine. But Wright had an opportunity to elevate the conversation. His speech Sunday was damn good. But 12 hours later, that's now dismissed, and he walked into the lion's den, thought he could tame it, and got mauled.

And he has no one else to blame but himself.

May 2, 2008

What Obama Needs To Do To Move Beyond the Rev. Wright

LET'S NOT KID OURSELVES. The Rev. Jeremiah Wright was going to be a part of this presidential campaign through November, whether Sen. Barack Obama smacked his former pastor upside the head or not.

Now that he has taken the necessary steps to separate himself from Wright, Obama must go on his most vigorous offensive to date and make it clear that he is running for president, not Wright.

Sen. Hillary Clinton is doing all she can to make the case to undeclared Democratic superdelegates that Obama is a wounded duck because of Wright; that she has a better shot at winning the votes of white working-class people; and he's not tough enough to take on Sen. John McCain.

With that said, Obama is leading among the pledged delegates and the popular vote. He also has closed the gap significantly between him and Clinton in superdelegates. Bottom line: He's winning.

But now it's time for him to ratchet up his message and take back the stage from

Clinton, McCain and, of course, Wright. One way to do that is to be far more forceful in advocating his position and direction for the country. Here are a few suggestions:

Let voters know that you will be calling the shots, not Wright. I've seen e-mails from voters who say they will not vote for Obama because of Wright. The junior senator from Illinois must challenge them directly.

Tell them that Wright doesn't have a hand in keeping their homes from foreclosure.

Tell them that Wright has absolutely nothing to do with gas prices doubling under the presidency of George W. Bush.

Make it plain that your name is on the ballot, not his, and you're the guy who has the right plan to transform the country.

Have your supporters increase the book sales of Alan Greenspan. McCain said last year that the economy wasn't his strong suit and that he needed to read up on the books of the former Federal Reserve Board chairman. I would put some of those young supporters to use and have them greet McCain at every campaign stop with a copy of a Greenspan book. Even print up some Greenspan masks and hound him to death.

Then you must back up that in-your-face campaigning with an economic message that speaks to the masses, especially those blue-collar voters. Show them that the Bush tax cuts that McCain wants to continue will benefit those same business owners who are shipping their jobs overseas. Tell blue-collar voters that the hedge fund owners who are snapping up companies and slashing their jobs don't care about them and will be happy to fund the campaign of McCain.

Make the case that McCain might be a good guy, but he's more concerned about the tax bracket of his wife (she's worth in excess of $100 million) than the middle-class voters in Ohio and Pennsylvania.

They say you've got a white problem? Tell those white rural voters that voting against their economic interests is political suicide.

Make it clear to women, especially white women, that *Roe v. Wade* will be extinct if McCain wins. The next president is going to choose three Supreme Court justices. If McCain is elected president, there is no way—no way—the religious right would let him appoint people with a moderate bone in their bodies. Remember Harriet Miers? Bush even said he knew her heart, and they told him to go to hell.

What Obama has to tell those women—who are supporting Sen. Hillary Clinton in huge numbers and will be disappointed if she's not the nominee—is that sitting at home on Election Day or crossing the aisle and voting for McCain virtually ensures that a woman's right to choose what to do with her body will be taken from her.

I would run an ad slapping a large "C" for conservative on the faces of Justices John Roberts, Samuel Alito, Clarence Thomas and Antonin Scalia and make it clear that three other justices likely will step down. If McCain chooses, the new justices will vote with the conservative bloc. That is a day the abortion rights movement never wants to see.

Make college tuition a cornerstone of your campaign. You and Michelle paid off your student loans three years ago; why keep that such a secret? Hit folks over the head with it. With Sallie Mae cutting back and being more selective on student loans, parents' ability to pay for their kids to go to school is a huge issue. Push it. Hard. Don't let it be just one of many items on the list.

Convene a panel in Indiana, North Carolina and Oregon of parents and young folks, and let them express their fears about not being able to go to college and get good jobs. There isn't a parent, aunt or uncle who isn't concerned with that issue.

The war still matters. On "Larry King Live," I watched Lanny Davis, a big-time Clinton surrogate, challenge Obama's judgment on attending Wright's Chicago church for 20 years. Obama must re-engage the electorate and say that the judgment of Clinton and McCain has led to a war that has cost us 4,000 lives and billions of dollars. Those costs are real. Don't let it slide by. Ratchet up the sound. Don't let voters forget for a second that the wrong choice was made by your opponents.

A lot of folks are assuming the doom-and-gloom scenario for Obama. Everyone is saying he's toast and this race is over. But we forget that conservatives really don't love McCain, and the evangelicals aren't in love with him, either.

Go back to who you are: Mr. Change. Drive the issues home in a more forceful manner. The election is a little more than six months away, and a whole lot can happen between now and Nov. 5.

May 7, 2008, Essence.com Blog

The End Is Near for Clinton

SHE NEEDED TO BEAT SEN. BARACK OBAMA in North Carolina. She didn't.

She needed a decisive victory in Indiana. She squeaked by.

Her campaign is running out of money and she loaned herself $6.4 million last month. Not a good sign.

For Sen. Hillary Clinton, her White House ambitions are fast fading, and there isn't much she can do.

With the remaining contests offering a total of 217 delegates, and Obama picking up more superdelegates than her, Clinton is hoping—praying—that something cataclysmic happens that will get them to switch.

It was sad watching her supporter, Lanny Davis, saying the new number to win the nomination is 2,209. That's what her campaign has been pushing by including Florida and Michigan.

I had to remind Lanny that the DNC makes that decision, and right now, it's 2-0-2-5.

He didn't like it.

Clinton's campaign is clinging to anything that keeps them in the game.

But folks, barring an earth shattering event, it's over.

Her focus now is to bow out gracefully. Anything less damages the party in November.

Surely that isn't what she or her supporters want, right?

May 9, 2008

Hillary, Dems Need More Than Hardworking White Workers To Win

EXCUSE ME IF A LOOK OF BEWILDERMENT continues to cross my face when a surrogate of Sen. Hillary Clinton starts off on the we-need-hardworking-white-workers-to-win-in-November mantra. In fact, the candidate herself now has made that the primary—and latest—argument to the superdelegates in order to convince them that she's the best person to beat Sen. John McCain in November.

"I have a much broader base to build a winning coalition on," she told USA Today. They said she cited an Associated Press article "that found how Sen. Obama's support among working, hard-working Americans, white Americans, is weakening again, and how whites in both states who had not completed college were supporting (her)."

Now, I know I'm not one of those hardworking white Americans she's talking about, but the reality is that hardworking white Americans alone will not put Sen. Clinton or Sen. Barack Obama in the White House.

African Americans alone won't do it.

Young people alone won't do it.

Seniors alone won't do it.

College-educated people alone won't do it.

Nonworkers alone won't do it.

Gays and lesbians alone won't do it.

Nonreligious people alone won't do it.

Veterans alone won't do it.

Hispanics alone won't do it.

Women alone won't do it.

In fact, Democrats alone won't do it. You also must take a good portion of independents.

No Democrats can win the White House, unless they are able to pull from all the various constituencies in the country, and it's downright silly for the Clinton campaign to continue to assert that when it's all said and done, hard working white people's votes are the only votes that matter.

Sure, they'll contend that's not what they are saying. But it sure sounds that way (and no, I don't agree with what's being said on blogs that this is playing the race card).

Is Clinton suggesting that the whites who voted for Obama in Iowa, New Hampshire (where she beat him by about 8,000 votes), Missouri, Iowa, Colorado, Connecticut, Delaware, Washington state, Minnesota and so many other states were phantom voters?

Were they not hardworking white voters? Were they only the "eggheads and African Americans" who Paul Begala referred to on CNN on election night?

Look, I get spin. And I get that Clinton must figure out some kind of argument that makes sense for the superdelegates to go her way and ignore Obama's lead among pledged delegates, the popular vote and state's won. But she is ramming home this notion that hardworking white Americans somehow are the bedrock of the Democratic Party, but that's just not true.

Clinton wants to make the argument that her white working-class support in Ohio and Pennsylvania—states the Democrats need to win in November—shows she's the best choice. But one major failure in Clinton's argument is the assumption that all of the traditional Democratic constituencies will continue to offer her broad support if she's the nominee. And considering her high negatives, she can't afford any erosion. Obama could make the case that she has failed miserably in the primaries in garnering young voters and African Americans, and without them, she loses.

Not only that, the Democratic Party has a chance to expand the map beyond the battleground states of Ohio and Pennsylvania. If you look at the presidential map, Democrats have a solid shot at winning Iowa, New Mexico, Missouri, Virginia, Colorado, Nevada and New Hampshire. Of those states, Obama won four of the seven and had narrow losses in New Mexico and New Hampshire.

Small states? Sure. Winnable? Absolutely. Their electoral votes count as much as the big states.

If the Democratic Party is serious about winning, it is going to have to put on ice this notion that white working-class voters, or any other constituency, are the be-all and end-all in November. Winning the White House, no matter the candidate, is about building a true broad coalition, and how else to judge that than who has done it in the primaries? If it's Obama, he's the nominee. If it's Clinton, she's the nominee.

That should be on the mind of every superdelegate, not the debate over which ethnic group reigns supreme at the ballot box.

May 13, 2008, Essence.com Blog

As Obama Gets Closer, The Bigots Come Out

DON'T ACT LIKE YOU DIDN'T THINK this day would come.

For all the talk about racial unification of an Obama presidency, the actions of a number of folks clearly show that they don't mind showing they are true racists to the bone.

And what gets me is when they try to suggest they are not being a bigot!

Take for example Mike Norman.

He's the owner of a tavern in the Atlanta area—Cobb County to be exact—who is selling t-shirts with a photo of a monkey peeling a banana and "Obama '08" underneath.

Yes, a monkey.

But Norman tells the *Atlanta Journal-Constitution* he meant no harm using the image of the monkey, "Curious George."

"Look at him . . . the hairline, the ears, he looks just like Curious George," Norman said, even giving the proceeds to the Muscular Dystrophy Association.

That has led a number of groups to protest his bar, saying they will do everything they can to shut his business down for being such a, well, you know what.

But the situation is even more egregious when you read a story by Kevin Merida in today's *Washington Post*.

Merida talked to a number of field workers for Sen. Barack Obama who said they have had to confront all kinds of bigotry on the campaign trail.

He writes: "Victoria Switzer, a retired social studies teacher, was on phone-bank duty one night during the Pennsylvania primary campaign. One night was all she could take: 'It wasn't pretty.' She made 60 calls to prospective voters in Susquehanna County, her home county, which is 98 percent white. The responses were dispiriting. One caller, Switzer remembers, said he couldn't possibly vote for Obama and concluded: 'Hang that darky from a tree!'

"Documentary filmmaker Rory Kennedy, the daughter of the late Robert F. Kennedy, said she, too, came across 'a lot of racism' when campaigning for Obama in Pennsylvania. One Pittsburgh union organizer told her he would not vote for Obama because he is black, and a white voter, she said, offered this frank reason for not backing Obama: 'White people look out for white people, and black people look out for black people.'"

Merida also writes about an Obama campaign office in Indiana being vandalized.

For their part, the Obama campaign doesn't want to focus too much on the racism they are encountering, choosing to be positive about the inroads they are making. And they should. His candidacy is forcing people to confront the reality of race, just like Sen. Hillary Clinton has forced folks to confront the reality of gender.

But there is no doubt there are people in this country who don't want to see a black man in the White House. The exit polls in Pennsylvania showed a sizable number of people who said race was the most important factor in their decision.

And as he gets closer to the nomination, they are showing who they are.

And more than likely, these are the folks who want to hold themselves up to be the greatest patriots. Of course, they don't mind African Americans shedding blood in Iraq; entertaining them on stage; or coming to their rescue in a time of need.

This is why we all—no matter our ethnic background or skin tone—must challenge our family, friends, co-workers and church members to remove the racial veil that covers their eyes and seeing their fellow American as one of them.

May 16, 2008

Make Wearing a Flag Pin the 28th Amendment to the Constitution

WHEN IS THE LAST TIME YOU WATCHED a mindless movie that had no redeeming value on you intellectually, but it made you laugh a lot?

That perfectly describes the raging debate among voters and the rabid television and radio talk show hosts who love to yell and scream at the top of their lungs, "I'm an American, and by golly, you better show as much appreciation for this country as I do!"

But once you finish listening to these high-minded bloviators—and yes, that includes the voters who have bought into this nonsensical issue—ask yourself: Does it really have anything to do with anything?

I've watched this debate reach the level of absurdity this year because journalists and commentators have raised the question to Sen. Barack Obama, "Why don't you wear a flag lapel pin?"

I really got a kick out of that one during the ABC debate last month because not one person on stage—Sens. Hillary Clinton and Obama, along with moderators Charlie Gibson and George Stephanopoulos—bothered to accessorize his or her attire with a flag lapel pin.

Sen. John McCain has been traveling the globe as the Republican nominee, and this former soldier often doesn't wear a flag lapel pin.

It has become sort of like bird-watching, as I've surveyed elected officials on the local and national levels and looked them over like a henpecked mother or a foaming-at-the-mouth military drill sergeant, studying their attire and deeming them insufficiently American because of their lack of decency and respect by refusing to adorn themselves appropriately with lapel pins.

So after listening to radio callers and the folks who e-mail various TV shows, maybe we ought to expand this need to express our Americanism even further. Shouldn't we insist that our politicians all begin to sport red, white and blue socks so we can feel good knowing they are walking as Americans? How about asking male and female office holders to sport the American colors as undergarments in an effort to show that their undying love for the country is so important to them that they want the flag pressed against their skin.

There have been times when the candidates—especially McCain, who has beaten back skin cancer—have worn hats on the campaign trail. I want to know, datgummit, why the man and woman running for the highest office in the land didn't cover their heads with flag baseball caps to express to the nation their love and affection for the U.S. of A?

Because it is clear that our nation has been paralyzed from being unable to close our borders, feed the homeless, develop businesses in the inner cities, and save people from having their homes taken by foreclosure because of ruthless mortgage companies—all because some folks don't wear a flag lapel pin—we need to lead a national movement to demand that Congress and the states make a 28th Amendment to the U.S. Constitution, requiring office holders to wear flag lapel pins.

See, if it is so important, then take it all the way. Don't make it optional. Don't leave it up to someone to choose to wear a flag lapel pin. Let's really show those politicians that nothing is more important to us than seeing them with the U.S. flag on their chests.

That's what zealots do. They take something so simple, so personal, so voluntary and absolutely lose their minds trying to force someone else to do as they do, and everyone else be damned.

Folks, the first year I ever cast a ballot for political office was in 1988. And in the past 20 years, whether it was mayoral, school board, city council or a statewide, congressional or presidential campaign, the thought of what was on a politician's lapel never entered into the equation as to whether they were worthy of office.

Those who will criticize me will say, "Well, Roland, if it's no big deal, then why not wear one?" And the reply is the same: "If it's no big deal, then why do you make it a big deal?"

Let me tell you something. When I'm on the golf course and I slip my wedding ring into my golf bag, the Rev. Jacquie Hood Martin is still my wife. When we shoot hoops and I remove my Texas A&M University ring from my right hand, I still love my school. The fact that I no longer can wear my 1987 class ring from Houston's Jack Yates High School doesn't mean I don't cherish the crimson and gold. I may not be able to fit into the shirt in which I pledged, but I will be a member of Alpha Phi Alpha Fraternity Inc. until the day I die.

I am an unapologetic Christian, but you won't see a cross dangling from my neck or a James Avery charm bracelet on my wrist. Why? Because my love of Jesus Christ is in my heart.

This debate is useless, tiresome and distracting. Why? Because if there are members of Congress who are wearing flag lapel pins but refuse to shore up our borders, aren't doing enough to stop the flow of drugs from coming into our neighborhoods, or eradicating the gaps between the haves and the have-nots, then are they truly fighting for the concerns of Americans or playing on the emotions of people by what's on their lapels?

We're better than that. We're smarter than that. It's time that we make decisions based on substance, which is what we say we actually care about. But maybe we're just lying to ourselves about that, too.

May 20, 2008, Essence.com Blog

Spouses Are Fair Game in Presidential Race

SEN. BARACK OBAMA DIDN'T HOLD BACK in an interview with Robin Roberts of "Good Morning America" yesterday, telling his critics to back off in their criticism of his wife, Michelle.

Sen. Obama called it a "low down" move by the Republican Party in Tennessee using comments by Michelle in a campaign ad.

Obama said it's fair to come after him, but not his wife.

I understand his position, and he was right to aggressively defend his wife, but it is within the bounds to criticize her.

I've always believed that when a spouse, child or friend decides to step into the public square and campaign, they are fair game.

Vice President Dick Cheney was wrong to assert that his lesbian daughter should not be discussed in 2000 when she was on the campaign trail. Who is giving money to Bill Clinton's presidential library is a campaign issue. The Clinton camp would allow no interviews with Chelsea Clinton. That's BS. If she's going to tell voters who to vote for, she shouldn't be declared off limits. And Cindy McCain should release her tax records. Again, she's in the game.

And when you're in the game, all bets are off. Be respectful, but don't think criticism won't come your way.

May 23, 2008

Clinton To Bow Out Gracefully? Forget About It

REMEMBER ALL THOSE WRESTLING "DEATH MATCHES," during which they talked about guys tearing their opponents' heads off in the ring? We all knew wrestling is fake, but the promotion was awesome because it always sucked us in.

Lest anyone think the race for the Democratic Party's presidential nomination is going to end peacefully in June, forget about it.

Sen. Hillary Clinton will do anything and everything to win, and the idea that Sen. Barack Obama should give in to her demands to seat the Michigan and Florida delegates is ludicrous. When you're ahead, you don't concede any ground. If the roles were reversed, she would do the same.

This race, regardless of what anyone says, is still airtight. Obama has the lead among superdelegates and has garnered a majority of pledged delegates, but they always can change their allegiance, per the Democratic Party rules, and don't think for a second that the Clinton camp doesn't understand that.

Her comments to The Associated Press that she may take this to the convention in August shouldn't be dismissed. I don't think Clinton cares about the party. Last week, CNN's Suzanne Malveaux said a Clinton source told her that their focus is Clinton first and the party second.

The only way Obama can truly focus on the next step is if he does everything to get to 2,026 delegates. If he gets there first, he wins. But Clinton will go to the mat to prevent that from happening.

Everyone talks about her running in 2012 if Obama wins the Democratic nomination but loses the general election or 2016 if he wins two terms. But nothing is guaranteed. She's 60 years old. This is her best shot at winning, and she'll leave it all on the table to try to get the nomination.

In the past few days, her surrogates, and even Clinton herself, have ramped up the talk about sexism. There is little doubt that she is trying to stir the ire of her female base and push them to demand that she either be the nominee or be given the VP slot. But it's really about the former rather than the latter.

The Primaries

In Florida Wednesday, she shamelessly invoked slavery and the epic civil rights battle against Jim Crow in her quest to count the vote in Florida as is.

Forget the fact that she once said the states wouldn't matter because they broke the rules. Forget the fact that many of her supporters on the Democratic National Committee's rules committee supported the stripping of delegates in Michigan and Florida. And forget the fact that her chief supporter in Michigan, Gov. Jennifer Granholm—a Democrat—is the bonehead who signed the bill into law that allowed the state to move up its primary.

Clinton and her supporters now discount all of that and act as if they were always champions of the "disenfranchised" voters in Florida and Michigan. But they weren't. And the record is clear. Only when it became apparent that she needed the states' delegates to close the gap with Obama did she change her tune. She said one thing in Iowa and New Hampshire and now is saying something else.

The Clintonites don't want any compromises in Michigan and Florida. They want the results to stay the same, even though Obama's name wasn't on the ballot in Michigan and all candidates signed an agreement not to campaign in those two states.

But *The Wall Street Journal* and other media outlets say the Clinton camp doesn't care. Her biggest backer, former President Bill Clinton, is telling her to stay in it until the end, hoping to persuade superdelegates to switch and give her the nomination.

The DNC rules committee will meet May 31. Expect a bloodbath. Trust me; there will be nothing nice about that meeting.

The Obama camp better not let their guard down. The Clinton camp is gearing up for a protracted battle. Folks, this is for all the marbles, and feelings—and party—be damned.

Only one thing is certain: If this battle goes to Denver, the Democrats might as well dump those inauguration tickets on eBay because supporters of Sen. John McCain will need them.

May 30, 2008, Essence.com Blog
Another Pastor Problem for Obama

FIRST THERE WAS REV. JEREMIAH WRIGHT. Then there was an endorsement by Minister Louis Farrakhan.

Now Chicago priest, Father Michael Pfleger, is on the hot seat for comments he made at Sen. Barack Obama's church, Trinity United Church of Christ.

You can see the clips below, courtesy of someone in the audience recording the sermon.

Pfleger is a white priest who is very close to Rev. Wright, and is a close friend of Farrakhan. He also has been a big supporter of Obama.

What makes this truly a hot media story has nothing to do with Father Pfleger's comments. It is the fact that Sen. Barack Obama is running for president, the comments were made in the pulpit at his church, Trinity United Church of Christ, and were made by a white Catholic priest who is an ardent supporter of him.

Had Pfleger made his comments in his church, and wasn't an Obama supporter, folks would summarily ignore what he said. Look at that fool Pastor David Manning out of Harlem. He has said some of the most vile comments imaginable about Obama, even alleging a gay relationship with Rev. Wright, and although he has often appeared on conservative radio shows-and even "Hannity & Colmes" TV show-he has largely been ignored.

Pfleger made his comments during a more detailed sermon at Trinity on the day the United Church of Christ on the same day the UCC wanted to have a dialogue on race. Will there be a broader discussion on what folks think is white entitlement? Nope. This will be caught up in a major political discussion.

What I'm shocked at is how Pfleger didn't realize that even mentioning Obama, Clinton or McCain would somehow be ignored. This is nuts. Absolutely nuts. I don't get why pastors who have chosen to get involved in the political process-knowing full well the toxic mixing of race, religion and politics-would even go there.

The comments were dumb to even make, even if he thought them! Have I heard them said before by whites and blacks about Clinton? Yes! Have I heard whites say blacks feel entitled to the president? Yes! But do you say it publicly? Of course not! The e-mails I've gotten from whites, blacks, males and females that are far worse than what Pfleger has uttered would never be said by a public person who has endorsed either candidate.

If he had referenced Clinton feeling entitled to the nomination, no one would have gotten upset. Why? Because that has been discussed for months on television and radio. But the mere mention of her being entitled to the nomination because she's white? Oh, yeah, this was easy to see it would blow up.

Pfleger's statement on the matter: "I regret the words I chose on Sunday. These words are inconsistent with Senator Obama's life and message, and I am deeply sorry if they offended Senator Clinton or anyone else who saw them."

Obama's statement: "As I have traveled this country, I've been impressed not by what divides us, but by all that unites us. That is why I am deeply disappointed in Father Pfleger's divisive, backward-looking rhetoric, which doesn't reflect the country I see or the desire of people across America to come together in common cause."

May 30, 2008

We Should Be Voting on the First Saturday in November

WHILE DEMOCRATS CONTINUE TO BE EMBROILED in their ongoing war over counting votes in Florida and Michigan, everyone else seems to be focused on Nov. 5, when the nation will go to the polls to choose a new president.

But why is Election Day on a Tuesday? Why in the world do we continue to insist on voting on a weekday when we are supposed to be encouraging as many people to vote as possible?

Most of the primaries and caucuses during the past four months took place on Tuesdays, but a number went to the polls on Saturdays. This Sunday, voters in Puerto Rico will head to the polls, and many expect a record turnout. What's better than going to church in the morning then making your way to the voting booth?

Officially, Election Day is the first Tuesday after the first Monday in November (depending on the year, it could be Nov. 2 through Nov. 8). Since 1845, this has been the standard practice in this country. Congress wanted a set date to elect a president and members of Congress, and because we were an agricultural society, this was the best day for farmers in rural America to get to the polls. That made a ton of sense. Then. But a lot has changed in the past 163 years, and it's time that our Congress change this unnecessary law.

The purists are likely to argue that everyone knows that a Tuesday in early November is set aside for Election Day. So with that in mind, just leave the election in November. Sure, it makes sense to go with a month during which it's warm in nearly all of the USA, but the consistency of the month makes sense.

But why not the first Saturday in November? If that date were chosen, the majority of voters wouldn't have to worry about trying to vote before going to work, hoping and praying the lines aren't too long so they can zip in and zip out. The same thing happens in the evening. Folks have to hurry up and finish their work, interrupt meetings, and shut down whatever else they are doing and head to the polls. They are likely to confront long lines, and that discourages some folks from voting. (Now, I don't have much sympathy on this one. We'll stand in line for a concert or movie; and that surely isn't as important as electing a president!)

Saturday is already a day of leisure, and there is no doubt that more Americans would head to the polls on a traditional day off from work.

Because of the excitement generated by this year's campaign, you can bet there will be long lines at the polls, and if there are not enough ballots, we can expect all kinds of delays. Folks will grow frustrated, be afraid to show up to work late, and likely will leave and not come back.

That's just not good for democracy. This is one of those simple decisions that doesn't require a ton of debate. I can't imagine there being major opposition to moving the election date.

In 2004, 71 percent of all eligible voters were registered, according to a story by the *Carnegie Reporter*, "Election Reform: Lessons From 2004." But of that number, 60.7 percent voted.

Someone is likely to say that with the number of people voting up in 2004 from the number in 2000, that's not bad. But when we see 90 percent of voters in Iraq voting—and we are trying to instill democracy there!—it's clear that impediments to voting in the United States aren't helpful.

It would be nice to see the presidential nominees weigh in on this and pledge to change the election date. Let's see a debate moderator ask this question!

Instead of putting up barriers for people wanting to vote, we should be the most open society when it comes to giving our citizens as many options as possible to vote, and moving Election Day from a weekday to a weekend makes a lot of sense.

We can't speak of our cherished democracy around the world if we aren't willing to improve it every chance we get.

Back Story: Breaking A Big Story From the #15 Hole at Wildcat Golf Club

ANYONE WHO KNOWS ME knows that I am a golf fanatic.

I have a set of golf clubs at my place in Chicago (the "A" set); another set at my brother's home in Houston (the "B" set); and a set at my home in the Dallas area (the "C" set).

So on May 31, when the Democratic National Committee were meeting in Washington, D.C. to decide the fate of the delegates from Florida and Michigan, all eyes were glued to the contentious debate.

It had been a furious battle after the DNC chose to strip the two states of their delegates after both broke party rules and moved their primaries. Florida blamed the Republican-led legislature, even though prominent Democrats were happy to see it happen. In Michigan, they were led by Sen. Carl Levin, who had tried to do this previously, but was rebuffed by then-DNC Chairman Terry McAuliffe, who threatened to strip the party of its delegates if it made the move.

So, while The Best Political Team on Television were in New York watching the proceedings, I was in Houston visiting family. I hadn't gotten a chance to see my family much because of the election, and the respite was needed.

Roland S. Martin

My brother, Reginald, and I headed to the Wildcat Golf Club near his home in Pearland, Texas. We met up with some longtime buddies, and were having a great time. My game was up and down. Not surprising since my move to Chicago four years previously totally screwed up my golf game. That's what happens when you it's freezing seven months out of the year.

So while we were on the 15th hole, I got a call that Sen. Barack Obama and his wife, Michelle, had sent a letter to Trinity United Church of Christ and resigned from the church.

I had gotten the heads up the day before that this was coming down the pipe, but it had not been made official. It was first reported by blogger Monroe Anderson out of Chicago, and it didn't take me long to confirm the news with several sources in the Obama camp, as well as the pastor of the church, the Rev. Otis Moss III.

So, I sent an e-mail to a large listserve inside CNN alerting them of the news.

And man, did my Blackberry blow up!

This was huge news, obviously, because of all the controversy surrounding the sermons of the Rev. Jeremiah Wright.

Our political director, Sam Feist, was all over me to come on the air, and my handler, editorial producer Stephanie Kotuby, was telling me to call into the control room—NOW.

This is all happening as we hit our tee shots on the par 3, 16th hole.

So as we approached the green, I'm sitting just off the green and have a nice, slightly downhill 20-foot put for birdie. I'm trying to line the putt up, and these guys at CNN put me on hold!

I put the speakerphone on and ask my playing partner, "Hold this. If Wolf Blitzer comes on, just yell and I'll come get the phone."

So I putt, and miss the birdie. I then hear Wolf introducing the story, and I run over to get the phone. But I still have my birdie putt. While I'm breaking the story down to Wolf and the millions watching on CNN, I'm putting and sink the par shot, get my ball, and walk off the green.

Now they are blowing up the Blackberry for me to get to a studio, but I really do want to finish my round! I hate unfinished rounds of golf, but we really have no choice. So my brother and I take off, leaving our playing partners and head to the car. We go back to his home so I could change and get my rental car, and head to a studio CNN booked for me to go on the air.

Since we had a little money on the golf game, I did send an e-mail to our Washington bureau chief, David Bohrman, Sam and CNN/U.S. President Jon Klein, asking them, "Since I missed the birdie putt while reporting the story, could I invoice the $1 I lost missing the putt?"

They all laughed at that one.

But I'm still waiting on my $1, guys!

June 4, 2008

WVON-AM/Chicago: Bob Johnson on The Roland S. Martin Show

Roland Martin: Join me in the phone line right now is BET founder, Bob Johnson. Bob, good morning.

Bob Johnson: Hey Roland, how are you doing?

Roland Martin: I am doing great. First question for you Bob and that is, it has not even been 24 hours since Senator Barack Obama has won the nomination for president. He has 2,156 delegates according to the latest CNN count. Why would you come out right now saying that you are going to press the Congressional Black Caucus but choose Senator Hillary Clinton as the VP? I mean, do not you think the guy deserves a moment to at least enjoy the moment versus automatically being pressed down and choose her as VP?

Bob Johnson: Yeah, but before I point into the question, Roland, may I do what I did on CNN and first of all is to congratulate Senator Obama and his family on this historic selection as a democratic nominee? It is obviously a personal triumph for him and his family and also a historic triumph for African Americans and like in his accomplishments... in fact, this... yeah, like I would say, it is more significant than the emancipation proclamation and that simply freed millions of slaves. This is putting a chance for the offspring of slaves to become the most powerful person in the free world and will give white and black Americans to demonstrate to the world that we have the capacity to live up the challenge that Dr. King left us with and that is to judge this young man, Barack Obama as the nominated democratic party based on his commitment to leadership, his integrity, and his ability to move the nation forward, and I hope the nation will live up to that and elect him as the first African American president. Now, to your question, we... I came out and asked, and there is no pressure. There is no urging. Barack is in charge of his party not part?

Roland Martin: Right.

Bob Johnson: And he will make that decision on his own at his own choosing. As you know, there were members of the caucus on one side of the primary or members of the caucus on the other. I am simply saying that I think what we want as African Americans is not to see Barack Obama just as party nominee. We want to see him in the White House on 1600 Pennsylvania Avenue... and the best way to do it...

The best way to do that is to make sure this party comes together, Clinton supporters and Obama supporters in a unified way to bring this party together and take the White House in November.

Roland Martin: You could have even waited 24 or 48 hours to make this announcement to allow him to bask in his glory.

Bob Johnson: Roland... but Barack Obama is basking and will continue to bask in the glory of the nomination, that is... and he will do receive that. He is allover the newspapers, allover the globe. He will be heralded for what he has accomplished and I will be the first to say it. I will say it on CNN. I was a democrat long before I was a Clinton supporter, long before I knew Obama and I will be a democrat when he is an elected president. I will be a democrat after that, because... and I believe that there is a need for this unity, but the real issue Roland... we know... you say we have time for basking...

Roland Martin: Yeah, we do... I mean, this is only... this is only June....

Bob Johnson: But we... we do not have...

Roland Martin: Bob, Bob, Bob... it is June 4th. I understand that. It is June 4th. He has got the number of delegates. I mean, all I am simply saying is, how is it the day after this historic win by Senator Barack Obama and the banner across CNN right now is you going on CNN talking about the Congressional Black Caucus is going to press Obama to choose Clinton as VP.

Bob Johnson: Yeah, Roland, see now... you are not being fair to me. You heard me on CNN and you... understood clearly. I did not say the word press Johnny King said press, I said urge. I said encourage.

Roland Martin: Okay.

Bob Johnson: So you are journalist. So now, be fair to me. So I said encourage. Barack Obama is going to make the decision as to what is in the best interest for his, as I said on television, not only for his election effort, but also for his government effort, and so, when you say we do have time. Well, the point is, there is a great urgency out there in this country. You have got $4. People facing $4 a gallon of gas, they do not want to have people waiting to solve that problem.

Roland Martin: I agree.

Bob Johnson: People who have kids dying in Iraq do not want to wait until we can figure out what this is… they want to know that we are going to have the best team the democrats can muster to win in November, so we can do something about Iraq, so we can do something about healthcare, so we can do something about high gas prices, so we can do something about putting more African Americans to work, and putting [overlap]…

Roland Martin: And Bob, if that is the case… if all of that is the case, then why did not Senator Clinton concede last night as a pole to say "I am going to keep fighting, I am going to keep going, and I want you guys to e-mail me and to let me know what you think I should do."

Bob Johnson: Now, Roland you got it… you are missing the messages…

Roland Martin: No, no, no… I hear you.

Bob Johnson: Senator Clinton…

Roland Martin: I heard the messages… I know what you mean last night.

Bob Johnson: Senator Clinton was talking to her supporter. She said some terrific things about the race that Barack Obama has won. She acknowledged his historic achievement. The simple thing she did not do was shut down the campaign, but we all know the fact that this election... primary election is over. Barack is the nominee. I went on television with the senator's awareness and blessings to say I want to move towards bringing this party together, and that is bringing about a unity ticket. So, I think if you get caught up in the theater, sure she wanted to have her last stand in the sun and maybe, what you are saying is you should have just turned out the lights last night.

Roland Martin: No, no... I mean, I think... Bob, come on. I think when... when you keep... when you keep on pressing the argument, that you are the stronger candidate, that you want more electoral count in the states, and that you want people to ride in, then they will know what you should do next, I mean... that sounds like you should try to campaign. The bomb blast is here. I absolutely agree that in order for the democrats to win, they are going to have to have a unified party, but the reality is this. It is that you cannot be in a situation where you have Clinton supporters out there who are angry, who are upset, and you even remotely give the impression that she is pushing them on to do that. Last night, even in her speech, folks start chanting, Denver, Denver, Denver, and she did not say "No, that is not party unity" it went on, and I just do not think...

Bob Johnson: But Roland, I am trying... here is what I trying to... I am trying to get people to stop fighting yesterday's battle.

Roland Martin: All right.

Bob Johnson: The battle is tomorrow and I posted this question, I posted it to the members of the caucus, and I posted it every time. If you have the certainty of wining, if you have the certainty of winning, why would not you move towards certainty... I mean, you...

Roland Martin: Well, first of all... Bob, Bob, Bob... you and I both know there is no... Bob, there is no certainty of winning here, because like it or not, you still have hot negative ratings, you still have the fact that she can indeed fire up the GOP base, there is no certainty in politics, because if that was a certainty in politics, Senator Obama would not be the nominee today because everybody is saying that Clinton was the inevitable candidate, so it certainty does not exist in politics.

Bob Johnson: Well, I will tell you, that certainty does not exist in anybody in the world, but if you got to move closer towards certainty, I believe fundamentally that if you put Obama at the... with Obama as the nominee, Hillary as vice president, Hillary brings those 18,000,000 votes that she brought to the democratic party. She brought those... the working class, white voters, she brings the seniors and elderly voters, she brings the Hispanic voters, she brings the people who have been supporting her. You amass that with Barack Obama's young people, with the independent, that is the closest thing to a slam dunk as Michael Jordan and Scottie Pippen were on the Bulls team.

Roland Martin: Well, I will say this to you. If there is one thing though I think in order for that to happen, Senator Clinton plays a critical role in being able to lower the volume, and she has to be able to show that she is willing to step back and allow his moments in the sun and recognize that he has indeed won, so how fast she closes this campaign out and profess this unity will say a lot.

Bob Johnson: I think that is going to be a nonissue. I think he will close this campaign out very shortly. If it is not today, within a short time after that because what Senator Clinton wanted to do was I said... to give a final salute and farewell to those people who were with her, to just as Obama would do is a really tough time in the campaign and doing and dealing with all the issues he had to deal with. She has to go and deal with all the issues, so she wanted a time. Her small sunlight on her face to thank her campaign supporters and everything else, she has now done that. It is over. She and Obama are probably going to be speaking to each other today in Washington at the Israeli event, the APEC event. They have... I have been in contact with Obama supporters who have told me personally that Obama would welcome a call from Senator Clinton at any time, any place, would love to meet with her at any time and place. These two historic candidates are saying to us as surrogates and us as passionate supporters, we have made history and we have another shot at making greater history, and that is why I say the ultimate end-game here is not for millions of us to celebrate just the tremendous historic achievement of Senator Obama as the nominee, that is winning the playoff championship.

Roland Martin: I got you.

Bob Johnson: You really want to win... you really want to win the Super Bowl and the Super Bowl that is in November, when we beat John McCain and he is the first black man to walk in and have the power of the whole free world in his hand...

Roland Martin: I got you... it just...

Bob Johnson: That can happen I believe when this unified ticket comes together. That is what I thought it could happen.

Roland Martin: Well, I got you… but at some point, she will have to get off the stage and allow him to be able to make his own decision.

Bob Johnson: You know what Roland, I will call her right now and say that she has to…

Roland Martin: Call her right… you call her right now… you call her right now and say the fastest way to unify…

Bob Johnson: I believe… you understand exactly what you are saying. A lot of these… some of these is theater, you know it as well as I. Some of it is theater, some of it is jacking and posturing, and again the good thing about it is, what I have observed of Barack Obama and both Senator Hillary Clinton, they know how to do the two step and do timing to step back and move forward. So I think that is in process now and like I said, whether Senator Obama select Hillary Clinton or not, I would be happy to think he should, but while he selects her or not, I can assure you…

Roland Martin: I do not think he will.

Bob Johnson: Well, I would like to say… I do not know… I do hope he will but…

Roland Martin: I do not think he will, and then trust me, that speech last night did not help Bob.

Bob Johnson: Well, like I say…

Roland Martin: Did not help.

The Primaries

Bob Johnson: It really depends on how he and she... say, I do not know if they are having it back down and with the talks already and he is telling him, "Senator Obama, I am going to have to say this" and he said "I understand Hillary" and he says...

Roland Martin: No... Bob, I can say it right now. I do not think that was a single discussion about that speech last night.

Bob Johnson: Yeah, I would not know, but I would like...

Roland Martin: I could see. I do... I do...

Bob Johnson: What I am saying is...

Roland Martin: I mean, Bob... I do, I know...

Bob Johnson: Okay, well... I am sure you do. I mean, you have been very close to him but I have been close to her and I do know her heart is in winning in November with Senator Obama at the top of the ticket. She will do it with whether she is the vice president or not, Hillary Clinton will help Senator Obama and fight for him as hard as she fought for her own primary nomination. I can assure you that regardless of whether she is at the ticket or some other person is selected at the ticket, but I will say this, have you... can you think about this from a philosophical standpoint, when a historical moment occurs and an African American comes to the top, the pinnacle of political power in a party, and he looks at what the significance of this, there is something in his mind and say "Where is the other class of people who have suffered the way my people have, who have been discriminated, who have been faced with...."

Roland Martin: Oh, he had been talking about Native Americans a lot of times.

Bob Johnson: Why could not you... why could not you say what would the world say if a black man reached out and grabbed a woman and said...

Roland Martin: A white woman... a white woman...

Bob Johnson: A woman...

Roland Martin: I got you.

Bob Johnson: We are above race...

Roland Martin: Oh no, well... well, now come on. Now, you know...he can grab a woman.

Bob Johnson: We are above... [overlap]

Roland Martin: No, no, no, no... I am just stating that he is the black man and she is the white woman. Bob, I understand your point. I understand your point.

Bob Johnson: [Overlap] a black man and a white woman sharing the power of the greatest nation on the globe.

Roland Martin: No, no, no Bob. Here is the deal... here is the deal. This is not the Apprentice where Donald Trump... actually brother will you share being the apprentice. No, this is not sharing power. He is the... he is the presidential nominee. She has to take a bet... and see Bob, that is my point right there. I have got Clinton supporters who e-mailed me who see this is power sharing. No... if he is the presidential nominee, he will be president, she will be VP.

Bob Johnson: Yeah, no... believe me... I did not say that...

Roland Martin: They say no co-presidency. Okay, I mean...

Bob Johnson: There is no such thing as co-president. There is only president.

Roland Martin: All right.

Bob Johnson: What I am talking about is this is a unique historical moment that can be even may more so, if two things happen, Barack Obama moves from this conversation of being a nominee to the other conversation, we will have January 20th and he is the president, then that is what I am aiming for, and I think the best to do that, the absolute and certain way to do that is to combine his forces with Hillary's forces, his inspiration with Hillary's inspiration and his courage and her leadership together for the democratic party against McCain.

Roland Martin: I say, well Bob, give her a call and tell her to get the hell off the stage, begin to repair those bridges, stop campaigning for the VP and then you might see that. Well I guess they are publicly pressuring Obama choose her to VP is the quickest way for him to say no.

Bob Johnson: You cannot pressure... you cannot pressure a man who has all of the power of decision making. You cannot pressure that.

Roland Martin: Okay, how about that...

Bob Johnson: You cannot fight with somebody.

Roland Martin: Well, you got Lanny Davis, a Clinton supporter talking about launching a petition drive to get Obama to choose. That to me sounds like pressure.

Bob Johnson: That sounds silly to me, but when I....

Roland Martin: Well why do not you call Lanny and tell her.

Bob Johnson: I just want your [overlap] to be clear. What I did was to urge and encourage.

Roland Martin: So you urge. Okay, alright.

Bob Johnson: Urge and encourage. There is no pressure... but Barack Obama knows that Charlie was for Hillary. Barack Obama knows that there are other caucus members. There is Jim collaborating over him. He knows that, so he has got to be... he has to recognize that they have different opinions about what they like... who they like to see if it is on the bottom of the ticket.

Roland Martin: So I take it... I take it...

Bob Johnson: and all I am asking them to do is to make that known to him about what they are thinking and at the end of the day, the next president of the United States, Barack Obama, has to make that decision and he will have to make in any critical decision years ahead.

Roland Martin: All right. I take it. You are the cut your check to the Obama campaign huh?

Bob Johnson: I have got... you know what?

Roland Martin: Yeah?

Bob Johnson: I will tell you something... if Senator Obama knows this, that when he first arrived in Washington, Bill Gray and I held the first fund raiser for Senator Obama and my restaurant in D.C.

Roland Martin: Yeah, but this campaign... you know Bob, you are going to write a big check this time now, you know that do not you?

Bob Johnson: You know what, if I am one of those people, then why do people call me and they say "that is where the money is", so.

Roland Martin: Yeah, you are going...

Bob Johnson: I am used to having people asking me for money and I believe you just stay to give. I mean, I think the most important thing to do is to make sure that all of us are united.

Roland Martin: Alright. Bob Johnson. I appreciate it. Thanks a bunch.

Bob Johnson: Alright man, take care.

June 4, 2008

Obama Insiders: Clinton "Unlikely" VP Pick

AS SEN. BARACK OBAMA ANNOUNCED his vice presidential search team today, campaign insiders say it is "unlikely" that Sen. Hillary Clinton will be one of the top names that will be chosen to be considered by the Democratic nominee.

Obama previously announced that Democratic Party honcho Jim Johnson will head his selection team. But two other members have been named to the selection committee: Caroline Kennedy, daughter of former President John F. Kennedy and

Eric Holder, a former top official in the Justice Department under President Bill Clinton. I've been told they will be "equal" members of the committee.

As supporters of Sen. Clinton make the case that she should be the vice presidential pick, sources inside the Obama camp say it's highly "unlikely" that she will be chosen.

The criteria for who would make for a good running for mate for Obama has yet to be fully established, but some of the traits the campaign desires is total buy-in to the vision of the candidate, namely his desire to be a change agent; and a "total" team player.

"But everyone is confident that she will work with Barack to bring the party together, whether she's VP or not," said a knowledgeable Obama campaign source.

If you read between the lines, what does that mean? Clinton will not be the vice presidential nominee. She won't be considered; won't be on the short list; and doesn't stand a chance of running with Obama in November.

June 4, 2008, Essence.com Blog

Oprah "Doing the Happy Dance" About Obama's Historic Victory

THERE HAS BEEN A LOT OF SPECULATION as of late that Oprah Winfrey has been cautious about being involved in the campaign of Sen. Barack Obama because white women have been angry at her for the decision to back him.

Not true, according to her best friend, Gayle King.

So after e-mailing her, and notifying her that media organizations were saying that she had no comment on his victory, her publicist released the following statement: "I'm euphoric, I've been doing the happy dance all day. I'm so proud of Barack and Michelle and what this means for all of us...the new possibilities for our country. And if he wants me to, I'm ready to go door to door."

Back Story: Vice President Hillary Clinton? "Highly Unlikely"

WHEN SEN. BARACK OBAMA AMASSED ENOUGH delegates to claim the Democratic presidential nomination on June 3, it really was a monumental moment. Here was the guy nobody gave a snowball's chance in hell of winning, and he had beaten the "inevitable" nominee—Sen. Hillary Clinton.

She was thought to have had the money, team, and pedigree—she was, after all, the former first lady and her husband, President Bill Clinton, was the most popular Democrat in the nation—but none of that mattered. Obama was giving the winning speech, while she gave a defiant and confusing speech.

And boy, did that set the Obama folks off!

The moment she told her supporters to e-mail her and query as to what she should do next in her campaign, we all looked at each other on the CNN set and were like,

"What the hell is she doing?"

It was clear that the campaign was over and she had lost. But some of her hardcore supporters just didn't believe Obama stood a chance of winning in November. They said he was soft and wasn't tough enough to withstand the ferocious GOP attack dogs. They said that Clinton had withstood their best and survived. And yes, him being black was a part of the equation. They felt America was not going to put a black man (even though he is really half-white) in the White House.

So when she finished that speech, no one knew what was next. Would she embark on a floor fight at the Democratic National Convention? Would she really take this all the way to a bloody battle and force a vote, calling in every chip she and her husband could muster?

As journalists, it was one helluva story, and we would play the sucka to the hilt.

The Obama campaign was putting out the smart political talking points, saying

Hillary Clinton would be on anyone's vice presidential short list. But on the afternoon of June 4, I knew she would never get close to being on the same ticket with Obama.

As I sat in my CNN office on the seventh floor, I was working the phone, talking to a variety of sources in the Obama and Clinton camps, when one of my solid Obama contacts called me with some news.

"It's highly unlikely that Hillary will be his VP pick," I was told. In fact, the source told me that the real answer was "there is no way in hell she's on the ticket," but they convinced Obama to give a more palatable political answer.

He had hit the roof after hearing her speech Tuesday's night.

"You have no idea how angry he is," I was told by the source.

Other Obama sources told of a similar story. Mr. Calm, Cool and Collected just couldn't believe that he did all he was supposed to do to win, and here was Clinton still refusing to get off the stage.

The situation was made worse when not even 12 hours after he claimed victory, BET founder Bob Johnson, a staunch supporter of Clinton, released a letter he wrote to members of the Congressional Black Caucus, asking them to push Clinton as Obama's VP choice.

That also angered the Obama camp, and it was clear this was going to be a long, hot summer.

Man, this was a great "get" for me. As journalists, we all like scoops. I knew where my information came from, who authorized the information to be released, and was confident I wouldn't be wrong about it. I was 100 percent sure Clinton would not be on the ticket.

This was *the* question everyone was trying to get answered, and I had it on lock.

I immediately posted the news on my Essence.com blog, and quickly dialed up WVON, where Cliff Kelley was on the air with his afternoon drive show.

There was nothing speculative about what I had. I knew where it came from, I know who authorized it, and I knew it was flat out the truth.

The next day, the *Wall Street Journal* had a front page, above the fold story with the headline essentially saying Clinton "highly unlikely" to be VP.

On August 23, 2008, Obama officially unveiled Sen. Joe Biden as his vice presidential running mate.

"Yes, We Can": Obama's Victory Makes Parents' Admonition a Reality

FOR YEARS, BLACK QUARTERBACKS could run and pass with the best of them.

Yet when it came to Division I-A colleges—called "the big white schools" by African Americans—they were ignored, having to showcase their skills at black colleges. If they were recruited, coaches would move them to the wide receiver or safety positions, and the implication was often that they didn't have the smarts to run the teams.

It really wasn't until the 1990s that it was the norm in college, rather than the exception, to see black quarterbacks regularly under center.

Today we can turn on the TV and see the likes of Vince Young, Donovan McNabb, Byron Leftwich, Daunte Culpepper, David Garrard and so many others doing what they do best in the NFL on Sundays.

See, when one makes it through the door, what was the exception eventually can become the norm.

Jackie Robinson proved that, as well, with Major League Baseball in 1947.

The parents of those college quarterbacks, Robinson and others often would tell their children that if they studied hard, worked hard and kept their noses clean, they could be anything they wanted to be.

Even president of the United States.

Black children for years would hear that, write essays in school saying how they want to be president, and live that dream.

Oh, how painful it must have been for their parents to say those words knowing full well in the back of their minds that it likely wasn't going to happen.

But that all changed Tuesday night.

When Sen. Barack Obama stepped on that stage at the Xcel Energy Center in St. Paul, Minn., that dream deferred for so many became a living reality, and tears were flowing all across the nation.

Bishop T.D. Jakes, not one prone to spend a lot of time commenting on political issues, wrote in a CNN.com column that he got "goose bumps" by seeing Obama claim the Democratic nomination for president of the United States.

Oprah Winfrey, who caught a lot of heat during the primary for backing Obama, said, "I'm euphoric. I've been doing the happy dance all day. I'm so proud of Barack and Michelle and what this means for all of us ... the new possibilities for our country. And if he wants me to, I'm ready to go door to door."

Sen. Barack Obama's clinching of the Democratic presidential primary, winning states east and west, north and south, clearly means that African American parents today truly can look their children in the eye and not hope their words of "yes, you can" will ring true one day, but know for certain that that barrier has been broken.

Sure, winning the primary is far different from winning the general election, but being one of the final two standing is an incredible achievement.

There will be many people who say, "Please, don't focus on his race. That's not how he won."

And they are 100 percent correct, despite Geraldine Ferraro's many ridiculous attempts to suggest he is where he is because he's African American.

But we can't ignore the reality that a major barrier was broken June 3, 2008, and what a joy it was to see history made.

Had Sen. Hillary Clinton won, we would be speaking of the same historical significance and reveling in how far we have come as a nation.

What also is gratifying to those who support Obama is that no one can put an asterisk by his name or even try to suggest that affirmative action—except for Ferraro, some hateful Clinton supporters and those on the political right—was the cause.

He began the campaign in the same position as Sens. Clinton, Christopher Dodd and Joe Biden, Gov. Bill Richardson, John Edwards and the others. The game says you must raise the money, build your team, travel to every state in the nation, and convince the voters that you're the best choice.

Nothing was handed to him. He didn't get to cut corners. The rules were simple: The first one to 2,026 wins the nomination. (Of course, that was changed to 2,118.)

And that's exactly what he did.

Obama has assured his place in history. But for the 46-year-old junior senator from Illinois, I'm sure the only history he's thinking about now is being called the 44th president of the United States

Reflections: The View From the Campaign Trail

TATYANA ALI

"I was in Philly. We were registering voters at a club, at a nightclub and one of the guys at the nightclub started breaking down and crying because of his own personal experiences, and we were trying to get him to vote and he just felt like it was not important and we just talked to him one-on-one as peers, people of the same age, and he started crying and talking about all of his experiences in his life and why he thought that the government couldn't work for him. It was incredible."

HOLLY ROBINSON-PEETE

"In Philadelphia, we walked the streets. We went to barber shops, and we're from Philly, so we went down there and we did a lot of great on-the-ground support. And then Rodney hosted a party in North Carolina where we had some good friends from Charlotte—our Carolina Panther base. He went down there and got our Carolina folks round up and he hosted a party there.

"And then of course, we were on and present with the campaign for everything that they did out in Los Angeles because we were here. We were very involved, not just monetarily, but we were as involved as we could be with our crazy schedule, four kids, and having to travel and what not, but we were there and we felt like the victory was part ours too. We felt like we shared it."

CHRIS TUCKER

"I went down to the Myrtle Beach (South Carolina) to the debate down there and I went to the schools. I went to, like, a couple of schools down in South Carolina, colleges, and it was just—man, it was like being on tour with like a comedy tour where the fans are excited. Every school we went to, they were waving and they were just—the energy was just crazy because everybody was excited about the possibility of Barack Obama becoming president and they just felt like it was happening and everybody was ready for a change and ready for something new. So I went to a few colleges and I did a lot of phone calls on the radio."

BLAIR UNDERWOOD

"Because I'm from Virginia, I went to Virginia. I went to a few headquarters and did some canvassing up and down I-95. My parents live in Petersburg, Virginia, so I went to our hometown, did some canvassing in the neighborhood, did some radio, went to the headquarters, did a lot of phone calls, just the phone banks, just getting people out and calling people out to get there and vote. I also did a local calls in New Jersey for the day of the general election. So I just started plugging wherever I could."

SPIKE LEE

"I was doing what I felt needed to be done. It's not like I was speaking on behalf of this campaign. I was independent you know.

"But there were just too many things that happened; this could not have just been circumstance. This thing was ordained, and I knew that at the same time it was not going to be cakewalk. But it wasn't easy. What is easy? Anything we have done as a people, it's been anything but easy? Destiny brought us here… to this country from Africa. It has never been easy and we have always had to make do with what we got. Make a lot from a little. You know, when things get a little rocky, they want to jump ship and start panicking. Obama was so cool. He kept telling people from the beginning from the get go, 'Do not get too happy, do not get the big head,' do not get you know, like in New Hampshire. People are ready like to commit suicide. It is not going to happen and then to think the white man ain't going to make it happen. The white man ain't going to let it happen. This thing was too big to be stopped."

KEVIN LILES

"I think it was Florida and it was pouring down raining and you would think that people will not stand in line, but people just stood there in the pouring rain, and we went out and said, if they can stand there to vote, we have to go out and encourage them to keep standing. You can either see history, or you can make history, and that's what we were doing was making history man."

Erika Alexander

"I was a national surrogate as well for Hillary and I went all over for her. I was the only surrogate they sent to Montana. (Black folks) were whispering to me, 'Don't wake up on the wrong side of history', and I thought, 'How dare they?' I thought that they thought that they were right and to had the moral high ground over me. They thought, I think, that we were turning away from history and what our ancestors had fought for.

"But I thought the opposite. I thought (the Rev. Dr. Martin Luther) King had taken a bullet for my content of character, not color of skin. I live in Hollywood so race is always around me, especially race and gender, so I tried to ignore them both. And in fact, I did ignore them both. I didn't care about her gender. I thought that was a bonus like I thought Barack Obama's skin color was a bonus. But I didn't think that's what I should look for or why I should support somebody."

Common

"I actually did some work really close to Election Day where I went to his campaign headquarters and made a lot of calls. I also did that for radio stations when it was getting close to that time. Every show I would do, whether it was at college or a public festival, I would campaign. I would mention Obama and say we got to go out and support. The campaign was grassroots on my end.

"When I was overseas a year ago, every question they asked me in an interview was about Obama. It was nothing about the music."

Hill Harper

"Since I was born in Iowa and my family goes back many generations in Iowa, the campaign wanted me to do most of my surrogate work there. We put all of our aces in Iowa's basket and that is what folks do not talk about in my opinion.

"Michelle Obama actually made that point where she said, 'Hey, it is Iowa or nothing,' and everybody said 'she was nuts,' but in retrospect, she was on the money.

"We spent so much time there to the point his family moved down there during the whole Christmas holiday. As a surrogate, I got to work all over that state that state and I really took Iowa personally, meaning I felt like I had to deliver Iowa. I felt like it was my thing and so I spent a great deal of time there and on caucus night, they assigned everyone to different areas in Iowa to work different caucuses and I got assigned to work Waterloo where there is a decent African American population.

"There is not a huge African American population in Iowa anyway, but there are some pockets and Waterloo is one. I went to work the caucus there and there was just so much chaos directing people to the right room…there was a lot of confusion.

"I think there was a lot of purposeful confusion to be quite honest by the State Democratic Party, which did not necessarily support our candidate, but supported a different candidate, and it was great to have so many people on the ground.

"As soon as we knew they are counting, as soon as we knew they were done, we were educating people on how to not leave your area and to recruit other people into your area, and we were educating people on how caucuses actually work. As soon as that was over, I jumped in the car with the staff and we started driving toward Iowa City and…just trying to get a sense of what was going on in the state through AM stations and the little localities.

"The small little towns were the first to start reporting locally and when we started to see that, we weren't very far behind even in the small little rural areas. We were like, we know we are going to get this, and I started to get more and more excited, starting to hear more numbers.

"By the time I got to the convention center in Iowa City…I went down into the bottom room and Obama got down there and the announcement was made that we won. He walked up to me and I looked him in the eye and I said, 'We did it. We are going to win this thing. We are going to win this thing.' He looked me in the eye and he said, 'We are going to win this thing,' and I said something like, 'We finished this thing strong.' And he says, "That is right. I am a strong finisher. Everybody is a strong finisher. We did this."

"I felt like there was no question in my mind that he was going to be the next president of the United States."

PART 3

THE GENERAL
ELECTION CAMPAIGN

The Shameful Sliming of Michelle Obama

I CAN'T STAND PUNK MEN who lay hands on women.

Any man who finds the need to hit a woman should make it his mission to stand up to a man and see what happens. Go *mano a mano* and then we can determine how big and bad you are.

When I examine the pathetic and sordid attempts of the Hate Barack Obama forces to malign and slime his wife, they all fit in that category. And instead of reveling in their pathetic behavior, every stand-up person should blast them at every turn.

In case anyone has forgotten, when voters go to the polls in November, they will be voting for either Sen. John McCain or Sen. Barack Obama. Cindy McCain won't be on the ballot, and no one will be voting on the policies of Michelle Obama.

But when you listen to some of these righteous conservative blowhards, you would think that Michelle Obama is the one who soon will pick a vice presidential running mate and stand before the Democratic Party in Denver and accept their nomination for president.

Don't misunderstand me; I have long maintained that people who go on the campaign trail and openly campaign for someone should be willing to face media scrutiny based on what they have to say. During the primary season, the Clinton campaign was dead wrong to have Chelsea Clinton stumping for her mom while she was treated as if she was still a teenager in the White House who needed to be shielded from the press. In 2000 and 2004, Dick Cheney and his wife, Lynne, were angry at the mere mention of their lesbian daughter, but when she was on the road speaking on behalf of Cheney and George W. Bush, it was absolutely acceptable for folks to question the Cheneys' views on homosexuality and public policy.

Yet what we are seeing right now from some conservatives and liberals is downright disgraceful, and it shows their lack of a moral compass.

Take, for instance, this whole discussion about "The Tape."

All this crap started with a Hillary Clinton supporter, Larry Johnson, who wrote an item saying the Republicans have a videotape showing Michelle Obama speaking in a derogatory fashion about whites. Then we saw the shock jock Mancow Muller, who wouldn't know what journalism was if it slapped the fool in the face, go on the Fox affiliate in Chicago and swear that the tape exists and will be released.

Even bumbling idiots such as Rush Limbaugh have openly discussed the contents of the tape, but there is one huge problem: It doesn't exist!

For all the bluster, blog postings of detailed transcripts and such, no one has come forward and produced the tape. Some have said it is being held as an October surprise by the GOP, but don't you think that if all of these nut jobs actually had seen the tape, someone would have leaked it to YouTube or the favorite channel of the conservative hate crowd, Fox News Channel, so that little ball of hate, Sean Hannity, could play it ad nauseam?

Without the evidence, this is an absolute lie, and any cable news network should order their anchors, reporters and producers not to allow this shameful rumor—and others that are false—to be mentioned on their networks.

This is the kind of despicable politics that people are tired of. Here is an accomplished woman who is tough, strong and smart, and they resort to such tactics just to try to bring her husband down.

Again, if she were the nominee, go at her full blast (within reason), but she's not; her husband is.

What I would like to see are these same God-loving conservatives stand up to the forces of hate on their side and tell them that their actions are not those of Christlike folks, but political terrorists. And yes, if there are political terrorists on the left who would make up lies about Cindy McCain, then they should be exorcised from our lives, as well. Call them out publicly; denounce them; and hold them up to ridicule and shame for their actions.

Civility is important, whether it's on the job or in a presidential campaign. We can hold candidates, their spouses and surrogates responsible for misstatements, contradictory proposals, or hypocrisy, but when we see the outright fabrication of events, any decent person should speak out forcefully against these political terrorists.

We had better take a stand now because if they are allowed to run amok in June, only God knows what despicable things they will say in the fall.

June 20, 2008

Obama Opting Out of Public Financing a Win for Him and McCain

WHEN IS THE MOST RECENT TIME A DECISION by a presidential candidate ended up being good for him and his opponent?

That is certainly the case with Sen. Barack Obama's decision Thursday to become the first candidate since public financing went into effect in 1976 to make the bold move of opting out of it.

The move is a huge help to Sen. John McCain because McCain has cast himself as the fierce independent who is all about reform, even to the point of opposing President George W. Bush on key initiatives. By Obama ceding ground on this issue, Obama goes against all of the signals he sent for many months on the issue of public financing of campaigns.

Obama made the decision in a video message sent to his supporters, and it didn't take long for the McCain campaign to jump all over Obama, decrying it as the clearest indication that the junior senator from Illinois is not the breath of fresh air that he has portrayed himself to be.

"Today, Barack Obama has revealed himself to be just another typical politician who will do and say whatever is most expedient for Barack Obama," McCain communications director Jill Hazelbaker said in a statement. "The true test of a candidate for president is whether he will stand on principle and keep his word to the American people. Barack Obama has failed that test today, and his reversal of his promise to participate in the public finance system undermines his call for a new type of politics." Obama's declaration in the past now allows McCain to call himself the candidate who is prone to keeping his word and not making the politically smart move. Don't be surprised to see McCain make this decision a significant part of his campaign, and he and his surrogates will hammer Obama repeatedly between now and November on the one issue that the senior senator from Arizona has made his calling card.

How does this help Obama? Easy: He likely will blow McCain away when it comes to fundraising, giving him a huge advantage in the fall election. Obama would have been absolutely nuts to accept public financing because that would have meant he would have been able to spend only $85 million. He already has raised nearly $275 million, and he will have the resources to dwarf McCain. No one thought he would be able to raise such vast sums of money, but with 1.5 million donors contributing to his campaign, he has amassed a formidable operation.

Had Obama stuck to his guns and accepted public financing, McCain's team would have lauded him publicly but laughed him off as a naive fool for doing so. And his fellow Democrats would have berated him to no end for taking away a victory in the one area they have lagged behind Republicans for years: fundraising.

This is a cat-and-mouse game, similar to McCain's decision this week to back offshore oil drilling in the United States despite years of saying he was against it. He knows it could backfire against him by making him appear to be a flip-flopper, but McCain hopes the voters will put the $4-a-gallon gas concerns over the long-term opposition to the drilling.

Obama's risky move could severely tarnish the image he has burnished of being a different kind of politician. Hard-core Democrats will welcome the decision, but independents might have a problem with it. He's hoping voters will accept his position that the Republican attack machine will blast him with unregulated funds. Obama also hopes that voters will take to his decision not to take funds from Washington lobbyists or political action committees.

Running for president is about taking risks. We'll soon see who was right in this area.

James Dobson Is *Not* an Evangelical Leader

DR. JAMES DOBSON, FOUNDER OF FOCUS ON THE FAMILY, is in the news as of late for ripping Sen. Barack Obama over a 2006 speech dealing with faith and public policy.

My issue isn't the speech or Dobson's criticism. I want to know why in the world we in the media keep holding Dobson up as an influential Christian leader or evangelical leader when the guy says with his own mouth that he is nothing of the sort?

In a radio interview discussing the speech, Dobson was critical of Obama for saying: "And even if we did have only Christians in our midst, if we expelled every non-Christian from the United States of America, whose Christianity would we teach in the schools? Would it be James Dobson's or Al Sharpton's?"

Dobson took offense to that and made this interesting comment: "I am not a reverend. I'm not a minister. I'm not a theologian. I'm not an evangelist. I'm a psychologist. I have a Ph.D. in child development from the University of Southern California. And there is no equivalence to us."

Yeah. I had the same reaction you likely did. Here is a guy who is often declared a religious leader who now says: "Nope. Not me."

Now, if the guy who is held up as an evangelical leader says he's not, then why do we even care what he has to say about religion? Why even play up his reaction to an Obama speech—or even his criticism of McCain—in a religious discussion, when that's where it shouldn't be?

This is part of the problem when religious conservatives and nonreligious conservatives try as mightily as they can to roll moral issues, family values and religious values all into one ball.

They are not.

For instance, the Rev. Jerry Falwell was the leader of the Moral Majority, which advocated a host of "moral" issues that didn't have a particular religious bent. This has been seen as a Christian movement, but you can be a moral person and not be a Christian.

Later, the Rev. Pat Robertson launched the Christian Coalition, which was much more religiously focused than anything before.

In the past few years, we've seen Dobson—by virtue of his radio show on Christian radio stations, columns and Web site—be seen as a major figure in the religious movement. But he's not, and it's about time that we stop associating him that way.

There are a number of people in this country who are religious and who choose not to identify themselves with either of the major political parties. And this is one of the reasons. The commingling of "family values" with religion seems to provide certain groups with a sort of authoritarian voice on such issues when they don't deserve the platform.

It's fine to call Dobson a family values leader, if you will. But don't insult those individuals in the faith community who are truly ministers, reverends, theologians and evangelists. They've earned it.

Dobson's just a psychologist with a doctorate in child development. So his views on religion are just his; he's not a faith leader of millions.

July 11, 2008
The Rev. Jackson Owes God, Not Obama, an Apology

GULF OF MEXICO—THERE HAVE BEEN TWO CONSTANTS in this presidential campaign: Sen. Barack Obama will discuss his faith openly and present some of today's most troublesome issues through a moral prism, and the Rev. Jesse Jackson Sr. will say something outlandish and stupid for which he will have to apologize.

First, he told a reporter in South Carolina last year that Obama was "acting white" in his response to the issues in Jena, La. Then the good reverend wrote an op-ed piece proclaiming that then-Democratic presidential candidate John Edwards was the only one speaking to issues of importance to African Americans.

Now, in his most vile and pathetic comments yet, Jackson was overhead telling a fellow panelist prior to an interview on Fox that he was going to cut Obama's "nuts off" for his speeches on morality and fatherhood in the black community.

Rewind for a moment. An African American reverend—someone who is called by God to speak to moral issues of the day—takes issue with an African American presidential candidate speaking about faith-based issues, the need for black men to take care of their children, and the need for parents to care about their children's health and to turn the television off and start reading more books?

If there were any further evidence needed to show that the Rev. Jackson has lost his moral compass and is far out of touch with the state of black America today, this is it. And it is clear that Jackson has forgotten that as a minister, his first goal is to address moral issues before anything else.

I am on a long-awaited family reunion cruise and was doing all I could to stay away from work after a grueling primary season. But when I saw this story and the lame excuses the Rev. Jackson offered, nothing could keep me from jotting down a few words.

Folks, I have written on numerous occasions what it was like as a teen to see Jackson stand before the Democratic national conventions in 1984 and 1988 and give two of the finest speeches in history (both are on my iPod). He has left a significant legacy by his work on behalf of civil rights.

But all of the good that he has accomplished is withering away because of his ego run amok and his unwillingness to step aside and allow the next generation of leaders to take their rightful place. He has long claimed the mantle of the Rev. Dr. Martin Luther King Jr. and has run with that baton as fast and as hard as he can. Yet what he continues to do is tarnish his legacy and leave a bad aftertaste in the mouths of folks today who were babes when "Run, Jesse, Run" was a rallying cry across the nation.

What is especially galling is that Jackson would make such an idiotic comment about a man who is trying desperately to advance the issues near and dear to African Americans—and all Americans—while also speaking truth to the major problems affecting the black community.

Jackson seems to want Obama to shut up on the issue of black men fathering children out of wedlock and not taking care of their responsibilities. Instead, he wants him to keep his sights on jobs, economic development and education.

And that nonsense about talking down to black people? That's the kind of BS I've always heard, and it's Jackson's way of saying Obama thinks he is better than other black folks. That's right. It's just another way of calling him uppity.

Part of the problem could be that figures such as Jackson have lost a lot of their moral standing, often by their own doing. The Rev. Jackson can't necessarily give the same speech Obama gave because Jackson committed adultery and had a child out of wedlock several years ago. He's taking care of the young girl, but another child being raised by a single mother—even if it carries the last name Jackson—is part of the problem in black America. (Yeah, I said it; someone has to stop dancing around the elephant in the room.)

The issue of the black family—and the destruction of it—is the main problem we face (something that will be dealt with on CNN's "Black in America" series, premiering July 23). We can talk ad nauseam about education and wealth creation, but when you have seven out of 10 children born out of wedlock, those single women having to raise those children all alone, and the rampant black-on-black crime—fueled by many of these same children—that proves we have issues that must be confronted, from the pulpit to the pew.

Instead of trying to tear Obama down or anyone else who is sick and tired of the moral decay in parts of black America, Jackson should be joining the chorus of those who say, "Enough is enough."

I was at the Essence Music Festival over the July 4th weekend in New Orleans, and more than 5,000 people crammed into the Morial Convention Center to hear Bill Cosby speak from the same template as Obama. He didn't hold back or mince words. He discussed domestic violence, the lack of educational achievement, and the need for black parents to raise their game. Jackson previously stood with Cosby, especially when Cosby caught heat for his words, so why isn't what's good for America's Dad good for the guy who wants to be America's president?

Instead of denouncing, Jackson and others should praise Obama, Sen. John McCain and other political leaders who are willing to raise their voices to moral issues today.

And if the Rev. Jackson or others have a problem with a politician speaking truth to African Americans, the hell with them.

As a child of God, I gladly will stand on the side of any man or woman, Republican or Democrat, who is willing to say what's right. Not what's popular.

July 14, 2008, Essence.com Blog

New Yorker Missed an Opportunity; But Still Go After the Real Haters

I'M SUPPOSED TO BE ON A PLANE TO ACCRA, GHANA right now, but my flight out of Houston was cancelled, so we're going to have to leave out of JFK today.

As a result, I've had a chance to read a ton of e-mails regarding a protest of the *New Yorker Magazine* because of their cover depicting Michelle Obama with an Afro and a gun slung over her shoulder, and Sen. Barack Obama dressed as a Muslim.

I was sent a copy of the *New Yorker's* cover of Michelle and Barack Obama in an e-mail, as well as a headline discussing the issue of fear. Then the editor of the *New Yorker* said the following to CNN: "The idea is to attack lies and misconceptions and distortions about the Obamas and their background and their politics. We've heard all of this nonsense about how they're supposedly insufficiently patriotic or soft on terrorism," said David Remnick, the magazine's longtime editor.

Except for one thing: Remnick is lying.

I wanted to see a hard copy of the magazine, and Barclay Palmer of the AC 360 staff obliged.

There is no headline on the cover of art. The flap on the cover says the following: "How Obama became a pol. Ryan Lizza on the candidate's first campaigns-and how Chicago's byzantine politics shaped him."

And the headline on the inside says: "Making It: How Chicago shaped Obama" by Ryan Lizza.

That's it. No article deals with the issue of fear, and the headline doesn't match it at all.

The *New Yorker* is saying one thing and is doing another.

And frankly, they missed an opportunity.

The real culprits are the people the *New Yorker* should have been ripping to shreds: the rhetorical bullies, mostly on right wing conservative and television, that have been the chief merchants in selling this mess to the American people.

With their twisted logic, adherence to removing any context, and just flat out lying, they have been the driving force behind the smearing of Obama.

I've heard these rhetorical thugs call Michelle Obama "militant" and offer nothing to back it up, hoping folks will envision Angela Davis and the Black Panthers when they think of Michelle.

You've had right wing windbags continue to speculate about Obama being Muslim, even though the evidence is against that.

From day one these nuts have tried to scare the hell out of America, whether it was trying to make Obama accept every word from the Rev. Jeremiah Wright; assert that neither Obama is a true American; all in an effort to make them both ungrateful to what America "gave" them.

Save your passion and anger for those fools, not a magazine that was trying to push the envelope to show the fear in which they choose to instill in the minds of the uneducated and easily impressionable. Unfortunately, the *New Yorker* failed.

Shame on them, but also shame on the fear mongerers, and they should be called out by name, no matter what network they work for, no matter what time of day their radio shows come on, and no matter which magazine, newspaper or syndicate they write for.

July 18, 2008

McCain Right, Obama Wrong on School Vouchers

"ALL I WANT IS FOR MY CHILDREN to get the best education they can."

That statement, along with so many others, has been a consistent one that I've heard on my radio show and in discussions with parents for years, especially those who are stuck with inner-city schools with decrepit buildings that lack critical resources.

And for the past 20 years, one of the most talked-about solutions is for parents stuck in dead-end, failing schools to have the option to use vouchers to allow them to send their children somewhere they could get quality educations.

Republicans have made vouchers a linchpin of their education overhaul initiatives. Democrats steadfastly have refused, saying it would take vital dollars out of the public school system.

This year's presidential candidates are lining up right along with their parties. Sen. John McCain, the GOP nominee, says vouchers are the right way to go to give parents an option for a better education, while Sen. Barack Obama says the GOP has talked and talked about vouchers and it hasn't amounted to much more.

But part of the reason vouchers have been denounced and dismissed is Democrats have been far too obstinate on the issue. They're not listening to their constituents, especially African Americans, who overwhelmingly support vouchers.

There is no doubt that on this issue, McCain has it right, and Obama has it wrong.

The fundamental problem with the voucher debate is that it is always seen as an either/or proposition. For Republicans, it is the panacea to all the educational woes, and that is nonsensical. For Democrats, they say it will destroy public education, and that, too, is a bunch of crap.

I fundamentally believe that vouchers are simply one part of the entire educational pie. There is no surefire way to educate a child. We've seen public schools do a great job (I went to them from kindergarten through college) along with private schools, home schooling, charter schools and even online initiatives. This is the kind of innovation we need, not more efforts to prevent a worthy idea from moving forward.

Obama's opposition is right along the lines of the National Education Association, and the teachers union is a reliable and powerful Democratic ally. But this is one time he should have opposed them and made it clear that vouchers can force school districts, administrators and teachers to shape up or see their students shipping out.

It is unconscionable to ask parents to watch as their children are stuck in failing schools and ask them to bank on politicians coming up with more funds to improve the situation. Fine, call vouchers a short-term solution to a long-term problem, but

I rather would have a child getting the best education now than having to hope and pray down the line.

McCain and Obama have presented comprehensive education plans, and those are noble. But leaving out vouchers does a tremendous disservice to the parents who are fed up with deplorable schools, and it allows school districts to operate with impunity and without any real competition.

August 1, 2008

Obama and McCain Should Help Fight Black AIDS

I INITIALLY WANTED TO WRITE ABOUT SEN. JOHN MCCAIN'S double talk on the issue of affirmative action. Based on his various statements, I'm not sure where in the heck he stands. Another potential topic was the silliness over getting a new press release each day about Sen. Barack Obama canceling a visit to troops in Germany. Another potential topic was each candidate's vice presidential pick.

But after logging on to CNN.com Tuesday and seeing the bold headline: "1 out of 2 with HIV in U.S. is black, report says," nothing else really mattered.

And as I thought about that startling fact, it only reminded me how little attention has been paid to this health crisis during this election cycle. It has been mentioned in two or three debates—on both sides of the aisle—but that was only in passing.

I shouldn't be surprised. Who can forget when, in 2004, PBS host Gwen Ifill asked Vice President Dick Cheney and then-Sen. John Edwards about AIDS affecting black women. Both of them spent more time discussing the problem in Africa than the problem in Alabama, Georgia, North Carolina and other states.

Cheney even said: "I have not heard those numbers with respect to African American women. I was not aware that ... they're in epidemic there because we have made progress in terms of the overall rate of AIDS infection."

While Sens. Barack Obama and John McCain go back and forth over who didn't visit troops in Germany; the impact of Obama's overseas tour; and who is best positioned to deal with the crumbling economy, critical domestic issues go unnoticed, such as AIDS.

Then again, we've been here before. Silence played a vital role in so many white gay men dying in the 1980s. But the reality is we knew less then than we do today, so our silence in 2008 is more shameful than anything that took place during the Reagan administration.

Now it's time to make it front and center. This is not an issue that will be addressed solely by politicians. It is a national health crisis that will kill a number of people and cost untold millions in health care. Sitting on the sidelines simply isn't an option.

Obama and McCain should speak specifically to this issue when they attend the annual conference of the National Urban League next week in St. Louis. Don't bother just talking about growing black-owned businesses or creating educational and economic opportunities. If black communities are decimated by AIDS, there won't be folks there to run those businesses.

Yet they aren't the only ones with some homework to do. Black religious leaders must stop sticking their heads in the sand and speak forcefully, truthfully and compassionately from the pulpit about AIDS. If they are against homosexuality and men and women having sex outside marriage based on biblical reasons, I understand that. But the reality is that women are dying in the body of Christ, and they are being infected mostly by men. Ignoring the issue because it makes us uncomfortable is not Christlike.

There has to be a serious reallocation of resources, and that means organizations that have targeted gay white men must share those dollars where they're needed most. I have heard from countless black AIDS activists who say doors routinely are shut in their faces when they try to move money for training, education and testing to largely black neighborhoods. There is an economic and political battle, and it's time to squash that to save lives.

And then there is the personal responsibility. It was sickening to watch the young lady in Soledad O'Brien's "Black in America" documentary fret about the results of her AIDS test. But what was horrible was realizing that she suspected her man of cheating yet chose to have unprotected sex anyhow. These folks need to be hit between the eyes with common sense. You can have all the fliers, e-mails, Web sites and PSAs you want, but if the two people lying in bed together—or even the IV drug user—don't do their part, we're just wasting time and money.

HIV and AIDS are 100 percent preventable. No one has any excuse today not to know what safe sex means. We must have the courage to say what needs to be said, even if it's painful to our sisters, brothers, friends, frat brothers, sorority sisters and church members.

I rather would have someone scare me straight today than face an early death tomorrow because of something I easily could have prevented.

Back Story: "Carl, We Don't Talk to the Same People"

AS I SAID EARLIER, conventional Washington, D.C. wisdom would not let go of the notion that Obama had to choose Hillary Clinton as his running mate.

But I kept saying, 2008 was an unconventional year and Obama was an unconventional guy.

So, on August 4, 2008, we were debating the "Will Obama pick Hillary" topic—AGAIN!—and I was on AC 360 with Carl Bernstein, the Pulitzer Prize winner who, along with Bob Woodward, is one of journalism's historic figures for their Watergate coverage.

Anderson asked, "Carl, Barack Obama's not hugely ahead in these polls that we're looking at. A lot of Democrats getting concerned about that. Does this make Hillary Clinton more viable as a VP pick?"

"Yes," Carl said. "It's very, very early, though. And—but I will go out on a limb and say, look, if Barack Obama wants to win the election with little risk, Hillary Clinton is probably the way to go."

I just sat on the set shaking my head, thinking, "You guys are nuts! She *will not* be the pick!"

For two months I had been saying this. A few weeks later I was on a panel on Martha's Vineyard hosted by Harvard professor Charles Ogletree, and CNN's David

The General Election Campaign

Gergen started on this he-needs-to-pick-Hillary line of thought. And I sat there, shaking my head, saying, "Ain't gonna happen. Hillary *will not* be the VP pick!" When it was my time to speak I said the same thing.

These guys may have been astute to the way things were done in Washington for all these years, but they knew nothing about this Obama guy and how he thought. What I was getting was the raw truth, and folks kept dismissing me.

So as I pushed back against Carl, he turns to me—on the air!—and says, "Roland, I talk to the same folks in the Obama campaign as you do."

"Are you sure about that?" I shot back.

He went on and on, and repeated the line.

And I shot back, again, "Are you sure about that?"

I finally said, "Look, I have talked to high-ranking Obama sources. It's very simple. She is not going to be the nominee. All the talk about, well, she might be there, what the polls say, it is not going to happen. Now, I don't know more definitive…"

Then Anderson says, "We're going to mark this tape."

Fine with me. I knew the truth.

When we walked off the set, I went to the makeup room to get a wipe to remove the makeup. Carl kept going on and on saying, "Roland, I've talked to everyone in the Obama camp except Obama."

I looked at him and said, "Carl, we don't talk to the same people."

He froze in his steps, and looked at me with a stunned expression.

"Are you saying Obama is your source?" he asked.

Knowing full well Carl and Bob protected Deep Throat for more than two decades, I wasn't going to reveal any of my sources to him.

I simply said, "Carl, we don't talk to the same people."

And I walked off. Leaving him there to figure it all out.

August 8, 2008

Bill Clinton Desperate to Get His Black Card Back

POOR BILL.

He's stuck in no man's land—no longer able to stand before adoring crowds of African Americans, who welcomed him as the "nation's first black president" with thunderous applause and all kinds of pats on the back—and he clearly is having issues dealing with the new world order.

Almost two months after Sen. Barack Obama captured the Democratic presidential nomination, the former president still is brooding about his wife's loss. And his chief source of anguish? That supporters of Barack Obama accused him of injecting race into the campaign.

Never mind that the Obama camp—loaded with white male advisers—was so afraid to bring up race that it wasn't funny.

When Bill Clinton compared Sen. Barack Obama's win in South Carolina to the Rev. Jesse Jackson's 1984 and 1988 wins there, it was seen by African Americans as an attempt to marginalize Obama. That always has been a fear of African Americans who achieve mainstream success, and it left even close friends of the Clintons' aghast.

That was the tipping point, along with other perceived slights, and we know a person's perception is his reality.

What Bill doesn't understand is that the masses of black people know what it feels like to be marginalized, and many saw that in those comments.

In an interview with ABC's Kate Snow, Clinton, when asked about regrets in the campaign, immediately threw out, "I am not a racist."

He kept insisting that he isn't angry, but we all have seen that stare, that change in body language, and the parsing of words. Even when Snow asked whether Obama is ready to be president, Clinton answered in the third person, never actually saying he's ready or not. The only thing left was the eruption, and he promised to share all in January, after the November election.

Bill, we get it. You still are peeved. At Obama. At Rep. James Clyburn. At the media. At anyone who you determined was against you and Hillary.

The General Election Campaign

Many have said Clinton wants his legacy intact, and a lot of that has to do with the reality that no group gave him more comfort than the black community.

When he was facing the end of his presidency, he called on black folks like no others, using the love and affection to get him through the Monica Lewinsky scandal. He relied on black support to keep his poll numbers high. And we all know it.

But what Bill knows—and we know—is that you don't have to be a racist to use race as a tool in a political campaign. An inference here, a comparison there, and you can send the right signal at the right time to the right people. He says he did nothing wrong. Yet perception is very powerful, and denying it doesn't make it go away.

Bill and the legions of Clinton supporters and former campaign aides are quick to act as if the comments made by African Americans—the regular folk—simply didn't exist. That was his bread-and-butter group, and its members were none too happy.

But what the Clinton folks also fail to grasp is that they did offend older African Americans, such as Clyburn, Dr. Johnnetta B. Cole and others who were always in the corner of the Clintons but could remain silent no longer.

It's clear that Bill can't deal with the fact that his black supporters didn't stay quiet. Many of them recoiled at what they heard and didn't offer the Clintons cover.

As for what's next, some Hillary Clinton fundraisers have said Obama should help restore Bill's reputation and show respect for both Clintons, according to *The Huffington Post*. But the truth is that there is nothing that Obama can do to salvage the reputation of Bill Clinton before most African Americans.

Bill lost that on his own, and he's going to have to get it on his own.

And the Clintons need to stop living in la-la land, listening to the same folks soothe Bill's bruised ego. They thought they would win the nomination and that blacks would fall in line. Harold Ickes said as much.

But in this new world order, when young black folks don't see Bill as the Great Messiah and really didn't have a love affair with his eight years, he needs to recognize that a lot has changed.

Bill, you clearly have issues with what took place, and sure, you can be angry. But denying you're angry doesn't help.

August 15, 2008, Essence.com Blog

Jackson in 1988 Makes Case For Nominating Clinton in 2008

LAST WEEK WHILE IN MARTHA'S VINEYARD, we had some major technical issues that knocked WVON-AM/Chicago off the air. I was just talking and talking until we were notified that we were not broadcasting.

So instead of talking for three hours for the online audience, I chose to play Rev. Jesse Jackson Sr.'s 1988 speech at the Democratic National Convention.

In a truly mesmerizing speech that still make tears well up in my eyes, Jackson spoke to the pain and success of his supporters and the nation, but also offered some critical words that explained why the name of the first African American to run all primary races should go into nomination.

"As a testament to the struggles of those who have gone before; as a legacy for those who will come after; as a tribute to the endurance, the patience, the courage of our forefathers and mothers; as an assurance that their prayers are being answered, that their work has not been in vain, and, that hope is eternal, tomorrow night my name will go into nomination for the Presidency of the United States of America," he said to rousing applause.

And later in the speech, Jackson told his personal story of being raised by a single mother, growing up with three last names, and the poor conditions he endured in South Carolina.

But he also offered a compelling reason why his name should go in nomination, which also can be used by the ardent supporters of Sen. Hillary Clinton today.

"Every one of these funny labels they put on you, those of you who are watching this broadcast tonight in the projects, on the corners, I understand. Call you outcast, low down, you can't make it, you're nothing, you're from nobody, subclass, underclass; when you see Jesse Jackson, when my name goes in nomination, your name goes in nomination," he said.

Women have waited years to see one of their own ascend to the presidency. While other nations have elected female leaders, America is 43 for 43 when it comes to white men. When her name goes in nomination, their name goes in.

And it's no different for African Americans. A nation that once enslaved millions of Africans could be on the verge of seeing the son of an African father and Kansas mother occupy 1600 Pennsylvania Ave. When Obama accepts the nomination, they accept the nomination.

Yet the difference between 1988 and 2008 is that Jackson and his supporters accepted the reality that he wasn't the nominee, and that continuing to champion his cause—and ignoring the nominee, Massachusetts Gov. Michael Dukakis—could spell doom for the party in capturing the White House.

"The only time that we win is when we come together. In 1960, John Kennedy, the late John Kennedy, beat Richard Nixon by only 112,000 votes—less than one vote per precinct. He won by the margin of our hope. He brought us together. He reached out…

"In 1964, Lyndon Johnson brought both wings together—the thesis, the antithesis, and the creative synthesis—and together we won. In 1976, Jimmy Carter unified us again, and we won. When do we not come together, we never win. In 1968, the division and despair in July led to our defeat in November. In 1980, rancor in the spring and the summer led to Reagan in the fall. When we divide, we cannot win. We must find common ground as the basis for survival and development and change and growth."

But when you have groups like Party Unity My Ass (PUMA) and MakeThemAccountable.com continue to assert that Clinton should be the nominee, and do everything to doom Obama's chances in November—that runs counter to the issues that Clinton and Obama stand for—health care, ending the war in Iraq, not having conservatives have a majority on the Supreme Court, and so many others.

Choosing to champion McCain as "payback" against Obama and the Democratic Party will do the one thing Dems say they don't want: guarantee a McCain victory.

Even conservatives have figured this out. Many of them can't stand Sen. John McCain for a litany of reasons (remember the right wing talkers saying they would vote for Clinton over McCain in November?). But if it's seeing Obama getting sworn in, they've decided to put their personal feelings aside to focus on winning. And in the end, that's all that matters.

Even Jackson spoke to this issue in his 1988 speech during the section where he made the case for Dukakis.

"Our ships could pass in the night—if we have a false sense of independence—or they could collide and crash. We would lose our passengers. We can seek a high reality and a greater good. Apart, we can drift on the broken pieces of Reagonomics, satisfy our baser instincts, and exploit the fears of our people. At our highest, we can call upon noble instincts and navigate this vessel to safety. The greater good is the common good.

"As Jesus said, 'Not My will, but Thine be done.' It was his way of saying there's a higher good beyond personal comfort or position.

"The good of our Nation is at stake. It's commitment to working men and women, to the poor and the vulnerable, to the many in the world."

August 22, 2008, Essence.com Blog

Top 15 Songs Played in the 8 Homes of Cindy and Sen. John McCain

IN THE SPIRIT OF THE BROUHAHA between the camps of Sens. John McCain and Barack Obama over McCain not remembering how many homes he owns, we had a little fun with the topic this morning on my radio show.

Here are the top 15 songs we played. The main requirement was that the song had to have house or home in it. And no, they are not in the order of what's the best song!

1. "A House Is Not A Home" by Luther Vandross
2. "Brick House" by The Commodores
3. "Take it to the House" by Trick Daddy, featuring Duece Poppi, Tre + 6 & Unda Presha
4. "Bring it on Home to Me" by Sam Cooke
5. "I'm Coming Home" by The Spinners
6. "When Johnnie Comes Marching Home" by the Texas Aggie Band

7. "Take Your Drunken Ass Home" by Big Al Carson

8. "Take It Home" by B.B. King

9. "Baby's Home" by Barry White

10. "Housequake" by Prince

11. Theme from the soundtrack "Animal House" by Stephen Bishop

12. "A Heart Is A House for Love" by The Dells

13. "Walkin' My Baby Back Home" by Nat King Cole

14. "In My House" by the Mary Jane Girls

15. "The House That Jack Built" by Aretha Franklin

August 22, 2008

Obama and McCain's Mantra Should Be "Just Win, Baby"

TO ALL THE OBAMAITES WHO CONTINUE to send e-mails asserting that Sen. John McCain was given the questions prior to Saturday's forum at Pastor Rick Warren's Saddleback Church, please give it a rest.

Even a child can figure out that if you are going to a church that is socially conservative, abortion and gay marriage are going to come up. I didn't even have to watch the two-hour "civil" forum to figure out what was going to be on the agenda.

McCain wasn't trying to have a conversation or offer deep insight into his views on faith and morality. All he wanted to do was talk to the white evangelicals who have been on the fence about his campaign and chew up the red meat they always eat: abortion, gay marriage, right-wing Supreme Court judges, and taxes.

Warren kept saying he did not want Obama and McCain to cite their stump speeches. Obama played to Warren's agenda. McCain didn't.

So should you be angry about that? Hell, no. That's what a candidate is supposed to do. When running for president, you don't give a flip about what the other person is trying to achieve. Your job is to win.

That's right. The real mantra of this campaign isn't "change." It's not "experience."

And it sure isn't "judgment." Al Davis of the Oakland Raiders owns the phrase for this year's election and for any election: "Just win, baby."

The Republicans never have cared about other people's feelings or whether the truth matters. Does Obama want to raise taxes for folks making $42,000, as a McCain ad claims? On NBC's "Meet the Press," I heard Louisiana Gov. Bobby Jindal say Obama wants to do just that. Of course, FactCheck.org calls the McCain statement "false," and *Newsweek's* Jonathan Alter blasts it and others as blatant smears that are consistent with the McCain camp.

But did Virginia Gov. Tim Kaine gut punch Jindal by calling it a blatant lie and chastising him with the truth? Nope. The moment I saw Jindal tap dance on Kaine's head, I knew the Virginia governor would not be Obama's vice presidential choice. When you need someone to do your dirty work, that's your VP nominee. If he can't even defend properly, why choose him?

To a certain degree, the same goes for Sen. Claire McCaskill. She went on "Larry King Live" Monday sounding positive about the Warren forum. McCain surrogate Minnesota Gov. Tim Pawlenty? He defended McCain and ripped Obama. Did McCaskill respond in kind? Nope. She just shook her head and defended, defended, defended.

Even Al Davis will tell you that if you're spending more time defending than going on the offense, you can't score points!

For McCain to win, he must keep up the pressure. Keep pushing Obama into a corner on experience, and stay on the attack. Look, the guy is behind in most polls. He has no choice but to blast Obama whenever he can.

He'll use his POW status as a shield and not let anyone question his background in the military, even if the less than stellar student may have gotten a helping hand from his four-star-admiral father and grandfather. (How about that affirmative action plan?)

Early in the campaign, when the right-wing hate machine had some crazy things to say about Obama, McCain was quick to denounce them as not being what he envisions for a campaign. Then he was ripped summarily by the likes of Rush Limbaugh and Sean "Little Ball of Hate" Hannity because that meant their antics would come into question, too.

The General Election Campaign

Now that he has been behind all summer, McCain has gone silent, not saying a word about the pathetic and lie-filled book by Jerome Corsi. That's like the Raiders issuing a late hit and the team not getting flagged. Do you think the coach is going to admonish his players for throwing in some extra hits? Call it dirty, but it's smart politics.

Obama must redefine the character debate and realize that it's not about the issues. The Republicans have been damn good about maximizing the character issue. What do Democrats do all the time? Respond that it's about issues. How did Bush beat Gore? Character. Bush beat Kerry? Character. How has John McCain closed the gap? Character. Yes, the economy matters. Yes, the war matters. But their way to victory is to attack Obama's character.

What Obama must do is emphasize his family and marriage. Look, he's got an awesome wife and daughters, and he's going up against a guy who cheated on his wheelchair-bound first wife for a rich youngster, whose money paved his political career. Bring up those family values, Tony Perkins.

Obama, hit McCain with your personal economic values. This dude lives in six houses and wears $520 shoes. You only own four pairs! Also, hit home that you paid off your college loans four years ago. In these difficult times, every parent is confronting this issue. Make it clear that you worked your way through school and got scholarships (and it wasn't the Cindy McCain Beer Drinker of the Year fund). This shows that you didn't have a silver spoon in your mouth. It's a values story that plays well on both coasts, Middle America and in the South.

Lastly, stop spending time trying to placate supporters of Sen. Hillary Clinton. You need to raise money to win in November and focus on McCain. If her folks don't want to get on board, go find new voters. If she's in the news, that means you have two opponents to fight in November. If they try to take over Denver, *shut them down*. If the convention isn't about you, then McCain is one happy man.

This is where games are won: the fourth quarter. What happened during the past 20 months means nothing. For the Obama and McCain camps, if you miss an opportunity or waste a day, you can't get it back. So don't screw it up.

Now we'll see what these candidates are truly made of.

August 29, 2008

Race Is Obama's To Win or Lose

DENVER—ALL THROUGHOUT THE WEEK, strategists, analysts and pundits were chirping and complaining that the party's convention was too soft in the beginning by not blasting away at Sen. John McCain and President George W. Bush.

My CNN colleague James Carville, one of the chief architects of Bill Clinton's victory in 1992, was among those leading voices, believing that the Democrats didn't have a consistent message to counter the GOP.

Yet that was never the view that struck me. As the week developed, I began to view the proceedings much like a sprint relay, with the speeches of the speakers prior to Sen. Barack Obama's focused on staying in their lane and properly passing the baton to give their anchor leg a chance to finish strong and race to victory.

On Monday, Sen. Ted Kennedy and Michelle Obama ran a good first leg by focusing on faith, family and values.

Tuesday brought the bipartisan focus of former Virginia Gov. Mark Warner, who was billed as the keynote speaker. But it was Sen. Hillary Clinton who was the main attraction of the night, and her call for healing of the Democratic base and uniting behind the Democratic nominee was vital to the party moving beyond the contentious battle between the Obama and Clinton camps. That speech, coupled with her putting Obama over the top during the roll call the next day, providing the opportunity for the Democrats assembled to put their differences aside and focus on winning the White House.

Leg two was solid.

Then came leg three, which was run by three speakers: Massachusetts Sen. John Kerry, who showed amazing fire and passion in his denunciation of Sen. John McCain and President Bush. He was followed by former President Bill Clinton, who made a strong case for backing Obama, even calling on his wife's 18 million supporters to put their full thrust behind the junior senator from Illinois. The hat trick was completed when Sen. Joe Biden spoke to the audience, and connected with them by virtue of his blue-collar roots.

Leg three, again, solid.

Then it came down to the anchor: Sen. Barack Obama. Anyone who follows track and field knows that normally, the person running the last leg of a relay is seen as the strongest and fastest. If a race is tied, their job is to take a lead and grow it; pull a team ahead if they are behind; or if given a lead, blow away the competition in a race to win gold.

That was clearly Obama's task. He needed to deliver the most important speech of his political life, and to speak to the lingering questions from his critics and supporters. Among them:

- Were his values consistent with other Americans?
- Did he offer a vision, laden with specifics, to lead the nation?
- Was he patriotic?
- Did he have the gumption to fight back and hit McCain hard on the issues?

The stakes were raised even higher because he decided to move the final act to Invesco Field and speak before more than 75,000 delegates and supporters. When you make a move like that, you better deliver.

And, oh, he did.

The stadium was already electrified by the reality of the historic moment: the first black presidential nominee of a major political party, as well as his speech coming on the 45th anniversary of the 1963 March on Washington for Jobs and Freedom, where the Rev. Dr. Martin Luther King Jr. delivered his famous "I Have A Dream" speech.

As my eyes panned across the massive stadium, all I could do was shake my head at witnessing an epic election event that had not been seen since then—Sen. John F. Kennedy held a similar acceptance speech at the Los Angeles Coliseum in 1960.

Obama was firm and decisive, speaking to the pain Americans are going through because of the faulty economy, but also taking McCain on when it came to national security. He didn't back down, nor did he offer nuanced answers. He truly delivered a speech that will go down as one of the most important political addresses in recent history.

But with all its brilliance, this wasn't the finals. It was the preliminaries. He may have had an awesome showing, but he must continue to run harder and faster and stronger over the next two and a half months if he truly wants to win the gold.

August 31, 2008, Essence.com Blog

With Palin, Does McCain Now Believe in Quotas and Affirmative Action?

I'LL HAVE MORE TO SAY ON THIS LATER, but please, give me a break? Does Sen. John McCain actually think he chose the most qualified—or even the second, third or fourth—person to be his vice president?

Sarah Palin may be the governor of Alaska, but prior to that, she was the mayor of a 10,000-person town.

This was all about being a woman. McCain knows it and we know it.

But the sad thing is that there are far more qualified women in the GOP. One that comes to mind is Texas Sen. Kay Bailey Hutchison. She clearly has the chops to do the job.

Then the McCainites say it's about her being a strong social conservative. Another ridiculous statement.

Name the one social conservative who grabbed a huge share of grassroots evangelicals, and was governor for a lot longer than Palin? Mike Huckabee.

But McCain didn't even bother to vet him.

So, let's look at filling a void for the key markers:

BATTLEGROUND STATE. The choice would have been Minnesota Gov. Tim Pawlenty. If he was on the ticket, the state likely would have gone in the Republican column. It will likely stay a blue state.

ECONOMY. Mitt Romney. The former Massachusetts governor ran a strong second to McCain, and is an accomplished businessman. He fills a serious hole in the McCain armor.

SOCIAL CONSERVATIVE. McCain is weak among evangelicals, so why not choose the southern Baptist minister Huckabee? He beat McCain in Georgia; held strong in Texas, and although big name evangelical leaders shunned him, the folks who get people to the polls-grassroots organizers-loved him.

APPEALING TO MODERATES. Palin may give Huckabee a run for his money on this one, but with his lighthearted manner, as well as sunny disposition, he never really ticked off liberals with his hard right positions. He still tops her on this one.

Guns, guns, guns. Who gave one of the best speeches at the National Rifle Association convention? It wasn't Palin. It was was Huckabee.

So, if you make a pick based on these issues, Palin doesn't fit the bill.

So what does that leave? Hey, she's a woman!

I'm all for history, but what I'm hearing from women is "don't insult me by picking anyone. Pick a qualified woman."

By any available measure, she doesn't make the cut.

Other than being a woman.

Way to fill that quota, John.

Back Story: "I'm Voting For Barack Obama"

AS JOURNALISTS, IT'S JUST NOT IN OUR NATURE to reveal our political interests, who we're voting for and anything that could show bias.

But the reality is that damn near every one of us votes, and we sit there, talking about both camps, knowing full well that in the privacy of that booth, we're going to cast a ballot. I've always believed that journalists should reveal their voting choices, political leanings and idealogy, so the viewer or reader knows exactly what they are getting, and can make their own determinations.

You have columnists out there who lean a certain way, and you can gleam who they will likely vote for. I'm just not that worried if commentators do the same. We are paid for our opinions and perspectives, so why not be open about it?

During the election, folks watching at home believed from day one that I was voting for Sen. Barack Obama. Seeing as how I was based in Chicago, had covered him, am black (therefore a Democrat), I must be the resident Obama guy!

Not true. Like many voters, I really didn't know a lot about Obama to determine how I would vote. I recall in 2004 that former Illinois U.S. Senator Carol Moseley Braun and the Rev. Al Sharpton sought the Democratic nomination. I didn't support their candidacies so it was silly to assume I would go for the black guy.

I made a smart calculation as the campaign began. I was signed to CNN as a contributor in February 2007, and Obama announced his candidacy the same month. I knew he was not considered a frontrunner, and a lot of journalists just didn't put much stock into his campaign. Most thought the smart money was on Sen. Hillary Clinton, and he was seen as the novelty candidate. I chose to go the other way.

I knew no one else at CNN knew as much about him as I did, and I surely had the inside track because of all of my Chicago connections, so I decided to become the one guy with the Obama connections. Whatever he did, I wanted to know first. Whatever he was planning, I wanted to be the one to say it. Bottom line: I needed to break through the dozens of people on The Best Political Team on Television, and the way to do that was to have information no one else had.

After Obama won the presidency, I remember hearing reports that he was considering tapping Eric Holder to be his attorney general because he got to see Holder up close when he ran his vice presidential vetting operation, and came away impressed.

I laughed at that. Holder and Obama knew each other for a long, long time. At the Congressional Black Caucus gathering in September 2008, who was sitting next to Obama? Eric Holder.

I was reporting on my radio show in June that Holder was a shoo-in for the job. When we were on Martha's Vineyard in August, Harvard professor Charles Ogletree kept knocking it down. Yea, right, I said. Holder would turn down being the first black AG in history? Not a chance.

Yet the rule of thumb is that people today, especially in Washington, D.C., think in terms of boxes. You're either a "D" for Democratic; "R" for Republican; "L" for liberal; or "C" for conservative.

I fought these labels because I refused to be pigeonholed. That had been my modus operandi my entire life. I casted ballots for Republicans, Democrats, non-partisans, white men, white women, Hispanics, African Americans, Asians, you name it. So why in the hell would I choose to be in a box because of this historic campaign?

I found it interesting that I would get e-mails from people calling me a liberal or a Democrat, yet no one called me a Mike Huckabee supporter when I pushed for him to stay in the race as long as possible! Oh, so I couldn't vote for a Southern Baptist preacher who was a pro-life Republican? You bet your ass I could! I liked Huckabee and felt he was a really good guy.

I remember getting an e-mail from a supporter of Sen. Hillary Clinton blasting me for agreeing with the decision by the Democratic National Committee to pull the delegates of Michigan and Florida for changing their election date. I was accused of taking the Obama position on not counting their delegates. I was like, damn Obama! I think those two states should be stripped because of their stupid actions. It had nothing to do with a political side. I have my own mind, and depending on the issue, you might call me an Obama person, a Clinton person, a Democrat or a Republican. When I ripped Obama on school vouchers, no one called me a turncoat. I just hate the silly political labels.

After the Democratic National Convention, I hosted three weekends worth of shows on CNN. And on the first show, we were dealing with race, age and gender.

As we tried to figure out how to open the first election special, which dealt with age, race and gender and the 2008 campaign, I wanted a way to make a strong statement out of the gate. Knowing my varied political choices in the past—my first vote was in the 1988 presidential campaign and I voted for then-Vice President George H.W. Bush — I decided to reveal my previous presidential choices. The goal was to show that as a black man, I had made choices based on the person and the issues, and not the party, ideology, ethnicity, gender or age.

I didn't do it to please anyone. It worked for the purpose of the special, and it was fine with me.

September 2, 2008

Pregnancy of Palin Daughter Cannot Be Ignored

IT DIDN'T TAKE REPUBLICANS LONG—or even some Democrats—to try to dissuade those of us in the media from focusing on the news that Alaska Gov. Sarah Palin's 17-year-old daughter is five months pregnant and plans on marrying the father.

Aides to Sen. John McCain quickly took to the airwaves to deplore any conversation regarding Bristol Palin, saying the issue is a private matter and we should look elsewhere. Even. Sen. Barack Obama made it clear that the children of candidates are off-limits.

But of course, that didn't keep some folks from trying to score political points.

"This is the pro-life choice. The fact that people will criticize her for this shows the astounding extent to which the secular critics of the pro-life movement just don't get it," Richard Land, president of the Southern Baptist Convention's Ethics and Religious Liberty Commission, told David Brody of the Christian Broadcasting Network. "Those who criticize the Palin family don't understand that we don't see babies as a punishment, but as a blessing. Barack Obama said that if one of his daughters made a mistake and got pregnant out of wedlock, he wouldn't want her to be punished with a child. Pro-lifers don't see a child as punishment."

Now, for everyone on the left and the right, please shut up for a moment and consider the broader issue here.

We have a crisis in America, and Bristol Palin exemplifies that. She's an unwed teenager who is now pregnant, forced to raise a child far too soon. She is a teenager who chose to have premarital sex, which I thought many of these same evangelicals deplore based on biblical reasons. She is a teenager who had unprotected sex and should thank the Lord that the young man she was with doesn't have a sexually transmitted disease.

According to The National Campaign to Prevent Teen and Unplanned Pregnancy, 46.8 percent of all high-school students say they have had sex, which is a decrease from 54 percent.

That's the good news. But we shouldn't be satisfied with almost half our children making the decision to have sex. Many of them are doing so without any protection, and we have seen an explosion of STDs among teens in the country. In fact, Alaska has one of the highest rates of sexually transmitted diseases among teens.

I can't forget the young woman in the CNN documentary "Black in America" who talked about having sex for the first time, only to be infected with HIV. That one decision has altered her life in a significant way.

It's worthy to examine the issue because Gov. Palin said in 2006 that she was dead set against any federal funding for sex education but was an avid supporter of abstinence-only funding.

But it's clear that teaching only abstinence didn't work in her household. So should she and her supporters re-examine their position?

On my CNN Radio show Monday, Rep. Marsha Blackburn (R-TN) wasn't too thrilled to discuss the issue of Palin's daughter but, when pressed, said she still supports abstinence-only funding, not sex education funding.

"I think that is the way we have to work with our children, and you have to engage parents in this issue," she said. "This is something you talk about at the kitchen table, and you sit down with your children."

But let's be honest. A ton of parents aren't having this conversation, so why not deal with it in the public policy arena?

Also on Monday, Bill Bennett, a CNN contributor and author of *The Book of Virtues*, said, "It's a perfectly legitimate issue to discuss in public policy.

"As an evangelical, I think liberals *and* conservatives are wrong on this issue. The situation is so dire and prevalent that it's wrong for liberals to dismiss abstinence completely, and it's wrong for conservatives to refuse to accept birth control and condom education as part of sex education curricula.

"We desperately need comprehensive sex education that incorporates all of these issues if we are to attack the problem. And enough of the blowhards on both sides who think their ways are the only ways."

While America harnessed its resources to tackle an emerging hurricane on the Gulf Coast, these same politicos and activists tried desperately to run away from a similar issue in St. Paul, Minn., involving our children.

I don't give a flip about politicians, pro-choice or pro-life activists, or the implications of this story on the presidential chances of Sen. John McCain and Palin or Sens. Barack Obama and Joe Biden.

What matters most—and should be the priority of all—are the thousands upon thousands of young women who are dealing with these issues every day, many of whom don't have supportive parents with great health care plans.

This is not a Republican issue or Democratic problem. We need to put aside the partisan BS and confront unplanned pregnancies. Let's do all we can to keep our kids from having either premarital sex or unprotected sex, and then we won't have to deal with them choosing to have abortions or not or, as the Palins noted in their statement, seeing our children "grow up faster than we had ever planned" and having to confront "the difficulties of raising a child."

September 5, 2008
Community Organizers Put Country First

THE REPUBLICANS HAVE MADE IT CLEAR where their focus is this week with their convention slogan, "Country First."

With the abundance of flags, chants of "USA, USA" and tributes to those in the military, they have been laying it on thick, which is traditional at GOP conventions.

Sen. John McCain often has talked about the need for Americans to dedicate themselves to service, namely military, and he is on the money.

But a line of attack that was used consistently Wednesday night by former New York Mayor Rudy Giuliani and Alaska Gov. Sarah Palin calls into question whether community organizers put their country first.

Palin focused on the issue in order to attack the Obama campaign for offering up Obama's community organizing work to counter her experience as mayor and governor.

But when you examine Giuliani's and Palin's community organizer jabs—and the subsequent laughter by the Republicans in the Xcel Energy Center—the Democrats could have an opening.

After praising Palin's speech, I said Republicans can expect the Obama-Biden camp to seize on that point.

This morning, I read an e-mail from Obama campaign manager David Plouffe, who incorporated the community organizer argument into a fundraising appeal.

Republican operatives I talked to said the lines were brilliant and that community organizers don't play to the GOP's strength.

I disagree. And so do the many folks who have sent me angry e-mails. They include white Republicans, black Democrats and people from Small Town, USA, and Big City, America.

At a time when Americans are losing their homes to foreclosure, trying to get by after layoffs, lacking health care, and facing pressing environmental issues, it's ludicrous to slam people who aren't asking the government for handouts but are doing what they can to make their neighborhoods and cities better.

I think of my parents. When I was a child growing up in the Clinton Park neighborhood in Houston, my parents were just regular folks trying to raise their five children (sounds like Gov. Sarah Palin). They were always present at our local elementary school (sounds like Gov. Sarah Palin) and were involved heavily in our church.

But our neighborhood was dying. Drugs were ravaging it. Older homeowners were dying, and their children didn't want to live there, so they began renting to people who really didn't care. We saw abandoned homes, weeded lots, no sidewalks, a park falling into disrepair, and a senior citizen center shuttered.

So my parents joined several neighbors and decided to form a civic club. Others called them crazy for trying to advance their ideas, but they didn't give up.

They enlisted their children in passing out fliers and putting up signs notifying people of the monthly meetings. Only a few folks showed up, but they kept going.

And going. And going. And going.

After months and then years, we began to see progress. Stepped-up police patrols. Crack houses raided by the Houston police, DEA and FBI. Abandoned houses torn down. Weeded lots cut. More heavy-trash pickup days. New streetlights. New sidewalks. New sewer pipes. A refurbished park.

Bottom line: These average, low-to middle-income people didn't have political power. They focused on people power. They organized a community to take action.

So when Giuliani and Palin mocked community organizers, they didn't just toss a barb at Sen. Barack Obama; they also were demeaning Reginald and Emelda Martin. They were degrading the women who fought for their rights. They dissed labor activists and immigrant-worker activists, such as Cesar Chavez. They dismissed those in the Civil Rights Movement, folks from small-town America who were sick and tired of being sick and tired. They thumbed their noses at the Nelson Mandelas of the world, who want better lives for their children.

It would have been perfectly fine for Giuliani and Palin to say Obama's community organizing days don't amount to enough experience to qualify him to be president. But when you openly laugh at and mock those hardworking Americans who are in the trenches every day, then you really don't care about "Country First" or service.

Will this be a major deal or a ripple? Likely the latter. But the one thing I know about community organizers is that they know how to organize communities. And if the McCain-Palin ticket wants to win, it better not slap those folks it will need to organize voter registration drives and pool systems to get folks to the polls.

Community organizers always are told they can't do certain things or are dismissed as meaningless. Yet they often have the last laugh.

Rudy, Gov. Palin and Sen. McCain might want to remember that.

September 12, 2008

Race, Age and Gender Are Taboo in This Election

ONE OF THE MOST INTRIGUING CONVERSATIONS I had at either the Democratic convention or the Republican convention was with a white labor leader from Ohio.

I can't remember his name, but he made it clear that he is going all around the Rust Belt looking his white union brothers and sisters in the eye and essentially shaming them into supporting Sen. Barack Obama for president.

No, he's not saying vote for the black man for president because he's black. He said he's telling them that it's shameful that as Democrats, they agree with Obama on various political issues but are refusing to cast ballots for him because of his skin color.

"We have gone to our black brothers and sisters for years to support our (white) candidates, and it's wrong for us to stand here and not support one of their own even though we're Democrats," he barked.

The General Election Campaign

There is nothing more in-your-face than to hear someone speak truthfully to the inherent racism that is at play in this election.

For all the talk about inclusion and the historic nature of this campaign, the true tribal feelings of so many people will come into play, whether we want to admit it or not.

We are seeing remarkable bias playing strongly in this election. Exit-polling data in the primaries showed some evidence of bias when it came to age, race and gender, but the great concern is whether people are as honest in talking to pollsters as they are in the voting booth.

Because Sen. John McCain is 72 and would be the oldest person to be sworn in as president, there is a lot of dialogue about how old this white guy is and how wrong it is that he's running. Age questions also have been raised about the 47-year-old black guy from Chicago and whether he is too young and inexperienced to lead.

While there is a lot of talk and excitement surrounding Alaska Gov. Sarah Palin being named as the first woman on a Republican ticket and what that may mean in terms of widespread female support coming the way of McCain-Palin, there are some voices who refuse to vote for a woman.

We also have seen a number of prominent women—including *Washington Post* columnist Sally Quinn and radio talk show host Dr. Laura Schlessinger—who have questioned whether the 44-year-old white mother of five children should be vice president, considering she has five children, including a special-needs child.

It's wonderful to talk about the economy, immigration, the war in Iraq, health care and education, but we can't be naive to the reality that when voters go into that voting booth, they will, as one person told me during an interview, "vote with their tribe."

That was one of the arguments we heard during the Democratic primaries, when Obama enjoyed overwhelming support from African Americans—to the tune of 90-plus percent—while Sen. Hillary Clinton had major female support, largely white, in the range of 65 to 70 percent.

So what should we do when it comes to our tendency to follow group identification?

- Stop dancing around the topic. When you watch TV and hear folks talk about Wal-Mart moms or small, rural towns, they are talking about white

Americans. These catchphrases never include African Americans or Hispanics.

- Confront bias where it is. Ask your friends, neighbors, co-workers and church members whom they are voting for. When they give you the "I really can't put my finger on it" line, press them. Hard. You know the real answer, so don't beat around the bush. The best folks to challenge Americans on their hang-ups regarding age, race and gender aren't the AARP, NAACP or NOW, but Y-O-U. Don't give in to the "That's the way I was raised" mantra. When someone suggests that flags and faith show that a candidate isn't one of us, drill down.

- Accept the fact that some people will not change. We all think that we have been gifted to the degree that our sane and logical arguments can get folks off their biased stumps. Some people just won't give in. Fine, move on. The goal is to rid our society of as much bias as possible. If someone is hardheaded, then you have to go on to the next person and try to change him.

It's critical that we be as honest as possible about the impact of race, age and gender in campaigns. A lot of people love to toss around the Rev. Martin Luther King Jr.'s quote that he hoped one day, people would be judged by "the content of their character." But it's still a reality that skin tone, gender and birth dates mean more than character to a lot of Americans.

September 17, 2008, Essence.com Blog

Major Clinton Backer—Huge Obama Hate—Supporting McCain

LATER THIS MORNING THE CAMPAIGN of Sen. John McCain will hold a news conference trumpeting the endorsement of Lynn Forester de Rothschild, a major fundraiser for Sen. Hillary Clinton and a member of the Democratic platform committee.

Forester, a CEO of her own company in New York who married a British billionaire, has been blasting Obama for quite some time, calling him arrogant, elitist and out-of-touch with the common man and woman.

Wow, someone named de Rothschild trying to call Obama an elitist.

Folks, I have interviewed Lynn and her rationale for backing McCain is nonsensical. What she should do is just be honest: she *hates* Obama and will never support this man.

She continues to be mad, angry and bitter at the fact that her candidate lost. Forrester will claim that Obama didn't attack the sexism against Clinton during the primary, and that McCain's experience is what's most important. Maybe Forrester is really ticked off because she had her sights set on being ambassador to England, and she knows all too well that she can give that pipe dream up if Obama wins.

When I interviewed her for my CNN radio show, I asked her her views on abortion, the war, the Bush tax cuts and a possible conservative majority on the Supreme Court. On *every* issue, she stands in stark contrast to McCain.

Not only that, how in the hell can you sit on the Democratic Platform Committee, and then support someone who stands in absolute contrast to that platform?

She should be ashamed of herself for the hateful and spiteful words she has tossed out about Obama. It's clear that she is a hater of this man.

Lynn, suck it up. Your candidate got beat by Obama. He won. She lost. And you just need to get over it.

Lastly, if McCain does win and puts into place policies that are counter to everything Forrester claims is important to her as a woman and as a Democrat, she should shut the hell up for at least four years because she would have played a role in making it a reality.

September 19, 2008

McCain and Obama Are Fighting for Middle-Class Voters

IF YOU ARE A MEMBER OF AMERICA'S middle class this election year, you are sort of like a blue-chip football recruit, lavished with praise, attention and adoration from fawning coaches and alumni who would love nothing more than to land the prized player to win the national championship.

For "coach" John McCain and "coach" Barack Obama, the title to win is president of the United States, and like the big-time football coaches, they will say and do anything to make it happen.

Tax cuts? Oh, absolutely, we don't want you to feel any more pain. Let the rich—and the poor—deal with carrying the burden.

You want more jobs? Sure, we're going to force companies that send jobs overseas to stay at home because we know you need those long-disappearing and high-paying manufacturing jobs that helped build this nation.

Can't afford to send your kids to college? Don't sweat it. We've got tax credits, Pell Grants, super-duper loans and all kinds of other options to make college a reality.

Are they cutting back on health care at your job? No big deal. Coach McCain says he's got some nifty tax credits lined up to tickle your fancy and ignite your soul. Coach Obama? He's going to go for the whole enchilada by pushing for virtually universal health care.

Oh, these guys are wonderful with their sales pitches. They have the ability to make everyone feel so special and loved; no one else is more important to them—at that moment.

I must admit, the pathetic pining for middle-class votes has turned so moronic that at times, it drives me nuts.

First, whom in the world are we even talking about? If you listen to the candidates and their campaigns, those in the middle class could make upward of $200,000 a year, while some suggest middle class means earning as little as $20,000.

I moderated a panel Tuesday for the National Black MBA Association and heard descriptions of the lower-middle class, the middle class and the upper-middle class. Someone even suggested that it's really about a "state of mind."

That's right. It boils down to how we feel and think. If that's the case, then even if you have $5 million in the bank but love your family, go to church and share the same values as others around you, you're middle class.

Please, can we just stop the lofty talk and plain-spoken, simplistic solutions and be as specific as possible?

There are really four fundamental issues affecting middle-class voters:

- **JOBS.** We've seen a loss of 600,000 jobs under President Bush, so how exactly would McCain and Obama create jobs? Is there anything in their past that shows they have the ability to do just that? I've heard "drill, drill, drill!" from McCain, and Obama says we're going to turn the old textile and steel mills into green machines by targeting wind and other sources of energy.
- **HOUSING.** Congress is providing a backstop for Wall Street—making billions available if cash is needed. What would McCain and Obama actually do to keep folks from losing their homes? Oh, I know a lot of people suggest that these middle-class folks should have read the fine print and not gotten in over their heads, but if something is good for Wall Street, why not Main Street?
- **HEALTH CARE.** This is no joke and a primary reason Americans file for bankruptcy. I know. My appendix ruptured in 2000 while covering the Democratic National Convention, forcing me to spend five days in a Los Angeles hospital, during which I accrued more than $70,000 in hospital bills. Yep, I didn't have health insurance. I was just a 29-year-old never-been-sick freelancer stuck out in the cold. The pressure of that led to me falling behind on my mortgage and the start of foreclosure proceedings. Bankruptcy was the only thing that saved me, and by the grace of God, my finances turned around, and this month, I'm making my final payment.

McCain says a $5,000 tax credit for health care would help, but the problem with that is you have to pay the dough upfront and then claim it on your taxes. But what happens when they want the money now?

Obama says the answer is his health care plan, but that switch won't be flipped immediately. So what happens while the laborious debate takes place? I just wait for my MRI until Washington finishes debating and the special interests pick the plan to death?

- **EDUCATION.** For many Americans, education is a ticket to the middle class and beyond. Much of the time, the candidates talk about vouchers. Look, that's not going to solve the education problem. What we should be hearing them talk about is the inequity of the school systems. Children living in wealthy school districts get tons of money and the best qualified teachers, while poorer districts are forced to make do with less qualified teachers and without computers or even basic amenities.

Remember those blue-chip players? Today they are telling coaches: If you want me to sign, promise that I'll start. No play, no sign. That's what middle-class Americans must tell the candidates. If you are unwilling to put your personal credibility and integrity behind your campaign pledges, then you don't get my vote.

If you give away your vote just because someone is a Democrat or Republican, a man or a woman, black or white and you end up getting screwed in the end, you have no one to blame but yourself.

So use the most powerful thing you have to demand real answers to your real problems from McCain, Obama, Joe Biden and Sarah Palin: your vote.

The power is literally in your hands.

September 29, 2008, Essence .com Blog

McCain Has Egg on His Face Over $700 Million Bailout Bill Bust

SEN. JOHN MCCAIN PLAYED LIKE JOHN WAYNE last week, offering up a faux suspension of his presidential campaign in order to ride shotgun during the negotiations of the $700 bailout plan sought by President George W. Bush's White House.

His staff claimed that he brought House Republicans to the table and had their concerns addressed in order for an agreement to be reached.

Yesterday, McCain's top campaign aide, Steve Schmidt touted his guy, saying he led both sides to the table. And today, McCain blasted Obama, saying he did nothing to help the deal along, and that it was his take-charge that made it all happen.

Except for one problem: the bill was defeated, largely because House Republicans voted against it.

It looks like the McCain camp counted their eggs before they hatched.

But that didn't stop them from trying to put the blame elsewhere.

"From the minute John McCain suspended his campaign and arrived in Washington to address this crisis, he was attacked by the Democratic leadership: Senators Obama and Reid, Speaker Pelosi and others. Their partisan attacks were an effort to gain political advantage during a national economic crisis. By doing so, they put at risk the homes, livelihoods and savings of millions of American families," said McCain-Palin senior policy adviser Doug Holtz-Eakin

"Barack Obama failed to lead, phoned it in, attacked John McCain, and refused to even say if he supported the final bill.

"Just before the vote, when the outcome was still in doubt, Speaker Pelosi gave a strongly worded partisan speech and poisoned the outcome.

"This bill failed because Barack Obama and the Democrats put politics ahead of country."

And the Obama camp didn't take long in firing back.

"This is a moment of national crisis, and today's inaction in Congress as well as the angry and hyper-partisan statement released by the McCain campaign are exactly why the American people are disgusted with Washington. Now is the time for Democrats and Republicans to join together and act in a way that prevents an economic catastrophe.

Every American should be outraged that an era of greed and irresponsibility on Wall Street and Washington has led us to this point, but now that we are here, the stability of our entire economy depends on us taking immediate action to ease this crisis," said Obama-Biden campaign spokesman Bill Burton.

Here is the reality: Both Democrats and Republicans voted against the bill, but far more GOP members didn't want it.

The final tally: 140 Democrats in favor; 95 against. There were 65 Republicans voting for; 133 against; and one not voting.

So it appears that Speaker of the House Nancy Pelosi delivered more of her troops, but McCain failed to do so.

But that didn't stop McCain spokesman Tucker Bounds from saying that McCain "delivered" 65 of the Republican votes through his direct action. So he's trying to get us to believe that before McCain came riding in on his white horse, only four Republicans supported the bill?

There is spin, and then there is delusion, and the McCain folks are the latter.

No matter how he tries to spin it, McCain failed miserably on this, and he has himself to blame for playing presidential politics with such a serious issue. This is not the kind of leadership we need.

October 3, 2008

Doing "Okay" in Debates Is Not Good Enough

WHEN SENS. BARACK OBAMA and John McCain step onto the stage Tuesday night in Nashville, Tenn., for their second presidential debate, Americans shouldn't expect to see two candidates praised for not making a mistake, stringing together a coherent sentence, or proving who can look into the camera more often.

This is the most ticked that I have been since this campaign started last century. And much of my anger resides with my fellow members of the media, who continue to utter some of the silliest commentary around.

Take, for instance, the debate between Sen. Joe Biden and Gov. Sarah Palin. We heard pundit after pundit talk about the low bar for Palin before the debate. And when it was over, she was praised to high heaven for being folksy and exceeding our wildest expectations.

Huh? Even a blind man and a deaf woman could have seen and heard that Biden totally dominated Palin, speaking with far more clarity and purpose than Palin ever could muster.

What was even more galling was seeing both vice presidential candidates praised for not causing a train wreck. Since when did we start giving people gold stars for not getting into accidents?!

America, we are failing you if this has become the standard. We are a nation growing increasingly dumb and simplistic because we've replaced actual intellect and ideas with who stands taller.

Call me idealistic or say I'm living in a dream world, but mediocrity should not be tolerated, and we all should be ashamed of ourselves when non-substantive stuff is used as the basis of true analysis.

Sure, I liked Palin's homespun language, but the "golly gee" talk got to the point that it felt contrived.

Frankly, I don't want an "average" American for president or vice president. I want someone above average, who can speak coherently to our issues, concerns and fears.

I debated one commentator who said that McCain lost the first debate because he never looked at Obama and that Palin won her debate because she looked at the camera all night. Not health care, education, housing, Iraq, Afghanistan or some other major issue. No, it was who looked at the camera.

This is absurd, and we know it. How in the world can I have high expectations for my nieces when it comes to education but have a low bar for the folks who want to run the nation?

Sorry, I can't go for this. It's time for all of us to demand more, not less, of these candidates. Demand real answers, not some poll-tested drivel.

If this is what we are choosing to accept, then we deserve whatever comes our way. Mediocrity is not what we always have preached. So why start now?

October 10, 2008

Why the Ayers Case Is Risky for McCain/Palin

DURING THE DEMOCRATIC PRIMARIES, I wrote a column about how easy it is for any candidate to tar and feather another about his associations with less than acceptable figures.

Sen. Hillary Clinton tried to blast Sen. Barack Obama for unsolicited comments made by Nation of Islam leader Louis Farrakhan, and folks such as Fox News' Sean

Hannity were happy to run with it, saying it was evidence that the junior senator from Illinois was unfit to be president.

But critics such as Hannity never bothered to raise the issue of former Republican vice presidential candidate Jack Kemp praising Farrakhan for his focus on self-help. Also, nearly everyone in the media was afraid to bring up the fact that Pennsylvania Gov. Ed Rendell had high praise for Farrakhan when Rendell was mayor of Philadelphia.

But blasting one person's associations can come back to bite you.

We now see Gov. Sarah Palin and the McCain campaign trying to stir the pot by invoking William Ayers, who was a major figure in the Weather Underground, a group that bombed the Pentagon and committed other unspeakable acts of terrorism against its own country.

Palin has been hammering home the point on the campaign trail that Obama and Ayers were friends, "palling around" the Windy City, even though the Weather Underground committed those crimes when Obama was just a child. And never mind the fact that Ayers and Obama were involved in a multimillion-dollar education grant that was funded by a right-wing Republican, media magnate Walter Annenberg. Do you hear any of them castigating this late Republican pillar?

The McCain camp, along with its right-wing media comrades, want to convince you that Obama should not have decided to serve with Ayers, who was named Citizen of the Year in Chicago in 1987 for his education work and who is a professor at the University of Illinois at Chicago.

Now, if someone was seen as an acceptable figure by business, political and education figures, many of whom support both Democrats and Republicans, should Obama be faulted for sitting on a board with the guy?

Let's use that same logic and apply it to McCain.

Rep. Jesse Jackson Jr., a Democrat from Chicago who serves as a national co-chairman for the Obama campaign, told me on the "Tom Joyner Morning Show" that if we are to use the association tag as evidence of a candidate being unfit for the presidency, what about McCain serving and working alongside people with virulent bigoted pasts, such as former Sens. Jesse Helms and Strom Thurmond and current

Sen. Robert Byrd?

Do we have evidence that those individuals committed specific acts against African Americans during Jim Crow? No. But we do know that their hateful words and willingness to uphold laws that were absolutely anti-American did not represent the best of this nation.

Thurmond ran for president as a Dixiecrat in 1948 with a platform of maintaining segregation. Based on Helms' policies, he didn't see blacks as full Americans.

Bombing the Pentagon is horrible and indefensible. But declaring yourself a patriot while you speak such hateful and venomous words against your own countrymen who just happen to be black and then trying to oppress them is just as indefensible.

So did McCain work with them? Did he not speak with them? Should McCain have declared that he would not work alongside those men because of their pasts? Should the self-described maverick who believes in integrity and character have taken the honorable stance of resigning from the Senate to protest those hateful characters serving in the U.S. Senate?

No. And that is why this association argument is so weak and impotent.

For goodness' sake, Byrd was once a member of the Ku Klux Klan, a domestic terrorist organization!

Now, if Ayers were involved in those despicable acts today—or Byrd and his late Senate colleagues—then it is fair game.

But no candidate should have to be held responsible for the actions of someone else that took place years ago.

I fundamentally believe that this is nothing but a smoke screen and an effort to ignore the real issues we face. People should not care about any of this when they are losing their jobs and having their homes foreclosed and finding themselves unable to afford to send their kids to college and to get access to health care.

What I find to be even more deplorable is that McCain's advisers are saying they want to turn the page to anything but issue No. 1—the economy.

If that kind of talk is coming from the camp of a guy who wants to be president, then that is something to be afraid of—not a candidate's association with Ayers or Thurmond, Helms and Byrd.

October 17, 2008
Time for Palin to Answer Tough Questions

DO YOU KNOW WHAT WAS SO GREAT ABOUT MAGIC JOHNSON, Larry Bird and Michael Jordan? They were three of the biggest trash talkers in the history of the NBA, but they had the game to back it up.

Somebody should tell that to Gov. Sarah Palin.

Sen. John McCain's running mate has been running around the country, firing up her—yes, her, and not necessarily McCain's—loyal supporters by blasting Sen. Barack Obama for "palling around with terrorists" and demanding that the American people know exactly when he learned about the past of William Ayers.

She has stoked the crowds by saying, "This is not a man who sees America the way that you and I see America." We all know what that is designed to do: portray Obama as a foreigner who isn't as American as she. Or you. Or Joe Six-pack, the hockey mom, soccer mom, Wal-Mart mom, NASCAR dad and the other coded words she uses regularly.

But what is truly pathetic is that Palin talks tough but is really scared of facing her own issues.

Because she is good at proclaiming that the American people need to know who Barack Obama is—an attempt to paint him as a shady figure who might occupy the White House—the American people deserve to hear Palin answer whether her husband, Todd, a former member of the Alaskan Independence Party, agreed with its founder, who wanted to secede from the union.

Is there anything more anti-American than wanting to sever ties with the country?

It's critical that Palin answer questions about whether she disagrees with John McCain's criticism of the Bush administration's decision to remove North Korea from the terrorist-nation list. She spoke in favor of it. McCain didn't. Are they on the same page or not?

The American people deserve to hear from Palin as to why she didn't say a word to rebuke the hateful, pathetic and degrading comments made at rallies featuring her, such as when someone in the crowd called Obama a terrorist, someone else shouted, "Off with his head," and others suggested he is a traitor.

Lastly, don't you think the self-described maverick needs to own up to what really happened with the firing of the police commissioner in Alaska? She was declared by a special investigator to have been within her rights in firing the commissioner, but she was blasted for abuse of power and violating the state's ethics laws.

So what did she say in a conference call with Alaska reporters—who were not allowed by the McCain camp to ask follow-up questions? That she was cleared of all wrongdoing, legally and ethically.

That's right. She repeated over and over and over an absolute lie, and we are supposed to say: "Hey, it's all fine. She winks at us. We love her hockey mom schtick. Don't worry about that abuse of power thing."

Well, after having to deal with Vice President Dick Cheney being accused of beating the drum for war by berating and pushing our intelligence apparatus to match his political views on Iraq, don't you think we should care about someone who has been accused in a report—authorized by Democrats and Republicans—of using her power and influence to get her way?

Sure, her supporters will say she's talked to the "media." She was questioned by Laura Ingraham, Rush Limbaugh and that self-described journalist—yes, he really called himself that—Fox's Sean Hannity.

Palin has done interviews with ABC's Charlie Gibson, CBS' Katie Couric and local TV folks. But why is she so scared of NBC's Brian Williams? And why is she so fearful of CNN?

Does she somehow think that big guns such as Wolf Blitzer, Anderson Cooper and Campbell Brown are just too tough in asking questions? My goodness; Tina Fey has actually done more interviews about playing Sarah Palin than Sarah Palin has done about being Sarah Palin!

Hmm. McCain, Sen. Joe Biden, Barack and Michelle Obama, Sen. Hillary Clinton, Cindy McCain and even McCain's 95-year-old mama and Palin's daddy all have done interviews with CNN, sharing their thoughts on the campaign. But Palin? Not a whisper.

It's clear that Palin really isn't a true frontier woman. See, when you tote a gun, carry a big stick and spit fire, you aren't afraid to take on all comers.

So, Sarah, if you want to talk big on the campaign trail to those audiences that don't talk back, go right ahead. But if you truly are the maverick politician you say you are, come and talk to us soft, coddled, elitist journalists. Surely we aren't as tough as the moose you like to take down with your Second Amendment-protected hunting rifle.

October 24, 2008
Republican Attacks Show Fear and Desperation

WATCHING SEN. JOHN MCCAIN and top Republicans swing wildly in their attempts to slam Sen. Barack Obama with less than two weeks to go before Election Day is like watching an old fighter—clearly out of gas, his legs turned to rubber, and all he can do is grab, hold, punch behind the back, anything to try to win.

McCain's campaign is no longer about issues. He and his supporters want to bring up anything and everything to derail Obama, and nothing is sticking, so they just keep returning to their old bag of tricks.

In the past two weeks, we've seen Rep. Michelle Bachmann (R-MN) make one of the most audacious statements ever, suggesting that Obama holds anti-American views, that other members of Congress have the same views, and that the media should launch a widespread investigation to ferret them out.

No, seriously, she said that on MSNBC's "Hardball."

It didn't take long for the folks on the left to get ahold of her comments. After the video spread like wildfire, Democrats across the country pumped $700,000 into the campaign coffers of her opponent. The normally talkative Bachmann is now on lockdown, not granting any interviews, as she has to work hard to hold on to her seat.

Then you have former Speaker of the House Newt Gingrich, who was caught suggesting that if Obama wins, Obama is going to put in place the policies of the Rev. Jeremiah Wright. Now, Gingrich has absolutely no clue what policies Wright advocated, but he wants to scare the dickens out of voters by literally making stuff up about Obama.

Cindy McCain, who barely has moved her lips during this campaign, now is accusing the Obama campaign of running the dirtiest campaign ever, and she is lighting up *The New York Times* and others for their viciousness. Never mind what's happening in her own backyard with all of the false and outlandish comments coming from her husband, his running mate (Gov. Sarah Palin) and their supporters.

They are now in full blame-the-media mode.

Then you have both McCain and Palin slamming Obama for essentially being a socialist. We shouldn't be surprised that it's come to this because we already had radio hosts such as Lars Larson, Glenn Beck and others trying to paint Obama for months as being a Marxist. Now the junior senator from Illinois is a student of Lenin!

This has gotten totally out of hand, but instead of trying to castigate Obama and tar and feather him, the Republicans should look inward at how their actions have seriously harmed this nation.

The Republicans ran Congress for six of the past eight years. The Republicans have held the White House for the past eight years. The Republicans have advanced the deregulation agenda that played a major role in creating the financial mess we are currently in.

The Republicans have led the foreign policy we have in place that has destroyed the moral authority we once held. Their president is one of the most unpopular in history, so bad that he and Vice President Dick Cheney can't even come out of the White House to campaign on behalf of McCain because they are so reviled by Americans.

Can someone please remind these folks of this?

Every campaign says they want the election to be about the issues, but when McCain's campaign manager, Rick Davis, made it clear that they want it to be about character and not issues, well, we should have realized we would get to this point.

That's why we're hearing so much about Bill Ayers. That's why they've spent more time blasting out statements about ACORN than about real policy points.

It's pretty sad, really. It's sad that instead of making it about a vision for America, they want it to be about the castigating of a good man. It's sad that McCain can't fully articulate an economic plan that encompasses all Americans instead of redistributing income upward to the very rich.

It's sad that his only answer to the economy is tax cuts when we need a much broader answer.

Much can happen before Election Day. I've seen campaigns won and lost with less time on the clock.

McCain will continue to throw jabs, swing wildly, ignore the game plan he came into the fight with, and hope something—anything—connects against the jaw of his younger, more fluid opponent. And like any aging fighter, as the rounds tick away, he could get even more desperate and fearful. So hold on to your seats. Lord knows what will come from the GOP side in the coming days.

October 31, 2008
Dean's 50-State Strategy Is a Plus for Obama

IF SEN. BARACK OBAMA IS ABLE TO PREVAIL over Sen. John McCain Tuesday, all of those Democrats who ripped Howard Dean's 50-state strategy during the past four years should call the head of the Democratic National Committee and offer a heartfelt apology.

First in line should be Sen. Charles Schumer of New York, Rep. Rahm Emanuel of Illinois and my CNN colleague and political strategist James Carville.

When Democrats were in the final stages of winning back Congress in 2006, those three were at odds with Dean, saying he should forget about his pie-in-the-sky plan to have the Democratic Party compete in all 50 states.

They reasoned that it was futile to spend money on get-out-the-vote efforts in non-congressional elections and that all the effort should be on reclaiming Congress.

But Dean resisted their suggestions, weathering repeated calls for him to resign after that election.

Dean's insistence on having a Democratic Party that exists in the heartland—not just California, New York and Massachusetts—was brilliant in that it made it clear that the party recognizes the rest of America.

The Democratic Party earned its liberal label because it ignored the moderate and conservative voices, which paved the way for the Reagan Revolution to win three consecutive elections. Yet the decisive wins weren't just on the national level.

Texas is a prime example. What used to be a blue-dog Democratic state now has Republicans dominating every statewide office.

But things are looking up. In Dallas County, all of the county positions except for a handful were in the hands of the GOP, especially judicial positions. That changed four years ago, and the party could solidify itself this time around.

The same thing in Harris County. The state's most populous county saw Republicans take everything in sight. This time around, Democrats are poised to take back Houston and surrounding cities.

Texan Democratic leaders used to cry the blues when an election was near, but after seeing the massive turnout during the primary, they have been able to build their voter database and cultivate a new generation of politicians to run for office.

Will the state go red? Sure. But with a rock-solid black vote, the ability to attract more Hispanic voters, and a growing appeal to whites, Democrats may make Texas a competitive two-party state soon.

If Democrats are going to achieve success on the national level, they must have significant enthusiasm on the local level. It's hard to get your supporters ginned up for a national campaign if they see no infrastructure, especially in local get-out-the-vote operations.

When Obama announced that he was implementing a 50-state strategy, he was laughed at. But here we are with a few days left in the campaign, and the Republicans are having to spend precious dollars on ads in Montana, North Carolina, Virginia, Missouri, Iowa, Colorado and Nevada, GOP locks in past elections.

Obama deserves a lot of the credit for this because his "change" campaign theme, along with the horrible leadership of Republicans nationwide, is helping his candidacy. But changing the attitude of the nation's Democrats was also vital, and that's where Dean played a role.

The former governor of Vermont saw firsthand the sorry shape of the party when he ran for president in 2004. Republicans, led by Karl Rove, perfected their voter-registration efforts, targeting voters down to the neighborhood, block and household.

They knew that in order to win, they needed a well-oiled machine that wasn't activated every four years; it needed to be active year-round and in every election cycle.

So Dean put the people and resources behind substantial voter efforts in a number of states, and they went about rebuilding a crippled party that had no central voter-registration effort, an outdated database of supporters, a fundraising arm that heavily relied on trial attorneys and Hollywood types, and a message that changed depending on the day.

In addition to seeing how Obama performs Tuesday, we also will watch and see whether Democrats are able to increase the number of governorships and legislatures they control.

That will be critical in 2010 because that's when the borders of congressional districts will be redrawn, and the party that rules the general assemblies, legislatures and governor's mansions will write the rules to the game.

Old pols always said that all politics is local, and the only way for a revitalized Democratic Party to expand its reach nationally is by re-branding the party on the home front. That takes time, money and leadership, and Howard Dean was willing to put his money where his mouth is.

Reflections: Denver and the Democratic National Convention

TICHINA ARNOLD

"I think my most encouraging moment was his acceptance speech when he was the Democratic nominee. His words were just very powerful and it just kind of sums everything up. And I never cry in front of people but I invited people over. I said bring whomever to my house because this is a moment in history that we will never forget, and I recorded it and I sat in front of the TV with my daughter. I explained everything to her that was going on and I just cried because it was just refreshing to see that okay, there is a possibility for change and there is a possibility for new beginnings."

HOLLY ROBINSON-PEETE

"Rodney has played in Mile High (Stadium) before and I used to tell him back in the day when he was playing and there were only a handful of black quarterbacks in the league. I would tell him, 'You really are a pioneer out there.' I remember him playing in a league with mostly white quarterbacks. I was just being very proud of him and mentioned that he really had broken down some barriers with that, and at that time, he was the most recruited football player in the country and yet, he wasn't drafted until the sixth round basically because he was a black quarterback.

"When I rolled up in there and I saw just the wall to wall of people and enthusiasm and then what a melting pot that place was, it was just mind blowing and it was just— it just made me feel as though—it felt dreamlike. It didn't feel real.

"Rodney was always complaining about playing there because he felt like he needed more oxygen on the sidelines. But there was something really giddy about the atmosphere. All of the speakers, the people that came on, how perfectly organized it was. If there were glitches, I never saw anything, and just that feeling that, for lack of—not to sound corny, but there was that Kumbaya moment that none of us, I think, in that whole place ever thought we would ever live to see.

"But I have to say it was the brotherhood that I think stands out the most to me. And I have this photo of me and my Mom and sitting there with her and then every minute, she would lean over, 'Remember I told you? Remember I told you?'

"I didn't mind her telling me, 'I told you so' that night."

ERIKA ALEXANDER

"It's bittersweet. I'm a very competitive person, so of course, I wanted my candidate to win for all the reasons that I stated. It was also bittersweet because there I was also wearing the buttons. And I think that people really felt that they could look down on you. They felt a certain pride to winning and feeling. So many were very excited about that, but they're also very scared, I think, at that point thinking, what if he doesn't win? So they had some of that sort of anger and fear for anybody that looked like they were against Senator Obama. There was no way that anybody that was supporting Hillary can honestly look at the convention and not support Senator Obama if what they said they were supporting her for was true.

"But if you came with that T-shirt and that button, it was like you were on another planet, and I had people come up to me and say, "Oh, sister, no. Come on, sister, no, no." And I thought that was extremely rude. I don't think that if they just flipped the script, they would have saw that if I came to them, say Hillary had won, I'm going like, "Oh, come on, brother, come on." That would be ludicrous. But I think black people didn't think of it that way. They didn't think of it that perhaps, there I was in support of my candidate and now trying to be a supporter of the Democratic nominee and that they would need the vote because I always say, "You didn't win because you voted for Obama. You won because Hillary's supporters voted for Obama." So I said you need to take that kind of pride and ego you have…and you need to put it in check because you're going to need other people in unity to win this.

"When I was at the Democratic National Convention, it was a moment that stood out for me that I realized that we had some time to go with unity when I went to a T-shirt store and I had seen a slogan that has been screamed at us several times, like "Bros before hos", and there was this picture of her and I demanded they take that down. I said, "That doesn't represent Senator Obama and it certainly doesn't represent Senator Clinton." And the women in there, they said, "No, some people like that message," and this was a Democratic National Convention official T-shirt store. They refused to take it down until we got all these people around and they still wouldn't take it down.

"And finally, a young brother, who was working at the door, walked up to me and said, "You're right. It is wrong. Here's the manager." It was difficult to sort of have those feelings and still look and embrace this historic moment for my, I should say, for my tribe's sake because that's how I put race."

Malik Yoba

"The thrill for me was being at the DNC, just being there and being in Denver and just feeling that energy and being at the Pepsi Center and all that stuff, that was bananas. I was doing an interview with Benjamin Chavis and he was reflecting on what it felt like for him walking in the '60s and marching and stuff and I'm listening to him, and my last time hanging with him like that was at the Million Man March, and I just started crying in my interview and just started bawling."

KEVIN LILES

"We were in Denver. Myself, Mary (J Blige), Oprah, Forest Whitaker, (and we were) all hanging out, and when the president comes (to Invesco Field), they shut down everything. It is not like you can walk around and anything. So he came, and everything got shut down, so we all looked at each other and said, 'There is no VIP guys. We got to walk.' We all walked to the stadium. No matter who you are, everybody does what they have to do, and that's what the state of mind was. We did not say who we were and what we are, we walked in, in the name of history, we walked in the name of being together."

COMMON

"I got feedback because I was in motion that day but I got a feedback from people of what was going on. I had people that were there and they said this and that, and that was just like one of the best experiences and they had never felt anything like that ever."

HILL HARPER

"Denver was amazing because you know, we were still in the midst of the campaign and still had to work, so you are really trying to look at Denver as to how can we utilize different moments and touch points to really push the campaign forward.

"Another brilliant decision I thought was fantastic was to have the convention in the stadium, because what it did was it allowed us in the campaign to have so many people from Colorado attend. Colorado is such an important state and to allow so many points of life, folks that could leave that event and go back to their areas in Colorado and say I was there and infect and affect so many other people. Brother, I think that was one of the best decisions. I think a lot of people were like he is making decision for the TV cameras, and all that, and that is great and obviously the powerful thing is to see it in a huge stadium, but I really think if you really want to drill it down, it was a great decision for us winning Colorado."

PART 4

VICTORY

Getting Out the Vote

WHEN AL GORE VISITS FLORIDA, I wonder if he passes people on the street and asks himself, did they bother to show up at the polls in 2000? Forget winning the Nobel Peace Prize, working on an Academy Award–winning film, and owning a cable network. Nothing eases the pain of coming close—600 or so votes close—to being elected president, only to see George W. Bush comfortably slide in to 1600 Pennsylvania Avenue. I bet Gore feels that pain. I've heard the reasons cited by any number of people as to why they don't vote. "My vote doesn't matter." "They'll steal the election anyway." "I put my trust in Jesus." "None of the candidates are worthy." I call those lame excuses used to justify lackadaisical behavior.

The fundamental truth is that every vote counts. None of us, not a single one, knows the outcome of any election. We may wake up on Election Day and assume that our candidate will win or is destined to lose, but until each and every vote is counted, we simply don't know. Monroe Anderson knows something about this. He's the journalist who penned a 1982 column for the *Chicago Tribune* arguing that then Congressman Harold Washington could beat two heavyweight White candidates and become the first Black mayor of Chicago. Fellow staffers laughed at Anderson for suggesting such a thing. But on election night, Anderson had the last laugh, as Washington narrowly beat his opponents, primarily because nearly 90 percent of the registered African Americans in the city voted. Now that's Black power!

Had a small number of Black voters chosen not to go to the polls because it was too cold or because they assumed Whites would never back a Black candidate, Washington—who put African Americans in key governmental roles that had been largely shut to them before—would have never won.

We can no longer be a complacent nation that is so jaded by politics that we think nothing matters. Don't buy the faulty argument that elected officials—presidents, congressmen, state representatives or water district reps—have no impact on your life. An elected official influences every facet of our lives, from what we eat and drink to how much we pay in taxes.

How many people do you know who complain about the war in Iraq, but chose not to vote in 2000? Those of you who hate that Clarence Thomas sits on the Supreme Court—did you vote in 1988? Did you want to see the U.S. Justice Department take more action in Jena last year? Understand that the person sitting in the White House was responsible. If you care about these issues, then you need to care who will win in November. Your decision to vote for Barack Obama or John McCain will greatly determine which policies—on health care, education, the war, energy and the economy—this nation enacts in the next four years.

When folks call my Chicago radio show, comment on my Essence.com blog, or respond to something I've said on TV, they naturally demand that the president or a member of Congress fix the problems that we as a nation confront. But who gets to do the fixing is contingent on whether the American people spend their time complaining or using the best weapon they have to determine the future course of this country. You matter. Your vote matters. Leaving a nation in tip-top shape for our children's children matters. So the question is: What are you prepared to do?

November 4, 2008

The Tom Joyner Morning Show: Sen. Barack Obama

Tom Joyner: He is on the phone yo… he just left the polling place.

Sybil Wilkes: We just watched him.

Victory

J Anthony Brown: We watched him. He was there a long time.

Roland Martin: It was a five minute show.

Tom Joyner: The president of the United States of America—Senator Barack Obama. Good morning...

Sybil Wilkes: We are in your house.

Barack Obama: Listen... is everybody working out there?

Sybil Wilkes: Oh yeah.

Roland Martin: Oh yeah, everybody is working.

Barack Obama: I want to make sure now... that everybody is on their best behavior in front of Tom Joyner.

Tom Joyner: And they got you on time, I did not think you are going to call, they said you are going to call at 8 o'clock. Here it is 8 o'clock central... and you have called, I was watching you on TV. It took you a long time to vote.

Barack Obama: Well you know in Chicago we got this judicial elections along with the other elections and there are probably... 50 judges then you got to make a decision whether they should be retained or not. So that ends up consuming a lot of time. But I will tell you what? There were long lines here, all across the country, you are seeing long lines. In some cases we got bad weather and rain and the key thing in this election is going to be who wants it more. Who is willing to stay in line, who is willing to put up with some of the inconveniences and I hope that our supporters and people all across the country recognized that this is one of those times where you are just going to do of what is required to make sure our ballots are cast.

Tom Joyner: You got to hold the line. Hold the line.

Roland Martin: Senator, there were a couple of things that were amazing to watch. One was your daughters assisting you in filling out the ballot. A couple thoughts what did it mean for them to be there to make it happen, and also the emotional loss for you of your grandmother who passed away and certainly our condolences go out to you.

Sybil Wilkes: I am so sorry.

Barack Obama: Well, I appreciate that. Look, I wish that my grandmother had been here to see this. I wish my mother had been here to see it. They are in a better place now, they are looking down on us. And to see my daughters be a part of this. And stand beside us when we were marking the ballot. That is something presumably that the will never forget, that the will carry with them. I hope that children across the country are going to the polling place with their parents who have that sense of civic obligation. Michelle seemed to really take a long time deciding who to vote for president. [overlap]

J Anthony Brown: We know how you lean over to double check... look mark the BO one now...

Barack Obama: Right. I just want to make sure. I was not sure.

Victory

Sybil Wilkes: But how cool was it that your grandmother was able to vote for her grandson Barry as president of the United States?

Barack Obama: That was pretty cool, I mean the fact, she had a chance to vote absentee and she told me, it made her very proud and I think that what we are seeing here today that makes me proud is just the historic participation all across the country, when you look at the early voting totals, in places like Georgia and North Carolina, people waiting five to six hours in line to cast their ballot. That is a sign of an awakening that I think that we have to just keep on driving home. But we are not finished yet, we are going to have to fight for every single vote out here. Everybody has got to make sure that we are as determined and as committed to casting our ballots as the people who have been standing in line in the rain in some cases, for early vote, I heard this powerful story of this woman in Florida who was early morning stood in line, her husband was in hospice and she got the news that her husband had passed away. While she was in line waiting to vote and she kept on, she stayed there to vote.

Roland Martin: She held the line.

Barack Obama: To cast her ballot and that is the kind of commitment that we are seeing throughout the country.

Sybil Wilkes: How is your day looking, what is up for the rest of the day?

Barack Obama: I am on my way to the airport, we are going to fly down to Indianapolis. Because we got a close race in Indiana, a Democrat has not won there since 1964 but we are going to see if we can go ahead and break that string of loses and I think it is going to be very close, so we are going to try to encourage our volunteers and shake some hands down in Indiana, but I will come back here, get on some television. Try to make sure that everybody is encouraged to get out to the poll. I do have my ritual of my election day basketball game.

Tom Joyner: When are you going to get that in?

Barack Obama: We are going to get it in the afternoon.

J Anthony Brown: Where are you going to play?

Sybil Wilkes: You can play the Pacers... you could win.

Barack Obama: I am not going to tell you where we are going to play, are you crazy?

Tom Joyner: You may have 80,000... sure like what you did last night in Virginia.

Barack Obama: Well, this is just me and my boys, and we are going to get a little game and then...

J Anthony Brown: Shirt or skins?

Barack Obama: What is that?

J Anthony Brown: Shirts or skin?

Sybil Wilkes: He is shirt.

Tom Joyner: What are you shirt of skin.

Victory

J Anthony Brown: Shirts or skin?

Barack Obama: I am definitely shirt...

Sybil Wilkes: Tell Reggie we said hello, would you?

Barack Obama: ...I will wear my 26-year-old Reggie love, the east skin.

Sybil Wilkes: Yeah, we liked that about him. Tell him we said hello, we like that. [Overlap] Okay, it is jus Sybil Wilkes. Would you just tell him Sybil Wilkes likes the skin part, okay?

Barack Obama: I will ask him.

Tom Joyner: Thank you, thank you, thank you again for having us here in your campaign headquarter, sir.

Barack Obama: I hope they are treating you right...

Tom Joyner: They are.

Sybil Wilkes: Yeah Corey has been wonderful, thank you very much and the rest of staff has just been fabulous.

Tom Joyner: And your machine, your organization is amazing, sir.

Barack Obama: It is the best ever. The best ever and I do not exaggerate that. I mean, my campaign folks, my volunteers they have just been outstanding. I am so proud of them. But obviously what counts is what happens today. So, I am going to let you guys go and hopefully I will go get back to work.

Tom Joyner: All right.

Sybil Wilkes: And you go make history.

J Anthony Brown: Senator just jump shots no drive down the middle.

Barack Obama: All right, just remember, everybody who is listening stay in line, do not get discouraged.

Tom Joyner: Hold the line. Hold the line. Hold the line.

Barack Obama: Hold the line, alright, bye, bye.

J Anthony Brown: Hold the line.

Tom Joyner: That is the next president of the United States Senator Barack Obama.

Sybil Wilkes: In his house.

Roland Martin: In his place. Yeah…

Tom Joyner: All right, now do not spill anything.

J Anthony Brown: Do not steal nothing, do not touch nothing.

Tom Joyner: Do not mess up his deposit.

Sybil Wilkes: Until we get to the White House.

J Anthony Brown: Tom, there will be body check anything in that basketball game today.

Sybil Wilkes: And J Anthony Brown would say, he is the truth.

J Anthony Brown: He is the truth. I do not get the truth that loud.

November 4, 2008, Essence.com Blog

A Truly Emotional Day For Black Voters.

Posted at 7:15 a.m

The e-mails are already pouring in from African Americans who are headed to the polls, and many are literally in tears.

One woman called the "Tom Joyner Morning Show" to say that she made all five of her kids get up in order to go to the polls.

My good friend, Roy Johnson, editor-in-chief of *Men's Fitness,* and his wife, Barbara, sent me the following e-mail:

"Took the kids. Got their asses up and said, Go ahead and tell your kids their grandparents were crazy, waking you up at 5:35am to pull a lever!"

He later wrote: "Some folks are crying on way to polls. This one came from a friend:

"My people like my grandmother aren't alive to take part in history today. So when you *vote* this morning take a moment of silence for those who died so u can *vote*."

Voting Problems Being Reported in North Carolina, Virginia, Florida

Posted at 10:51 AM

TOM JOYNER CONTINUES TO BROADCAST his show and Ken Smuckler is here at CNN as they monitor voting problems being called in from across the country.

Thus far, Smuckler says they have received 3,000 calls this morning, and it is averaging nearly 800 an hour.

If you have any issues at the polls, call 866-MYVOTE-1.

The issues being reported are mainly in North Carolina and Virginia.

Donna Brazile reported: "The voter hotline is reporting long lines in our key precincts in all battleground states."

Key States Are About to Close, Virginia is the Biggest One for Obama

Posted at 07:05 PM

ELECTION 2008 IS UNDERWAY and critical states are about to close. The results in these states could give us a great indication as to whether Sen. Barack Obama wins tonight. The key states closing at 7 P.M. eastern is Georgia; Indiana; Kentucky; South Carolina; Vermont; and Virginia.

Virginia is the biggest state for Obama. His entire strategy is predicated on how that state goes. If he wins Virginia, he will win the presidency.

His strategy from day one was to win Virginia, then take the western states of Nevada, Colorado and New Mexico, then he had to only win Ohio or Pennsylvania to win the presidency.

Folks, forget the blowout. All he has to do is win 270 electoral college votes and he's president. That's the ballgame.

CNN Calls Vermont for Obama; Kentucky for McCain

Posted at 07:07 PM

THIS IS EXPECTED. Vermont is a very liberal state—Howard Dean was its longtime governor—and Kentucky is a bigtime Republican state.

DEMS Now Control Virginia; Warner Declared Winner

Posted at 07:14 PM

IN THE BATTLE AGAINST FORMER VIRGINIA GOVERNORS, Mark Warner has dusted Jim Gilmore for the U.S. Senate seat being vacated by longtime Senator John

Warner, who is of no relation.

Mark Warner was up by as much as 30 percent and Gilmore had virtually no chance of winning.

Democrats now control by U.S. Senate seats as well as the governor's mansion.

CNN Projects South Carolina's 8 Electoral College Votes Will Go to McCain

Posted at 07:57 PM

We only have 1 percent reporting, but based on exit polls, we are calling that state.

CNN Calls Eight States for Obama; Two for McCain

Maine for Obama (3 of its 4 electoral votes—no call on 4th)

Connecticut for Obama

Delaware for Obama

Washington DC for Obama

Illinois for Obama

Maryland for Obama

Massachusetts for Obama

New Jersey for Obama

Tennessee for McCain

Oklahoma for McCain

CNN Projects Obama to Win New Hampshire

Posted at 08:30 PM

SEN. JOHN MCCAIN SCORED AN UPSET against George W. Bush in the 2000 Republican primary, but it didn't come to pass eight years later.

The state and its four electoral votes will go to Sen. Barack Obama.

CNN Projects Pennsylvania for Obama

Posted at 08:41 PM

FOLKS, THIS RACE IS O-V-E-R.

Sen. John McCain needed to win Pennsylvania to have a remote chance to win the presidency, but that will not happen.

Sen. Barack Obama is projected to win the state's 21 electoral votes.

CNN Calls West Virginia and Alabama for McCain

Posted at 09:27 PM

CNN Calls Ohio for Obama

Posted at 09:34 PM

THIS IS GAME, SET MATCH. By winning Pennsylvania and now Ohio, Obama doesn't need Florida or Virginia. He can win the western states and win the presidency.

CNN Calls Louisiana for McCain

Posted at 09:48 PM

CNN Calls New Mexico for Obama

Posted at 09:56 PM

WITH A HUGE LATINO POPULATION, and Obama winning them 2-1, he wins New Mexico. That is one of the three Western states he targeted. Now we wait to see if he can pull out Arizona and Nevada.

CNN Calls Iowa for Obama

Posted at 10:00 PM

HE WINS THEIR SEVEN electoral college votes.

CNN Calls Utah, Kansas for McCain

Posted at 10:00 PM

CNN Calls Arkansas for McCain

Posted at 10:11 PM

CNN Calls Texas for McCain

Posted at 10:23 PM

HE PICKS UP the state's 34 electoral votes.

CNN Calls Mississippi for McCain

Posted at 10:24 PM

HE WINS THEIR six electoral college votes.

CNN Calls Virginia for Obama

Posted at 10:59 PM

FOLKS, THIS RACE is truly, truly over.

SEN. BARACK OBAMA IS THE PRESIDENT-ELECT OF THE UNITED STATES

Posted at 12:03 AM

AS I WRITE THIS, I FIGHT BACK THE TEARS that are falling down my cheeks. I think of the countless men who were hung from trees. I think of the many African American children who sat in one-room schoolhouses, desperately trying to get an education.

I think of the black soldiers who fought Hitler and Mussolini, but were treated as second-class citizens in their own country. I think about the fact that in 2009, the NAACP will celebrate its 100th anniversary. The same NAACP that was launched due to a race riot in Springfield, Illinois.

How fitting that a man who cut his teeth politically in Springfield, Illinois, and who launched his career in that same city, would rise to the presidency in the centennial year of the National Association for the Advancement of Colored People. Now, I can tell my nieces with certainty, that yes, even you can grow up to be president of the United States.

Sen. Barack Obama, thank you. The ancestors thank you. America thanks you.

Back Story: Shedding Tears on Election Night

FROM THE MOMENT I WOKE UP ON NOVEMBER 4, I knew Sen. Barack Obama was going to win. In fact, I had the feeling the previous two weeks. Barring something crazy happening, it was clear Sen. John McCain was not going to be giving a victory speech.

The day was amazing. I was on the air most of the morning doing the "Tom Joyner Morning Show." We were getting reports of voting issues all over the country. Yet at the same time, we were also hearing about truly stunning turnout in largely black areas.

I had voted the previous month in Texas, and the polls opened at 7 A.M. I arrived at 6 A.M., and folks were already in line. It was an amazing site to witness, and I knew Election Day would be just as electric.

Victory

There was nervous anticipation all around CNN. We all had the feeling that we were about to witness history later that night. Sen. Barack Obama was planning to speak to thousands in Chicago, and some estimated more than 1 million could turn out to hear his victory speech.

When we got closer to our prime time telecast, Obama had come a long way, and so did I. For a guy who started the campaign sitting on the sidelines on the first primary night, this night, I was sitting on the front row, so when the cameras panned to The Best Political Team on Television, I would be front and center. I didn't get there because of my looks, how I dressed or my skin tone. It was all about the work and the impact on the audience. And Obama didn't get to where he was because he was clean and articulate (Sorry Joe Biden, I couldn't resist).

My partner in crime, Donna Brazile, was only going to be with us a short time. She also worked as an analyst for ABC News, and with me holding it down on CNN, she was headed over there.

When we sat down on the set, she said, "Roland, I've got my tissues."

We both knew tears would be flowing that night; all around the world, and especially in black America.

I was seated next to conservative Bill Bennett, and try as he might, he knew the election was over. As the results came in, it was clear McCain had no chance of winning.

I was bouncing back and forth between CNN and another studio to do TV One. Our political folks weren't happy about that; they wanted me on CNN's air non-stop. But I was being paid by TV One long before CNN came along, and with TV One airing their own election coverage, I was not going to short them.

As the results rolled in, I told my TV One audience around 9:30 P.M. that the election was over and Obama was our new president. I remember hearing a producer say in disbelief, "Did Roland just call the race?"

I didn't "officially" call it, but breaking down the numbers, I said McCain had no chance of winning. Knowing full well how the West Coast states would vote, I said that as soon as Obama won Ohio and Pennsylvania, McCain would have to win California, and that wasn't going to happen.

Around 10:30 P.M., our pollsters whispered in our ears, "We're calling the election at 11 P.M." Again, the numbers don't lie. Once Obama reached 200 delegates, and Washington state, Oregon and California accounting for 77 delegates, he would get the magical number of 270 and would be the new president.

The final 30 minutes were a bit anti-climatic. But when 11 P.M. struck, and we played the music signifying we were calling it, and the wall flashed those words, "Senator Barack Obama is the President-Elect of the United States", I cupped my hands over my mouth and just watched the jubilation in Chicago.

As it happened, the tears began to form. I would switch my eyes between the wall and the monitor, wall and the monitor, wall and the monitor.

A black man had been elected president of the United States. The land of slavery. The land where a civil war was fought largely over keeping people like me enslaved. A country where black men, women and children were denied their birthright.

As all of these thoughts went through my mind, I didn't want to talk or even look at anyone. I just wanted to take it all in. I remember Jeff Toobin patting me on my left shoulder, and Gloria Borger calling my name. Others tried to call my name. But I didn't want to speak to anyone.

Was I thinking of Obama at that moment, his wife, his children or his campaign team? No. To be honest, I thought of the black soldiers who returned from World War II and were lynched in their uniforms. I thought of the black children long denied an education—before and after *Brown v. Board of Education*—forced to learn in one-room schoolhouses, a stove in the middle of room, and decrepit books, clawing their way to an education. I thought of the nameless and faceless African Americans who had master's degrees and Ph.Ds who couldn't get a job better than a janitor or maid, all because of the color of their skin. I thought of the ancestors and what they endured for Obama to be able to stand on that stage in Grant Park as the president-elect, and a white man playing second fiddle to him. And yes, I thought of the African Americans who made it possible for me to sit on that set on the most influential media operation in the world. Ida B. Wells. Frederick Douglass. Vernon Jarrett. Lerone Bennett. Mal Goode. Ethel Payne. So many black journalists who fought for the right of African Americans to, in the words of the founders of the first black newspapers, Freedom's Journal, founded in 1827 by Samuel Cornish and John Russworm, who wrote in their first editorial, "We wish to plead our own cause. Too long have others spoken for us."

Here we were, 181 years later, and a 39-year-old black journalist born and raised in Houston, Texas, spent two years laboring in the fields, covering the most historic presidential campaign in history, pleading the cause of the voiceless, framing the issues within the context of so many, especially African Americans.

There were certainly other elections where black journalists had a voice. But this campaign, with a black man leading the way, was the first time African American journalists were truly at the table, unfiltered and ready and able to speak for the masses.

With all of that, folks, there is no way I could not have shed tears at the sight of Barack Hussein Obama becoming the 44th president of the United States.

NOVEMBER 7, 2008

Thank You, President-Elect Barack Obama

THE DAY AFTER SEN. BARACK OBAMA was elected the 44th president of the United States, my mom sent me the following text message: "I woke up this morning, did my prayer time and then turned on my TV to see if anything had changed. Thank God it hadn't."

That was the feeling among many African Americans and others Nov. 5. Yes, indeed, the first African American was elected to the most powerful position in the world. The world didn't implode. But I can assure you that a lot of folks stood a bit more upright and walked differently after watching such a historic victory.

A few folks have said that they always thought Obama would win. Count conservative commentator John McWhorter in that camp. I saw him at CNN the day after the election, and he said he always thought it would happen.

Sorry, I wasn't in that group.

Did I think it could happen? Yep. Was it likely, considering how messed up President George W. Bush has left the economy? Absolutely. But the doubt was there because we were venturing into uncharted territory. In fact, while doing an election special on CNN two days before Election Day, I was asked to give my prediction, and I essentially said:

"Forget 300 or 350 electoral votes. All it takes is 270. Everything else is gravy!"

And at 11 P.M. Eastern time, when CNN called the election for Obama, all I could do was look at the video wall and see a black man as president. Then I focused on the monitors to see the cheering crowds in Chicago's Grant Park—black, white, Hispanic, Asian, men, women, children. There were folks from all walks of life, and they were experiencing something none of us ever envisioned.

What went through my mind? The countless black men who returned home from the war and were lynched in their military uniforms. They courageously fought Hitler and Mussolini to protect the American way of life, only to have their lives taken by so-called American patriots who didn't want their racist way of life changed. I thought about the millions of black children who had to huddle in one-room schoolhouses clawing their way to an education because separate but equal, even when overturned, ruled the day. My mind thought of countless African American men and women who went to work every day having to sit in the backs of buses, drink from colored water fountains, get their food from the backs of restaurants, unable to stay in the very hotels they sang and danced in.

I literally felt our slave ancestors breaking the chains and yelling, "We are truly free now!"

But I also wondered what Viola Liuzzo would say.

She was the white 39-year-old Michigan mother of five who was shot and killed on an Alabama highway after the Selma and Montgomery voting-rights marches. She was one of many whites who gave their time, money and, yes, lives in order to see that full rights and privileges were provided to African Americans.

They, too, should celebrate this victory because their blood also was shed to see a day when a black man could walk into the Oval Office.

Lastly, I guess it's only fitting that Obama would be the president in 2009.

In the same year, the National Association for the Advancement of Colored People will celebrate its 100th anniversary. What many may not realize is that the NAACP was created after a race riot in Springfield, Ill., the same city where Obama served as a state legislator for eight years and where he launched his presidential campaign.

Some may call that coincidence. Others may say it's divine order.

Whatever you want to call it, all I can say to President-elect Barack Obama is "thank you." Our ancestors thank you. And America thanks you.

November 14, 2008

Sarah Palin Is Not the Future of the GOP

AFTER PRETTY MUCH IGNORING THE NATIONAL MEDIA during her 2.5 months as Sen. John McCain's running mate, Alaska Gov. Sarah Palin has been willing to sit down and chat with any man or woman with a pen, pad, audio recorder and video camera as of late, talking and talking and talking and ...

It's been hilarious to watch as she says that she doesn't want to rehash the campaign but then launches into a litany of issues that doomed the McCain-Palin ticket. She even chose to talk about William Ayers, as if that worked the first time she kept bringing it up.

Then there was that bizarre "news conference" at the Republican Governors Association meeting in Miami, where she held court with the national media and was flanked by her fellow governors, many of whom looked like kids forced by their mothers to go to church on a Saturday afternoon. At one point, I thought Palin was going to break out and starting singing a medley of hits from Gladys Knight and the Pips. Sorry, that's what it looked like!

Everyone seems to be stuck on the notion that she is the titular head of the party, the most visible face on a Republican Party that is looking more anemic by the day.

Don't count me among that group.

In fact, instead of being jealous of all the attention that continues to be lavished on Palin, her fellow governors should be happy because the coverage isn't showing her off as a policy wonk. Instead, she appears to be someone who can't get enough of the limelight. I say let Palin be Palin and cause the public to get so sick and tired of hearing from her that it won't even want to see her in 2012.

Yet the real reason Palin will not be the Joan of Arc for the GOP is that despite her best attempts, she is not the moderate voice the party needs right now. She is seen as a hard-right Republican who makes that arm of the party swoon but does nothing to appeal to the growing number of independents and moderates who populate the countryside.

Those who live in Palinland threw roses at her feet, saying she excited the base, especially the white evangelicals who run the party. But you can't win a national election by making the base happy. The map has changed from the typical win-the-South focus of the GOP of old. Today Republicans have to counter younger voters, a growing Hispanic base, and Western states, which are now in play for both parties. That requires having someone who appeals to a generation of folks who weren't alive when Ronald Reagan was elected in 1980.

It may be sacrilegious for this group to think that reincarnating Reagan isn't a good idea. But truth be told, the GOP must realize that it's a new day.

The one thing that President-elect Barack Obama didn't try to do was be President Bill Clinton Jr. He knew that in the 16 years since Clinton was elected to the first of two terms, the nation has changed. And if you don't think a lot has changed in the 28 years since Reagan whacked incumbent President Jimmy Carter, you're delusional.

What the GOP needs is not a lurch to the right. Now is truly the time for a moderate uprising in the party so they can take away the influence of the hard-core right. The hard-core right-wingers have dominated the party, and their crucifixion of McCain was evidence of the need for change. Many of them hated McCain because he wasn't like them, so they berated him into not being himself. The one man who could have appealed to moderates was turned into a Rush Limbaugh-Sean Hannity acolyte, and trust me; Americans are sick of those two, and they summarily rejected McCain.

It will be like giving castor oil to the GOP, but just as the Democratic Leadership Council forced the liberal wing of the Democratic Party to open their eyes to a whole new world in 1988, the same must hold true for the Republican Party.

If not, they might as well get used to Democrats enjoying festive inaugurations, because a move further to the right will alienate swing voters, who have tired of the Republicans' usual rhetoric and outdated ideas.

Sasha's Smile Could Be a Guide to Our Future

THERE ARE SO MANY THINGS that we could take away and remember forever regarding the inauguration of the first African American president in the history of the United States, but I'll always remember the laughter of a little girl.

Shortly after President-elect Barack Obama finished the oath and became President Barack Obama, he joined hands with his family and waved to the cheering voices of 1.8 million people packed from the Capitol to the Lincoln Memorial.

People cried, others hugged, celebrities and everyday folks snapped photos to capture the moment.

There really was an amazing energy that permeated the crowd as we all witnessed a barrier come tumbling down before our eyes.

But what stood out for me was a moment when President Obama looked down at his 7-year-old daughter, Sasha, and she said something to him, and then let out this huge laugh.

I don't know whether it was her statement or his response, but the bubbly child was having the time of her life. The sheer joy that was on her face as she grinned from ear to ear caused me to just start laughing as I watched her reaction.

I was shooting photos from the CNN platform just across from where he spoke, and one of the many images was of a beaming Sasha alongside her mom and 10-year-old sister, Malia.

Can you imagine what was going through this young girl's mind, to see her father stand there and take the oath of office?

As I saw her that day, and later bouncing along a sidewalk as she walked with her father, my niece Anastacia came to mind. Their smiles and bouncy walk are so much alike, and both are the same age.

These young girls, and countless other black children, among others, will grow up in an America where what they can imagine is backed up by what they see. Despite the reality that racism hasn't left us, these children have the advantage of not being burdened with being separated by race.

So much has been written about today's generation living in a world where hip-hop music brought them all together in one room, coupled with the diverse images on television and movies. Their reality is not the reality of their parents, and we will see that play out a lot in the future.

What also is most compelling about this age of Obama is how he has been received thus far internationally. Many political experts are simply stunned that a man who has only been on the national stage for five years would have so much good will across the pond.

Of course, a lot of that has to do with the fact that President George W. Bush and his team were seen as running roughshod over their international partners, praising them when they needed something, and savaging them when they disagreed with the U.S. position.

Yet what we also can't ignore is that Obama's skin tone also plays a central role. Americans may be shocked to find out that people of color make up two-thirds of the world population.

They know all too well about America's pathetic and violent history of enslaving and later oppressing African Americans, and it was always seen as ridiculous for U.S. officials to condemn human rights abuses abroad while racial and other forms of discrimination existed in their own backyard.

Obama's election sends a powerful signal to the world that Americans are backing up their rhetoric and ideals with action, and Obama serves as that powerful symbol.

Barack Hussein Obama now has the opportunity to show those who voted for him—and those who didn't—that the change he often spoke about can come to pass.

If he is able to fulfill many of the promises he made during the campaign, he will go down as one of America's most successful presidents, looked at fondly by the American people.

And if he does, maybe we'll end up having the same smile he received courtesy of Sasha.

PART 5

WHAT'S NEXT

January 2009, Essence Magazine

So What Now?

AT 11:00 P.M. (EST) ON NOVEMBER 4, 2008, I had a prime seat on the CNN Election Center set and witnessed the network call the presidential election for the junior senator from Illinois, Barack Hussein Obama, making this Black man the president-elect of the United States. As my eyes darted back and forth between the huge video wall with his smiling face and the thousands of cheering, crying and screaming supporters assembled in Chicago's Grant Park to mark the occasion, I was overcome with emotions. Forget the nonsense about journalists not getting personally invested in a story. There is no way you could be Black and not get teary-eyed at the sight of a Black man being selected as the forty-fourth president of the United States. We were all caught up in the moment—walking taller, smiling more broadly, and relishing the fact that we are alive at such a phenomenal time.

From the moment Obama announced he was seeking the presidency before more than 10,000 people who had braved single-digit weather in Springfield, Illinois, on February 10, 2007, to that balmy evening of November 4 when he made his victory speech before 240,000 people in Chicago, he has often reminded us that it's not about him. It's about us. His campaign's theme was change, but the slogan was Yes We Can. And 47 times in his victory speech he invoked the word we to convey the importance of each of us assuming a role in the Obama administration.

This call for community action reminds me of the biblical figure Nehemiah, who wanted to rebuild the wall of Jerusalem. He had the vision, but it wasn't until the people said, "Let us rebuild," that it came to fruition. President Obama cannot on his own rebuild the desolate parts of the Black community in Chicago, Detroit, New York, Oakland and every other urban and rural town. Just like we held the line on November 4 despite long wait times, we must hold the line to prevent the decay of our communities.

Obama has given us the vision, but we must stand up and ensure that our children are being educated, and reverse the trend of what the Education Trust says is one in three U.S. students failing to graduate on time. We must stop complaining about the need for more investment in our inner cities, but begin to put away $5, $10, $100 or whatever we can to build our personal savings. We must make the effort to buy Black at every turn, and not just talk about it. So, when was the last time you got your clothes cleaned by a Black-owned dry cleaner, ate at a Black-owned restaurant, used a Black-owned accounting firm, consulted with a Black-owned law firm, or hired a Black-owned janitorial service to clean the office of your small business?

We must fight crime in our cities, and that means working with police to start citizen patrols, creating more civic and neighborhood associations, and putting an end to the "no snitching" mandate that rules supreme in too many of our communities. We must learn to build healthy marriages and end the devastation wreaked by domestic violence. If we sit back and wait for President Obama to do all of this by himself, our communities will look the same four years from now. And our election night celebration will have been nothing but a fleeting moment, as opposed to a commitment to everlasting change.

As of 12:01 P.M., January 20, 2009, Obama will be the president of the United States. That's when he begins to fulfill his vision of change for America. He needs us to encourage him and pray for him, but also to hold him accountable. He has promised to bring our troops home, expand health care, and commit additional resources to make college affordable. We also need to see more African Americans and Latinos holding the coveted positions in the White House and not the second-tier jobs that we've always been relegated to. We came through at the ballot box, and he must come through in the Oval Office. Why don't you do as he will and put your hand on your Bible (or Koran or Torah) and swear to work to be a part of the Obama

Revolution to transform our homes, our streets, our neighborhoods, our cities and our states, and then our nation. If we truly voted for change, we shouldn't just see a change in presidents, but also in our minds, hearts and souls.

June 2009, Essence Magazine

A Long Way to Go

I'VE GIVEN NEARLY TWO DOZEN SPEECHES across the country since Barack Obama was elected the forty-fourth president of the United States. African Americans are still basking in the glow of this historic accomplishment, but I'm a bit perturbed with this sense that the election of a Black president is the culmination of the dream outlined by the Reverend Martin Luther King, Jr., in his famous address 45 years ago.

First, let's put things in perspective: The last 614 words of the speech—the "I Have a Dream" portion—must be understood within the context of the entire speech. Powerful words, but focusing on the last portion does a disservice to the rest of his text, which served as the true message of the day and his mission from that point until his death—achieving economic parity for African Americans.

Second, that historic march was not just a March on Washington. It was organized as the March on Washington for Jobs and Freedom. That distinction is important because without the jobs and freedom part, we could simply see that day as more than 250,000 mostly Black folks taking a walk in the park. Dr. King understood that for African Americans, full equality had nothing to do with whether his children could hold hands with white kids or go to an amusement park. He wanted his children to have the means to own that park one day. The real understanding of Dr. King's vision was that he wanted African Americans to be on a level playing field so that we, too, could partake in the riches of this vast nation.

So what does this have to do with President Barack Obama's being elected president?

It's simple. The election of a Black man to the White House is a huge triumph. But while we praise, worship, and wear our Obama buttons and swear we have overcome, barely more than half of our kids are graduating from high school, according to

America's Promise Alliance, the children's advocacy organization founded by retired Gen. Colin Powell and his wife, Alma. We know that the pathway to economic equality is determined by an education, so how could Obama's election mean Dr. King's dream has been fulfilled when we have these sad statistics to deal with?

Think about these numbers: As the national unemployment rate climbed to 8.5 percent early this year, joblessness among African Americans reached 13.3 percent, higher than any other ethnic group.

And speaking of dreams, a 2008 survey conducted by the Black-owned mutual fund company Ariel Investments and investment giant Charles Schwab reported that "for many younger African Americans, saving for retirement is more of a dream than a priority." The survey says whites have twice as much saved as Blacks, and we contribute about 50 percent less to 401(k) plans than whites. I'm not looking to pour cold water on Obama's accomplishment. But we desperately need a reality check to understand that with 95 percent of African Americans voting for Obama, going to the polls was the easy part in this effort to change America. Now it's time for us to get to work to achieve not just Dr. King's dream but the American Dream.

Reflections: What's Next?

Kevin Liles

"Roland, when you look at what this means for the next generation, I said this to you, we had several conversations, the new cool now is to be presidential, to act presidential, to walk presidential, to talk presidential, to demand excellence, and that is what I think we did when we elected Barack Obama as president, he is a symbol of not only hope but a symbol of standards."

Tatyana Ali

"I think it's spring cleaning time. I think it's time to clean house and to really reevaluate our priorities and our values, I mean, real values, like, is it okay to beg other people for money? Is it—you know my phrasing, but is it okay to buy ten handbags because it's cool, even though you can't afford it. I think on all levels, it's really time to clean house and start doing what we have always done best, which is making things, being creative, being imaginative, like knowing that you have to build things from the bottom up and also being willing to do it. I feel like that's what's going on right now."

Vanessa Williams

"As much as I was in the glory of it and feeling the ecstasy of it, I knew that what we were birthing was a beginning, and at least, it felt to me that it wasn't like a sit-on-your-laurels and like, "Oh, yes, Obama got it." It was, like, no, this is a reckoning for all of us to have the audacity to hope, to really be the change you want to see in the world, to live out all these axioms and all these beliefs that any and everything is possible. And certainly, the stars aligned and Obama was ready and the right man at the right time.

"And I thought back to Shirley Chisholm. I was a really little girl at that time when those trucks and those vans were going out when Shirley Chisholm also had that sort of audacity to believe that she would even campaign. And so knowing that he was standing on the shoulders of all of those candidates before him and all of those ancestors who lay in the bottom of the ocean, who came here not as immigrants but as cargo, it was a great amazing, amazing just manifestation of so many things simultaneously."

Jessica Alba

"Healthcare and mental healthcare and maternal healthcare for all children. We must make sure all kids are covered in this country.

"I think people really understand it and this is happening to tax-paying citizens, that they made too much money to get Medicaid and for whatever reason. They are getting comprehensive healthcare. They do not cover certain cancer treatments and it is unfair. Not in this country, of the 30 industrialized countries, we rank number 27 in providing healthcare. That is totally insane."

Cash Warren

"I think we redirect a lot of those privately-funded initiatives, whether they were clean water initiatives or whatever it is, I think we should start focusing a lot of that tension here and fixing our own issues. So, in particularly for me what makes a lot of sense, gang violence and the way we try to rehabilitate our youth."

COMMON

"I think we got to really get into getting a good educational system going because you know, education is still a key to developing our society. If we just start at the root of things with the children right now, then we know we are building a better future. We all know that we are dealing with tough economical times, but we've got to go out and try to create jobs and look at the resources that we have within our community and support those institutions."

HILL HARPER

"We need volunteerism. We need it on the community level. We need everyone who is not engaged and involved to take whatever effort they had and redouble it and volunteer. I can tell you what my charge is and that is education. I just did a talk in Baltimore city schools, and the graduation rate of African American males was just 27 percent. If I am an investor in a restaurant and the government showed up in my restaurant, and I had 27 percent success rate with the food, they would shut me down. We at the community level are allowing our kids to be undereducated.

"I do not care if you do not have kids in that school or even in that school system. We need you to make your presence felt, volunteer, show up, and volunteer whatever you are motivated by, but everyone that was part of this Obama movement, we need you to stay engaged, stay involved. Do not wait until 2012 and break out the t-shirts again.

"At the end of the day, if we do not show up, if we do not do the work, it is just like the campaign, he cannot do the work, right? We have to do the work. President Obama did not get himself elected. Let us be very clear. The people elected him. He did a great job, stayed on message, had a great message, he was at the right time, the right candidate, extremely intelligent, great people around him, great supporters, but I like to say it this way, he was the surfer on the surfboard. The people created the wave and brought him to shore. The wave is what is powerful, so all of us needs to continue and do the work we need to do because I guarantee you this, if we do not continue to do the work, there is no way he can be elected in 2012 because it would be seen as if the progress was not made and the only way we are going to make progress in all these ambitious areas is for us to do the work.

"That is why whenever people call me and talking about why they want a job and why they want to work for the White House, I am saying "stop, hold up!" if we want to reach his goals of 3 million new jobs, we need the best of the brightest out here, being entrepreneurs, being business people, making and creating things. Not all the best can work in the government, we are not going to be creating jobs that way. People always come to me asking, are you going to take a job in the government? No, I am going to volunteer and continue to do whatever I can do.

"I just did a trip to the state department. I am going to do another trip to the state department in two weeks. I am going to continue to volunteer and do what I do best, but I am going to keep being an entrepreneur and I am going to make movies and I am going to produce shows. I am going to get people's job and so staying engaged, being the best business people, entrepreneurs, taking risks, but also volunteering in whatever capacity. We need both."

SPIKE LEE

"We got to do something about young black, our youth; young black men killing each other; these young black men who do not expect to pass 18 years old, like that is okay. Black women having babies having babies. My wife told me something like 80% of African American woman are obese. We got it. We have serious issues within our community. Hypertension, heart disease, obesity, life expectancy. If it wasn't for the Native Americans we would be number in a whole lot of stuff.

"This is crazy. And a lot of stuff we cannot expect the government to (do it all). I'm not absolving them from blame, but what are we going to do as parents to try to turn this thing around? Here is the thing Roland, young black men did not stop killing each other November 5th. That shit still continues; with a black man in the White House; with an African American woman and family in the White House. We just keep doing the crazy shit we are doing and when those other guys were in there.

"So somehow we got tricked into that with Obama in the White House, a switch was flipped and everything is going to be all right. And that's is not the case. Of course it would be worse if McCain would have been elected. There is a lot of work to do.

"We have not been delivered. We have not been delivered. We are not in the promised land."